WHY WORKERS BEHAVE THE WAY THEY DO

WHY WORKERS

BEHAVE THE WAY THEY DO

DUANE BEELER
BINYAMIN LEBOVITS
JAMES BISHOP

other books

HOW TO BE A MORE EFFECTIVE
UNION REPRESENTATIVE
Beeler and Kurshenbaum / *$3.95*

ROLES OF THE LABOR LEADER
Beeler and Kurshenbaum / *$3.95*

UNION PROFESSIONAL
The Staff Rep In Action
Beeler / *$3.95*

SPEAK UP TO MOVE UP
Beeler / *$3.95*

LABOR LAW FOR THE UNION OFFICER
Beeler / *$3.95*

ARBITRATION FOR THE LOCAL UNION
Beeler / *$3.95*

DISCIPLINE AND DISCHARGE
Beeler / *$5.95*

NEGOTIATING THE CONTRACT
Beeler / *$4.95*

CREATIVE USE OF FILMS IN EDUCATION
Adapting Films For Union Use
Beeler and McCallister / *$1.95*

PREFACE

This book differs from the previous nine books in the Union Representative series. The others are "how to" books which deal with specific functions of union leaders.

This book focuses more generally on people and behavior. Its insights will help clarify your daily experiences in working with people; it will also help you understand yourself as well.

The basic question is, why does a worker behave the way he does? The answers come from the most important concepts in the disciplines of psychology, sociology, and the sociology of work. Psychology, because each of us is a unique individual whose behavior and development must be understood; sociology, because we are members of various groups which influence our actions; and the sociology of work, because we are all members of specific work groups which affect our lives in many important respects.

Each of these has been summarized in an easy-to-understand style by an expert in that area at Roosevelt University in Chicago. Binyamin Lebovits is a Professor of Psychology; James Bishop is an Assistant Professor of Sociology; and Duane Beeler is the former Director of Labor Education. Drawing on their studies and experiences, they present three valuable approaches to the world of work.

TABLE OF CONTENTS

ACKNOWLEDGMENT

The authors wish to thank the following persons who read the manuscript: Daniel Krause, Michael Fishbein, Jonathan Smith, Tony Audia, Bill Bork, Paul Hampel, Roy Ockert, Seth Roberts, and Ben Shouse.

CREDITS

PAGE 79   Reprinted by permission of *Journal of Psychosomatic Research,* Vol. 11, pp. 213-218, T. H. Holmes and R. H. Rahe, "The Social Readjustment Rating Scale," 1967.

PAGE 141   *The Hidden Injuries of Class,* Richard Sennett and Jonathan Cobb. Reprinted by permission of the publisher, Alfred A. Knopf, Inc.

PAGE 143 *Opinion News,* Vol. 9, No. 4, September 1949, published by the National Opinion Research Center, Chicago. Near identical results of a later test appears in *American Journal of Sociology* Vol. 70, No. 3, November, 1964.

PAGE 162, 163, 164, 165   *The Wealth of Nations,* by Adam Smith. Published by Random House, Inc.

PAGES 166, 167, 168   *The Principles of Scientific Management,* by Frederick Winslow Taylor. Published by W. W. Norton and Co.

PAGES 191, 192   *The Lincoln Electric Company,* a pamphlet printed by the company August 1977, pages 361, 362, and 369. This was reprinted by permission of the publisher, Richard D. Irwin, Inc. of Homewood, Illinois, from *Policy Formulation and Administration,* by Christensen, Berg and Salter, Seventh Edition, 1976.

PAGES 211, 212   *Job Stress and the Police Officer,* a paper delivered by George Kirkham at a symposium held May 8-9, 1976 at Cincinnati; HEW Publication No. (NIOSH) 76-187.

PAGES 229, 230   *Democracy on the Shop Floor?* Eric Einhorn and John Logue, Kent Popular Press, Kent, Ohio, by permission of the authors.

book design • bernstein design group / chicago
printing • delaney printing company / hammond

INTRODUCTION

1 | MAKING SENSE OF OUR WORLD

THE NATURAL SCIENCES DEAL IN PRECISE INFORMATION such as the distance to Mars at a certain moment or the molecular structure of salt. But the social sciences do not supply us with such specific answers. While any grain of salt looks and functions the same as any other grain of salt, no two humans are exactly alike or behave exactly the same way in every situation. That's why any generalization about people must be taken with a grain of salt.

EXPERIENCES

Each person's personality and behavior are shaped by the millions of experiences he has had during his lifetime, although he may remember only a few unusual, coincidental or insightful experiences that made an indelible impression on him. Many of our basic attitudes toward ourselves and toward others are formed during infancy, so we are unaware of the experiences that influenced them.

Through the years we push out of our minds the unpleasant things that happened to us: the storekeeper catching us taking a candy bar, the time we backed our car into another car at the parking lot and didn't report it. Selective recall enables us to maintain our self-esteem and retain our sanity.

We usually do whatever comes naturally. When we face a problem, we rarely sit down and analyze the factors and choose the most suitable behavior. Instead, we continue to do whatever has served us well in the past; thus, the experiences that are crammed into our unconscious dominate our behavior.

However, I can't experience your experiences, and you can't

experience my experiences. In this sense, we are strangers to each other. Consequently, personality clashes are too often inevitable.

We are sensitive to the way others see us. If others think we are clever, so do we; if others are impressed by our athletic prowess, we picture ourselves as budding athletes.

What we think of ourselves influences how we behave. We would hardly expect a self-conscious and embarrassed youth to be the hit of the high school party. A person who is disappointed in himself is disappointed in the world.

We learn by doing. We learn by our mistakes. And what works well, we use again and again. Take the man who comes home late at night with no good excuse, and picks a fight with his wife about her housekeeping ability—because he has learned that the best defense against her complaints is a good offense.

Failure can teach us a lesson and lead to self-improvement— but it usually doesn't, because it is hard for us to change. We have to reverse the history of our previous experiences. We have to take a serious look inward and become convinced of the need to change. Typically, a man who is unhappy with his marriage does not change his behavior; he nags his wife to change hers. We finally realize if it is hard to change ourselves, it is a lot harder to change the world.

Self-interest is a prime motivating factor in behavior. When someone faces a situation that can affect his welfare, his first thought is about the impact it will have on him.

In some cases, what is best for our self-interest is so obvious that there is no other logical alternative. But in other cases, we have a range of options—and cannot proclaim any one alternative to be the true self-interest solution.

Take the 40-year old man who is offered a challenging new job in a distant city at a big salary increase. At first thought, why shouldn't he grab the opportunity? However, he has grown up where he is, and has many friends here; his wife has close bonds with her nearby relatives; and the children are all socially established in high school. Money is a powerful motivator; yet, recognizing his responsibilities as a husband and father, where does his true self-interest lie?

Human nature isn't always logical. We love our son very much, but he makes us angry because of the stupid things he does. We admire our union steward because of his capabilities, yet we dislike him because we envy him. We divorce a wife who constantly carps at us, and then marry the same kind of woman.

We try to understand the people we deal with by using the cues they provide—the words they speak, and the way they behave (which is often more revealing than the spoken words). If someone says he likes your dinner, but eats only part of it, or asks you how you feel, but doesn't listen to your answer, you know his true feelings.

If a person is insulted, he will get angry—but he may conceal his anger, or express it in various ways. He may attack the person verbally or even physically. Or he may smile and remain silent— then the next time he meets the other person, explode at him. It is human nature to get angry—but how a person responds depends upon his experience and training.

If a person moves into a position of higher status, he may enforce the standards of his new group more vigorously than do the other members. The new foreman follows all the rules to the letter; the newly rich man is ostentatious with his wealth; the recent convert is more pious than others of his faith.

CONCEPTS

Our senses reveal a world crammed with a continuous stream of experiences. Unless we can somehow categorize and label the events and ideas we experience, our brains would become overloaded by an avalanche of details.

By grouping things, we make it easier to deal with the complex world of sensation. We can then quickly react to new experiences, instead of being overwhelmed by the immense range of choices available.

When we group and label sensory data, we create concepts. Concepts are two or more distinguishable objects, events or ideas that are grouped together and set apart from others. Concepts are ways of packaging events in our environment into smaller, manageable categories. Once concepts are created, we can apply them to the complex new events we experience.

While no new situation is an exact duplicate of one already experienced, many situations differ only in insignificant ways. By classifying new situations in the established categories, we can behave as if they were the same as the old ones. Whenever we ask "What it that?", we are looking for a category in which to place a new experience.

Concepts are mental images that summarize our observations. Concepts are an essential part of communication and interaction; you and I, to agree, must use concepts that refer to the same mental pictures. The more we have in common, the more likely it is that our concepts will involve the same mental pictures, and the more likely it is that we will understand each other.

People are constantly categorizing and labeling information, even if they are unaware of doing so. Things that are different are frequently treated as equivalent: all the animals in the zoo are labeled wild animals, and thereby treated as being the same.

Some people can distinguish between a dangerous dog and a barking dog. A dangerous dog doesn't wag his tail and doesn't jump; he growls, and the hair around his neck and shoulders stands up. In contrast, a boy bitten by a dog may be afraid of all dogs; his concept is formed by one bad experience. To him all dogs are the same: he is afraid of all dogs, no matter how small and friendly they may be.

When people have no concept for what they encounter, anything can happen. A stranger in Africa, seeing a crowd of natives rushing toward him, may think they want to attack him; actually, what they want to do is to sell him something. A New Yorker, driving through Texas and seeing a big impediment on the road, might swerve to avoid it unless he knew it must be a tumbleweed.

Suppose a friend tells you that he's late because he lost 20 minutes in a gaper's lag—and you don't know what a gaper's lag is. He might explain that after an accident, drivers still slow down and look about, even after the damaged cars have been moved off to the shoulder. Or, you could figure it out if you had been caught a few times in a gaper's lag; then you could understand the concept in terms of your own experience.

Concepts are considered to be the building blocks of thought. They make it possible for us to go beyond the infinite number of stimuli we experience, and to create a structured and predictable world. Only by using concepts can we take advantage of the recurring regularities that run through our constantly changing sensory patterns. Concepts make it possible to formulate general rules that help us make sense out of specific situations.

When we group objects and events, we do so on the basis of their relevant and irrevelant characteristics. This is easiest to do when physical objects are involved; it is easy to distinguish sizes, shapes and colors.

ABSTRACT CONCEPTS

When we go beyond physical characteristics, we run into trouble. Physical characteristics lend themselves to simple, general and easily understood concepts; but abstract concepts can be learned only by reference to other basic concepts—that is, through verbal explanations. Justice is such a concept. In 1969, a student was given a 20-year sentence for having been caught with a marijuana cigarette on his person. Thousands of others have been stopped by the police for the same offense, yet released. Is this justice? What words would you use to describe the concept?

Consider the concept of love. Parents complain eternally that their children don't love them, because the children won't listen when the parents urge them to take certain jobs or certain spouses. Even an abstract concept such as love can evoke much argument.

Consider the concept of a good job. What shall we consider relevant or irrelevant in defining a good job? Is travel time to and from work an important feature? Is responsibility important? Variety? Possibility of promotion? Neither workers nor psychologists can agree on the elements of a good job.

Concepts can be classified in many ways. The most important types are class concepts, sequential concepts and relational concepts.

Class concepts are the easiest to deal with. Some common ones are chairs, cars and books. A child between the ages of 1½ and 6 averages over six such new words each day. He learns, for example, that the object in the kitchen is a chair. Later, he learns the limits of the concept: high chair, rocking chair, folding chair, overstuffed chair—but not love seat or sofa. Since it is impossible to learn all of this when young, concepts are fuzzy, and near-misses occur until maturity (and. often, beyond).

Sequential concepts are not very difficult to grasp; they involve series of elements; for example, the alphabet, the number system, and a series of squared numbers (1, 4, 9, 16, 25).

Relational concepts are the hardest to learn because they specify the nature of the linkage between different things. A simple example is the child who calls all men "daddy" until he learns that he has only one daddy; later, he learns that other men may be a daddy to other children. "Uncle" is still harder, because an uncle may be a brother to either the father or mother.

Concepts are complicated because each one is associated with a rule that indicates when it can be used. If the rule is not understood, concepts can become harmful and cause arguments.

As an example, consider the number of employed alcoholics who claim that they have no serious drinking problem. Most people would scoff: "He's eternally potted and still he says he's not a drunk?" But such critics fail to understand the rule the alcoholic uses. To him, the determining factor is that a drunk can't hold down a regular job. So when he blacks out, he doesn't regard that as a drinking problem. In his eyes, holding down a job and being an alcoholic are incompatible.

Concepts enable us to make generalizations about the world around us. By establishing concepts and categories, we reduce the number of discriminations that we must make. As we walk down the street, for example, we immediately fit the people approaching us into classifications, such as people going to work, housewives, school children, and senior citizens. By using such categories to sift out similarities and distinctions, we size up the people we meet. We decide if we will pass without acknowledging them, or smile, or say a word of greeting, or stop and talk.

STEREOTYPES

Stereotypes are concepts that do not allow for individual differences. They take one or more features and apply them to everyone in a class; they are often used to stigmatize people different from us. Thus, someone with stereotyped views might picture all Blacks as shiftless, all women as emotional, and all old people as boring.

If such a prejudiced person encounters contradictory information (for example, an eminently successful Black, a poised, controlled woman, a witty senior citizen), he has problems. If the stereotype is important to him, he may ignore the contradictory information or treat it as an exception to the rule.

This illustrates an important rule of human behavior: a fact is treated as a fact only if we accept it. We do not all see the same world out there. We create and represent the outside world using pictures in our head. It is not surprising that people frequently disagree about what the facts are. This is why our concepts can force us to distort what people are really like.

We need all kinds of concepts—even stereotypes. But why should we want to use such concepts when they often distort and stigmatize what people are really like?

Nobody has the time and patience to study people in a scientific fashion. We have to make some assumptions about what others are like. And these assumptions are built into stereotypes. The problem doesn't lie in the use of these social concepts; it lies in (1) a rigid attachment to them, and (2) a tendency to glorify ourselves by picturing others as being inferior.

When we limit our social concepts to negative traits, and refuse to test them against real life, then we caricature and dehumanize people. A Black person may have in common with all Black people the effects of racism and a distrust of white institutions. But to understand a specific Black person, we must find out what is unique about him and judge him for what he actually is.

Each of us is like others in some respects, and different in other ways from everybody else. To understand us, both facets of our personality must be accurately presented.

Ideally, stereotypes ought to help us anticipate what different categories of people have in common; adolescents and elderly; women and men; Catholics and Jews; Poles and Irish. They should help us figure out what to expect of others, how to treat them, and what we can take for granted. Just because stereotypes are wrongly used is no reason to ban them; they should be used in responsible and fair ways.

Categorizing people can help us determine the nature of our problems and suggest solutions for them. Suppose, for example, we find a high rate of tardiness and absenteeism at our workplace. We might categorize the workforce into men and women, old and young, skilled and unskilled, production and maintenance. Using these categories we can look for relationships. We might discover that the rates are highest among younger workers and women workers. Further analysis might reveal that the women are working mothers who have difficulty getting children off to school, and that the young workers are young adults who behave like typical adolescents—they stay up late at night, don't know the kind of work they want, and are not disciplined in the work ethic. Thus, knowledge of the characteristics of each group enables us to explain the high rate of absenteeism of certain groups. Armed with that knowledge, we can devise remedial programs.

Similarly, if we were to analyze the high turnover rate, we might discover that it is the newly hired workers who often leave within six months. We can interview these workers before they leave; investigate our hiring practices; and examine our orientation program. After collecting and analyzing such data, we may come to conclusions about how to select and treat workers so they will stay with the company. Again, by classifying workers and understanding their problems, we can move on to solutions.

The way we categorize the physical world, the social world, and the task world can facilitate or impede our understanding and problem solving. If we use too few categories, we may overlook important differences; if we make too many fine-grained differentiations, we may fail to see common features. If we blindly force concepts and stereotypes on things and people, then we misperceive, distort and destroy the reality of our world; if we try to preserve uniqueness and treat everything as different, then we get washed away in a flood of disconnected experiences.

We must strive for a balance that allows our concepts to create for us a stable world—one that mirrors the important similarities and differences among objects, events, and ideas in our experiences.

Then our inner world—because it now reflects reality—will help us treat people fairly, and successfully solve the problems we encounter.

DRAWING CONCLUSIONS

Concepts are not sole determiners of thought and action. Another factor is the process of drawing conclusions. If their reasoning is faulty, people can torture themselves. Unfortunately, many people are very self-destructive, as the following examples show.

ARBITRARY INFERENCE   Depressed people distort their experiences because of their low opinion of themselves and so are very self-destructive. For example, if a depressed person is at a boring party, he may stubbornly insist that it is his presence that is preventing others from having a good time. He arbitrarily misinterprets situations, makes himself feel miserable and inferior, and destroys his chances for happiness.

SELECTIVE ABSTRACTING   When a supervisor criticizes a single feature of a worker's performance, the worker may conclude that the supervisor is dissatisfied with all of his work. By focusing on that one feature and ignoring most of what happens, the worker can become convinced that he is being treated unfairly, and ruin his relations with his supervisor and fellow workers.

OVERGENERALIZATION   A person may draw broad conclusions on the basis of an isolated set of incidents. For example, a mother visits a friend, notes that her own children aren't as well behaved as her friend's, and concludes that she isn't a good mother. Her feeling of inadequacy may be so strong that she may even consider giving up her teaching job because she is not capable of properly educating children.

MAGNIFICATION AND MINIMIZATION   A worker may picture a simple task as impossibly difficult (magnification), and ridicule his abilities to carry it out (minimization). Clearly, a person must perceive his abilities accurately so that he will take on jobs at which he can succeed, and not waste his time on discouraging tasks that are beyond his capabilities. If he doesn't, he'll never reach his potential for success.

ABSOLUTIST THINKING   Many people think in absolutes; they believe that a person is either happy or unhappy, good or bad, rich or poor, successful or unsuccessful. But the world consists of gradations; most of the people fall between the two extremes. People are happy *some* of the time, but they are also unhappy some of the time, too. And so it goes with any trait.

SELF-SABOTAGE   When a person fails to achieve a goal, his self-esteem is threatened by the failure unless he can logically explain it away. However, many people don't do a good job of accounting for their failures, and lose their self-respect. Suppose, for example, that a man fails a civil service exam. He can conclude that he is incompetent, stupid, lazy, or suffers from any number of other inadequacies. On the other hand, his explanation can focus on external features: the test was unfair, the room was too noisy, or he was hampered by other unfavorable circumstances. The explanations chosen affects his mental health and motivation to a substantial degree. When the explanation alleges that he suffers from permanent defects, it can cripple him socially and in the workplace. His self-confidence can be so weakened by such explanations that he becomes a helpless pawn of fate.

Explanations of failures may be even more important in social interactions. Say a woman is spurned at a singles bar by a man to whom she has made overtures. Her possible explanations of the snub: "No one likes me"; "I just didn't get on his level of conversation"; "Men don't like intelligent women"; "I'm not his type"; "He's one of those who think they are superior to all women"; or "Under other circumstances, we really could have hit it off." Her confidence and self-esteem would be affected differently by each of these explanations. Which one she chooses will determine how she will view men—and, more importantly, how she will view herself.

When people structure their experiences in self-defeating ways, they need to substitute more realistic patterns of thinking. This is not easy; once self-destructive patterns are firmly established, they're hard to change.

All in all, our thoughts and perceptions are very important. They determine how realistic we can be about ourselves, about other people, and about the outside world in general. And they help us understand why workers behave the way they do.

PSYCHOLOGY

2 | TECHNOLOGY: FRIEND OR FOE?

THE MOST SERIOUS PROBLEMS WORKERS FACE are (1) the threats to their jobs from rapid change in technologies and the increasing competitiveness of imports, and (2) threats to their health from the high level of occupational stress.

A hundred years ago, a worker might have lived and worked under much harder conditions than today—but he could at least expect to get a job and (barring major depression) spend his working years in one kind of work.

Today, as is shown by the increasing numbers of unemployed blue *and* white-collar workers, no one can assume that his job is secure. Even seniority is of little value. New technologies and growing industrialization are making whole factories and occupations obsolete in the United States.

The new economic pressure of international competition is being exploited by company management. The companies are pressuring trade unions to turn back the clock to the condition that existed before the Wagner Act, and are attacking OSHA on economic grounds, although occupational cancers, skin diseases, neurological diseases, and lung diseases—to name a few—have sickened, crippled and killed large numbers of workers.

We only have to go back to the early days of the railroads and the mines to see how dirt cheap the life of a worker has been considered, and how it can be wasted for the most *trivial* of economic gains. Substantial progress was made during the middle of this century, but now this progress is being seriously endangered.

Thus, it is important to take stock of the situation. Let us begin by examining what human beings are like, how they are affected by the things that happen to them and how environmental conditions act on them.

As human beings, we have certain strengths and weaknesses; we have various needs; and we have great potentials which we ought to realize and take pride in.

But relatively few workers feel that their lives are as rich, happy, and satisfying as they should be. Dissatisfaction and misery are so extensive that the papers constantly talk about alcoholism, violence, mental illness, and drug abuse—and these are only the tip of the iceberg.

What went wrong? Why aren't we expressing and developing all the goodness and capacities that we possess? It has been frequently said that life is precious. But if this is more than a cliche, why are so many of our talents and capacities left unused?

Apparently, the families in which we grew up, and the workplaces in which we spend most of our waking lives, have failed us.

For many of us, our homes and families have not made it possible for us to bloom. And, where the family and home have succeeded, the workplace has frequently buried our capabilities under a mountain of bureaucratic rules and a suffocating hierarchical organization.

The typical manager's behavior appears to proclaim: "When you enter our company, check your brains at the door and leave the thinking to us." Complementing this attitude is the protective reaction of the typical worker: "I only work here; ask the boss."

Can either managers or workers be faithful to their human nature under these conditions? Is a person more than a person if he lacks a heart *or* becomes an appendage of either a machine or a system? Probably not.

For too long we have ignored the spill-over of the workplace into the home and community. It's very difficult for a person to remain unaffected by his job and by the way he is forced to act while on the job. People who are given no opportunity at work to show initiative, to participate in decision-making, or to rise to the level of their competence are seriously affected. People who follow orders 40 hours a week can't easily become analytic problem solvers and fully involved citizens upon leaving the workplace. And if their stressed bodies have accumulated potentially harmful biochemicals, these chemicals aren't thrown out of their bloodstreams when the workers go home.

Fatigue, tension, impatience, and even a tendency to violence are the workplace burdens that many of us are forced to carry home with us daily. These psychological burdens are no different from what we might carry home in our work clothes. Just as the invisible fibers can contaminate the furniture and rugs at home and other clothes that are being washed, gradually sickening other members of the family, so the psychological strains can have long-term harmful effects. For example, stress diseases such as coronary heart diseases, ulcers, and hypertension can be created by exposure to these harmful states. It is a heavy price to pay for the right to hold a job.

The workplace affects us not only because we have to perform certain types of work and remain within certain kinds of environments, but also because it imposes certain patterns of relating to people. These patterns are hammered into us when we are formally required to function in certain ways and when—to protect ourselves—we form unofficial, informal social groups. Once crystallized, we adapt these patterns to the community as well.

After all, a person isn't a pie; his life can't be cut up into pieces, with each piece comprising a separate lifestyle. What happens to us all through the day affects the way we think, act and treat our family, friends and co-workers.

Let us examine doctors. Their divorce rate is relatively high. One reason may be that in their offices and in the hospitals, doctors are top bananas. They learn to expect the nurses (typically women) to cater to their whims and to automatically carry out their orders. Many nurses hold doctors in awe, treating them as if they were some kind of savior.

Not surprisingly, when a doctor comes home, he may continue to act as if his wife were another kind of nurse—a woman who is supposed to obey, cater and respect. Moreover, the ads in doctors' journals suggest that his women patients typically have psychological components to their illnesses. Frequently a doctor may not take their complaints seriously. Instead, he may turn on his bedside manner, and quickly get rid of the woman by writing out a prescription for some drug.

By the time a doctor's day is finished, he's frequently sick of sickness, especially sick women. If he comes home and finds his wife isn't feeling well, she may find that her doctor husband has no patience for the patient at home. His wife might get neither adequate treatment nor gentle sympathy. His day at work has burned out the doctor; his quota of sympathy, kindness and consideration has been used up.

Some doctors' wives say, half-jokingly, that the only way they can get proper attention from their mates is by making an apponntment in the office. Children of doctors sometimes say they never get to know their fathers. Their doctor fathers were either treating patients, reading journals at home, or just too damned tired.

As you can see from this example, it is important to know what people are like, and what the world of work does to them. We need to be as realistic as possible about our personalities, our families, and our workplaces. We need to examine how our experiences affect us; only in that way can we understand ourselves, our co-workers, and our place in society. But most of all, we must be aware of the new world that is fast closing in on us.

In this book, we talk first about personality development. The early family and school influences nurture the seeds that finally bloom into the persons we become. These institutions largely determine the way we relate to our family and co-workers, and the kinds of things that make us happy and that cause us grief.

After examining the early chapters, you will understand better why each of us is a unique person who can't be treated in a mechanical and uniform way. It's not just that our goals and needs are different; our strengths and weaknesses vary. It is ironic that while we recognize that all complex machines can't be treated in the same way, we often fail to recognize that all people can't be treated in the same way. Their abilities and failings are too special to be lumped together.

In the workplace, individual differences are grossly ignored. You are probably already familiar with the general philosophy of organizations in the business world. But you may be surprised to learn the costs that these bureaucracies impose even on their managers and executive leaders. While they rarely suffer from the occupational diseases from which their workers do, they often suffer from psychologically crippling team-playing.

Managers must be highly motivated to optimize profits and power. To get ahead, they must bend their wills to the corporate goals. Generally, as Maccoby's study shows, that means frequently discarding empathy, compassion, generosity, idealism and even honesty. As one manager put it: "I'd never get anything done. It would be impossible to deal with people if I were concerned about such things!"

Managers, in Maccoby's words, are in danger of losing their *hearts:* the ability to be deeply loving and to show the kind of interest and personal support that goes with the ability to rise above self-centeredness. Both at work and at home, managers tend to erect a wall around their feelings which makes it hard for anyone to touch them. Emotion and feeling are equated with being a bleeding heart, a sucker who lets others manipulate him by arousing feelings of guilt.

When organizations seek mechanical, impersonal efficiencies, everybody pays a price. When workers are treated as being less valuable than equipment and profits, everybody loses—from those at the top to those at the bottom.

It thus becomes important to consider leadership styles, hierarchies of power and authority, and the degree of participation open to workers. The organization is a tool—and, like any tool, can be beneficial or horribly misused. Thus, we must examine how procedures and methods of operations of modern organizations affect workers.

The most widely cited justification for the modern organization is the constraining effect of its technologies and machinery. People, it is often claimed, must adjust themselves to the machines: the machines are too difficult and expensive to replace and change. And, even if we could afford it, the technologies of today can't be discarded or significantly changed without losing our ability to compete with the Japanese, the Germans, and others.

Of course, the argument is also used that people can take it; we can even get used to working in temperatures of 120 degrees. In contrast, a computer would jam and be down much of the time if it had to operate in that kind of temperature. But who can say that the people don't suffer too? Machines, technologies and conditions do affect us; we challenge the notion that machines must come first.

History has shown that societies have become resigned to terrible conditions. As late as the 1800's, small children in England worked in mines and mills, suffering early deaths. In the early days of railroading in the United States, the rails spanned the Rockies on human bodies. The early railroad switchmen and brakemen had a life expectancy of seven years on the job. It is only recently that we have learned of the terrible effects of gases and dusts on the worker. "That's life!" people said, as they resigned themselves to years of painful physical disabilities.

In the past, the artistic, the creative and the wealthy were the only ones who were treated as having the right to develop themselves fully. The common man was supposed to work and suffer—and work and suffer he did. Eighteen hour workdays and the most cruel and inhuman work conditions were defended then as being part of the Lord's plan.

But recently the idea of self-development has been broadened to apply to the common man. We insist that machines *can* be adapted to meet our needs as human beings. People *can* come first. And *everybody* has a right to a life that is free from both physical and psychological crippling.

Let's look at people, organizations, and technologies—the heart of the workplace—and see what they're really like.

3 | GROWING UP

THE FAMILY IS THE MOST IMPORTANT SOCIAL INSTITUTION. Here, future citizens are created and trained. But our development isn't limited to the family years; between birth and death, we are constantly changing. These physical and psychological changes, whether they occur inside or outside the family, are the ones that concern us here.

People move through various stages in the life cycle from birth to old age. Knowing about these stages will help us understand what people are like, the kinds of problems they experience, and the consequences of their treatment in the different phases. While the phases are broken up into age groupings, they are not fixed in concrete. The important thing we want to stress is how the *effects* of the different phases are reflected in our adult behavior.

THE BABY

Babies—especially boys—are very vulnerable. Their homeostatic mechanisms (internal processes that compensate for environmental changes) are poor. Babies need all kinds of protection which only caretakers can provide.

Not surprisingly, how a baby is treated is of crucial importance. If babies are treated roughly or allowed to stay wet or hungry too long, what they learn is this: "People don't care whether I am comfortable or suffer. The world must be a very bad and dangerous place."

But, you might say with skepticism, we're talking about *babies*. Babies are pretty stupid creatures; what can such creatures know and learn?

True, babies can't think or talk, but they can *feel* intensely everything that affects them. Just watch a baby cry and scream when left hungry for very long. Feelings cause babies to develop automatic reactions to people and to the things that go on inside them—for example, being hungry. Such emotional learning and conditioning develops in all animals and even plants; it's not necessary to be a brilliant adult to be affected by the way we're treated.

Problems can develop for children at this early age for two basic reasons:

• Parents may not be sensitive enough to recognize how their baby needs to be treated. Children are very different; one may want to be fed every four hours, while another is hungry every two hours. Some are very active and want company much of the time, while others are inactive and just seem to enjoy looking around or sleeping.

• Parents may try to hurry the maturation of their children. For example, some children can be weaned to solid foods rapidly while others need much more time. Parents can be too impatient to accept their baby's rate of change.

Parents are only human. They make mistakes in handling their children, and they become angry and frustrated. Ideally, parent and child adjust to each other in a process called mutual regulation. However, parents have much more capacity to change and control themselves than children do, so most of the responsibility for pacing falls on the shoulders of parents. If parents accept that responsibility, then they can teach their babies a most fundamental attitude toward life: people and the world are safe places to be in and around; even when you're miserable, don't be discouraged—better times are around the corner.

When parents are rough and mechanical, they can lay the foundation for mental illness. Well-adjusted people are those who can say that horrible times and experiences will pass, that happier times await them in the future. This kind of attitude develops only if a baby is handled effectively; his bad times must be followed promptly by good times. A baby who suffers and suffers can't develop such an attitude of hoping for better times; his parents didn't come through in the right way. Mutual regulation and a capacity for hope are critical elements of development at this time.

THE CHILD

One of the most important responsibilities we have as parents is the socialization of our children. Among other things, we are expected to toilet train them, teach them to speak well, and instill obedience. Adults believe that such learning is logical and straightforward. Going "to potty" is so reasonable in our eyes, as opposed to continuing to mess the diapers, that frequently we get very annoyed with our children until they are toilet trained. It is a nuisance to have a child in diapers, and we take it as a reflection on our competence as parents.

The important idea to keep in mind is that socialization (toilet training, obedience) makes sense to us, but *not* to two and three-year-olds. Let us look at toilet training through the eyes of the child. If he relieves himself in the potty, he is praised as if he did a most wonderful thing. But when he does the same thing on the front-room rug, the whole house falls in. This confuses a child: how can feces be both good and bad?

The "crazy" rules we force upon the child make as much sense to him as do many of the bureaucratic rules that are imposed on us. But just as we learn to knuckle under and obey these onerous rules because it pays, so does the child. Given time and reasonable incentives (love, attention and rewards), the child will memorize the stupid rules.

Some parents are infuriated by what they consider rebellion. They see no reason why toilet training or instilling obedience should take so long. In some cases, their anger and resentment build up until the child ends up battered and bruised.

The reasons for the delay are basic. Children are limited in their ability to understand rules. Also, they have a very important need: the need to begin to act independently. The words "no" and "don' wanna" seem to be used all the time at the ages of two and three. Parents who want to be ruler of the roost are particularly aggravated by such negativism and attempts at autonomy, and they are tempted to let their fists do the socializing.

Remember that a child must develop a feeling of being his own man. Just as a tree evolves slowly from a sapling to a full grown tree, so a child must develop independence little by little. Within limits, children need to do things the way they want.

This point is extremely important. *Nobody,* not even children, accepts being told what to do all the time. Think about your work; would you like it if your supervisor gave you orders all day long on every single thing? Adults hate that kind of dictating—and so do children.

If a child is allowed to grow at his own rate, he can successfully learn and accept our rules and regulations. He makes the rules part of his way of thinking—the way he himself wants to act. Under these conditions, problems with negativism and obedience fade away.

Sounds simple, doesn't it? All we have to do is let a child develop at his own pace. Suppose a child persists in opening the gas jets on the stove. The parents stop him, lecture him, and finally hit him. The next day the boy walks toward the stove while saying: "Don't put on the stove," then opens the gas jets. Many parents would conclude that the child is being maliciously rebellious and would want to teach him a lesson. On the contrary, though, it simply takes a long time for a child to learn to stop (inhibit) himself from doing something.

As children mature, they become more skilled in performing their activities and want to demonstrate their new abilities to an appreciative audience. Now, instead of "no" and "don't wanna," we have "myself, myself." (Don't do it for me; I want to do it myself.) Also, "Look mommy; me do it too." (I am capable of doing things and want you to applaud when I do them.)

Parents, unfortunately, are frequently bored and very busy. It's much easier to *do* things for a three or four year old, and it's much more entertaining to talk to adults or watch TV. Children, therefore, develop techniques to attract and hold the attention of parents. To avoid being left to his own devices, a child might have to ask questions, beg his parents to read to him, or constantly talk about how much he loves his mommy and daddy.

The importance of the child-parent companionship can't be overestimated. Parents are the most important figures in the world of the child. His relationship to them is deeper, continues over a longer period of time, and is reciprocated. Thus, parents, by interacting frequently with their children during the day, can nurture language skills and role learning, something that is critical at this stage.

The family is like a little society, and makes it possible for children to learn roles. The traditional family, which includes a mother, father and children, provides the best set of models. A child can observe the activities of the two sexes and the different age groups. The child sees what others do, and tries to imitate them. He or she can play at being a mommy or daddy, a grown-up, or a child. By testing his observations in play, a child can practice the roles of the family members and cut them down to his size.

Just as actors use the stage to master a play, so children must play to make sense out of their observations and interpretations. In play, children enact the roles of mommy, daddy, adults, man and woman. Frequently they try to play the same roles with the parents themselves.

Sometimes this imitation is humorous. A child might say: "Mommy, when I grow up I'm going to marry you"; and parents smile. What a ridiculous and funny idea! However, when a child tries to drive the car just like daddy, it might not be so funny. Children aren't objective and realistic. They don't yet recognize their limitations. Part of our task is to teach them about expected behavior: what's right for a child to do; what only parents and adults can do; and what's appropriate only for boys or girls to do. We must teach them about the masculine and feminine roles (sex roles), the age roles, and the parental roles.

It's not an easy task, as you may have discovered yourself. Moreover, a child's need for attention can incite jealousy. Evenings and weekends are precious hours parents may want for themselves.

One parent may actually become jealous because of all the attention the spouse shows to the children. The parents may fight and even hurt each other. When that happens, a child can be caught between the parents and suffer a great deal. Most adults find it hard enough to compete in the outside world; to compete in their own homes with their own children—that's too much!

When parents respect each other's needs, show love and affection to a child, and set realistic limits for the child's imitations, then social roles can be made part of the child's thinking and behavior. Under these circumstances a child says: "I want to be just like mommy or daddy," something we call identification. When that happens, a child has accepted the values and behavior of his parents as the ones he will enact.

Note that we use the plural, parents. Both boys and girls must identify with both parents. Why are both necessary? Think of a baseball team; can the shortstop play his position without knowing the tasks and behavior of the other infield players? No. Neither can we be effective in our relations with the opposite sex without knowing how they think, how they value things, and how they act. We must be able to think of ourselves in their position. This capability for empathy is based on a child's detailed and long-term observation of his family.

SCHOOL EXPERIENCES

During the elementary school years, children are exposed to a new environment and a whole new set of rules. The school and the peer group (persons of the same rank) become very important and decrease the influence of parents on children.

At home, children are important; parents ooh and ahh over little things a child does. But the classrooms are filled with many of these "stars" who want special treatment and recognition; the primary problem of a teacher becomes discipline. However, no teacher can be deeply concerned with all of her students—so children have to learn to get along in a competitive, impersonal world.

To adjust to the school atmosphere, children are forced to learn the three C's: how to compete, cooperate, and compromise. Children must learn to share the teacher, to take turns at getting and holding her attention.

If a child can do this by achieving, fine. But if a child is not academically successful enough to capture the teacher's attention, then he may have to resort to attention-getting trouble-making. Because order is so important, no teacher can afford to ignore a trouble-maker. Such children obtain attention by being yelled at and by obstructing. It is ironic that by making a fuss about misbehavior, teachers can encourage it.

The school also teaches cooperation. In team play in the gym, and in such competition as spelling bees, children learn to work together to achieve goals. They learn to share defeat as well as victory, to ride with the team. Each member, facing what he did or failed to do, feels proud or ashamed because of his contribution. Such analyses and experiences teach children the nature and limits of their abilities.

It is during the school years that children realize that their parents' rules may be arbitrary and unfair. As a child becomes friendly with classmates and visits their homes, he sees how other parents treat children.

His parents may, for example, insist that eight o'clock is bedtime. But a child may find that others go to bed at nine o'clock. So he says: "John and Bob never have to go to bed till nine o'clock; why do I have to go at eight o'clock?"

Parents are toppled from their pedestals as their children compare their families with others. A child can begin to correct any peculiar ideas held by his own parents. He discovers that many rules are based on convention (how others do it) and power motivations (I'm the boss).

In short, students develop more realistic attitudes about their parents, learn to size up their mates, and develop a reputation for themselves. By working with others, they see what they're good at and where they fail. They learn to accept some failure, and to overcome it under the gun of competition.

Such objectivity is possible because the school system and peer group evaluate the child more objectively than does the family; a child's awareness of his strengths and weaknesses improves markedly. The danger lies in his not finding enough to be proud of, and perhaps in being rejected by others if he is too different. That is most likely to happen when stereotypes, prejudice, and bias make it impossible for a child to be viewed as he really is.

Up to this point, children have had many experiences, but they haven't become skilled at putting many of them into a proper perspective. Parents, too, for the most part, don't take to heart the embarrassments, failures, and frustrations of their children, and are of little help.

To compensate, a child needs a chum, a special friend who is trustworthy and can keep a secret. With such a friend, a child isn't afraid to open up and pour his heart out. When he does, he is surprised. He finds that his embarrassments, failures and frustrations are similar to those of his chum. What he once pictured as unique to himself, he finds is common; and by talking over his problems he feels better. Such exchanges and confidences are crucial. Through them a child comes to experience a concern for a chum that he never fully felt before. This new feeling is compassion, the ability to consider others' feelings as being as important as—or more important than—your own.

By focusing on someone else, a child learns how his actions can affect others; how he can make them happy and ecstatic, or can even shatter or demoralize them. Without a chum, children tend to grow up feeling they're very different from everybody else, and that others do not have the problems and feelings they do. Adults who have such attitudes may need psychiatric care.

ADOLESCENCE

Once an adolescent enters puberty, his physical and sexual development spurts forward. In a year or two, a boy or girl can gain inches of height and many pounds of weight. Girls are, on the average, about two years ahead of boys.

As the growth spurt emerges, the adolescent's body changes markedly. Physically, the adolescent must learn to maneuver his larger arms and legs. Most do this successfully; a few go through an awkward phase, knocking over glasses at the dinner table and tripping over their own feet. Psychologically, the adolescent must become accustomed to his new look. To do so, adolescents spend a lot of time examining their bodies in the mirror and comparing them with those of other people.

These body changes are stressful, and it requires time to become adjusted to them. Given time, most learn to live with their new bodies. However, acne and delayed menstruation can make adolescents so uncomfortable that emotional problems arise and can require treatment.

Adolescents also go through a number of changes that relate to secondary sexual characteristics. Boys develop beards and deeper voices; girls develop breasts and pubic and underarm hair. Such changes occur within a wide range of times.

Adolescents tend to worry a great deal about these changes. If the changes occur *later* than typically found in his group, the adolescent is worried. When the change occurs, the adolescent worries. And, if the change occurs *earlier* than typically found in the group, the adolescent is concerned. But, as you might imagine, the early bird is emotionally better off than the late bloomer.

The adolescent's examinations don't stop at his skin and body form. He also starts analyzing his beliefs and assumptions, and evaluates the conclusions that flow from them. Suppose his parents claim to live by ethical standards, with his father insisting that he is law-abiding and honest in his business dealings. But at the dinner table, the father brags about how he put one over on the union, and how he is chiseling on taxes. The son is indignant: "How can you call yourself honest, and then cheat?"

His father might be bewildered and incensed: "You don't understand life; you always have to be practical and make the best deal." To which the son might reply: "Hypocrite. You say one thing and do another."

It is not surprising that an adolescent eventually attacks the social system, the family, and all kinds of beliefs. In fact, he may very well be attracted to off-shoot political ideas—even the Moonies—anything that appears to be honest and not hypocritical. To the adolescent, one is either honest or a crook, religious or a faker, good or bad—at least at this particular time. For this reason, the adolescent is vulnerable to revolutionary groups; they know he is looking for a cause and is willing to die for it. Capitalizing on this vulnerability, many extremist groups find it easy to recruit adolescents.

Boys and girls find they have a keen interest in each other, in talking, in having physical contact, and even in sexual interactions. These needs can be very strong, and the adolescent has to learn to integrate them into his social relations.

Our society seriously complicates sexual relations. Masculinity is defined in terms of being sexually active: a male is supposed to use his line and proceed to make out. If he fails to get aroused and successfully employ his line, the implication is—heaven forbid—homosexuality.

Picture the adolescent couple who are insecure and uncertain about themselves. The boy feels he must demonstrate that he is a real male and must go as far as he can. A girl, according to the social stereotype, must be attractive and sexy, but still keep the boy within the limits she has set.

Today, with sex described as a natural phenomenon, limits are difficult to set. Because many high school students have sexual relations with minimum use of contraceptives, an epidemic of abortions and unmarried mothers has broken out.

The problems the adolescent faces in regard to sexual maturation are twofold:
• How can I define myself as a male or female? How must I behave to show I'm a genuine male or female?
• In my relations with the opposite sex, how can I be popular and still stay within the limits I want to set?

With reasonable upbringing, good social relationships, and a harmonious family life, the adolescent can come through this period successfully. But many parents don't have the kind of influence on their children that makes it possible for their children to avoid being pulled into peer group fads and fashions.

Whether the adolescent is lured by drugs or sex or by more worthy endeavors, depends upon the values and reference groups he accepts. It is these groups that determine the identity an adolescent shapes for himself: the kind of person he believes he is. Included in his identity are his ideas about his physical appearance, abilities, motivations, values, and the roles he wants and must assume. However, the adolescent identity is inaccurate and incomplete; it takes adult experiences to make the necessary corrections.

4 | ADULTHOOD

ADULTHOOD CAN BE DEFINED IN TERMS OF AGE, the accomplishment of certain tasks, or psychological characteristics such as maturity. However, none of these three alone is adequate. Adulthood can begin at 18, 19, 20, or 25; the traditional developmental tasks of marriage and child-rearing don't apply to many people; and few people can agree on what maturity actually means. Therefore, we define adulthood as some combination of the three: the period when an individual does such things as completing school or leaving home, taking a full-time job, or getting married. These life events give entry into the adult world. Because many of them are now occurring very close together, the pace of living has accelerated in recent decades.

YOUNG ADULTS

A young adult is expected to break the strings that tie him to family, peer groups and pre-adult institutions, and to begin to carve out a niche for himself in the adult world. To be successful, he must consolidate his identity and apply his decision-making skills to three crucial areas: values, interpersonal relations, and career orientation. However, he doesn't feel completely independent; he seems to be half in and half out of the nest.

For a number of years, the young adult may experiment with various options open to him in the three basic areas.

In regard to values, he soon discovers that his idealism isn't practical, and must be adapted to real-life dimensions. He must analyze and understand the rules by which our society operates. In particular, he must come to terms with the relativism of our everyday transactions. Whether he adheres to a rigid code, or concludes that there are no right or wrong answers—only the practical and the unrealistic—depends heavily on his moral and religious commitments. In any case, ethical co-existence is essential to acceptance and advancement in the adult world.

In the interpersonal arena, dating can be a source of fun and recreation—or a serious matter, a means for selecting a mate. If fun and recreation are the goals, the young adult stresses his line, and seeks to develop sexual intimacies without getting bogged down in commitments. Sometimes he finds that difficult; many women demand some kind of commitment before accepting sexual arrangements. Whether the fun and games last for any period of time is dependent upon the conditions set by the party who is least interested in maintaining the relationship. If serious goals are pursued, then the young adult must seek a broad enough range of social contacts to find and woo an appropriate partner. In general, unless significant efforts are made, a person is likely to marry someone from his or her own social environment.

While marriage isn't the only basis for a continuing family arrangement—there are now over a million non-legal "husband-wife" homes—marriage is still the most popular basis for family living. Ideally, the spouses learn to develop a shared identity as well as to sharpen and strengthen their individual identities. If either spouse is insecure (has a weak identity), can't give up the options open to single people, or rejects the values of the other, the marriage is in danger of breaking up. In fact, almost half of all new marriages break up within the first few years. With the current rejection of the traditional value system, people have all kinds of options—from the positions in intercourse to fulltime careers without children. Not surprisingly, it's more difficult to find the common ground and compromises that can keep both spouses happy.

If the couple decides to have children, then the birth of the child creates stress. Sleeplessness and inexperience are problems, and the new responsibilities and modified schedules can magnify pre-existing tensions. The exclusiveness of the husband-wife relationship is shattered, and many parents find this period an especially difficult one. Fortunately, most parents can find enough satisfaction to compensate for the burdensome bundle of joy. Ideally, too, the birth of a child serves to strengthen the love bonds that tie the parents together.

The area of work and career involves one of the most important tasks that young adults face. Both uncertainty and reality shock represent significant problems. New occupations keep appearing;

the supply and demand for workers in old occupations keep changing; and training and experiential requirements keep increasing. It has become very hard to plan ahead effectively; from year to year, the job market changes.

In any new job, a trainee must acquire technical skills and interpersonal behaviors, and must learn to fit into the authority relationships that regulate the work group. A young adult may find one or another of these features distasteful or beyond his capacity. Consequently, he may wander from job to job until he can make a mature choice. He must determine whether he possesses the skills the job demands, the degree to which improvement on the job is possible, and the extent to which the job will provide pleasure and satisfaction.

In short, finding the right job frequently turns out to be much harder than expected—and adjustment to the job more extensive than had been anticipated. One very acute danger is that a young adult will commit himself too early in order to avoid searching for the best fitting job; or, repelled by the unpleasant aspects of every job, he will continue to wander until the "perfect" job is found—although it doesn't exist.

A family life style must be integrated with the demands of the job. In a large percentage of cases, the job demands are treated as primary and the family demands as secondary. However, the family members have to live with such an arrangement. If not, the job must be changed or the tension may lead to divorce or illness of one kind or another.

Men and women evaluate this stage differently. A woman, once committed to marriage and a family, finds the adjustment relatively easier. She has previously played a dependent role, can derive a sense of accomplishment from her management of the household, and has successfully met the traditional society's criteria for being a successful woman—she has proven herself.

In contrast, a man has not yet proven himself; the masculine criteria of independence, occupational competency, and being a good provider are not yet achieved. Thus, women tend to become warmer and more nurturant; their cost is their independence and the chance for a career. Men, in seeking to fulfill the role of provider, stress independence and competence; their cost is dependence and emotional sensitivity.

What about the ERA woman and the two-paycheck family? Everything depends on the understanding that develops in the family. Arrangements can be successfully worked out; these can range from palimony patterns to supportive arrangements that make it possible for both spouses to create career lines for themselves. The costs? That remains to be seen. Clearly, more families will have one or no children; and in many families, children are spending much less time with parents and more time with TV and electronic games.

By his 30's, an adult has learned to respond to people without becoming anxious; to make decisions on the basis of his own personal experiences and values; to apply values and appreciate their relationship to social settings; and to broaden his commitments to the family and workplace. He has established a new home base for himself, explored and committed himself to adult roles and responsibilities, and has more precisely defined the kind of person he is. His self-concept has been expanded to include the effects of his encounters with the real world of courtship, marriage, parenthood, work and community.

In the mid-30's, however, questions frequently surface about the wisdom of previous decisions. Many people have the uneasy feeling that they have been doing the wrong things; their behavior and personal relationships seem to lack that oomph, that Tony the Tiger *great* feeling. As life becomes more serious, many people wonder whether they ought to change life styles, jobs, spouses, etc., in order to live really happy and full lives. Sometimes the result is a job or career shift or even a divorce. But more frequently people, after analyzing their lives, conclude that they're on the right track. When that kind of conclusion is reached, the person has reaffirmed his decisions and treated them as wise and responsible ones.

MIDDLE AGE

In introducing middle age (40-65), one author of a book heads the chapter "Health, money, love, and the time to enjoy them." He referred to the fact that people in the middle years are basically in good health and financially more secure; in many ways, they have attained the prime of life. Middle-aged adults constitute an influential segment of the adult population; they are the most powerful and wealthy age group in the United States.

Our society frequently talks about the 20's and 30's as being the best years. In reality, however, young adults are under extreme pressure to achieve everything; their theme might be described as: "I better make it now before aging cripples me." Not surprisingly, many people try to stretch out the period of young adulthood by thinking and acting young.

The middle-aged consider themselves—and are considered by others—to be happiest. The middle-aged can get things done; they feel confident and effective in almost any situation; they are skilled in using others when necessary to accomplish tasks; and they give advice and aid to others of all ages,. Still, they do experience crises and trials. Let's examine some of the most important ones.

Biological changes take place all through our lives. The cumulative effects of our gradual aging begin to be noticeable by the middle years. Each person possesses a cellular clock which determines such things as when our hair becomes greyer and thinner; when our skin loses its natural oils, becomes less elastic and appears wrinkled; when the fatty deposits under our skin decrease, making our faces sag; and when our muscle tone decreases, causing us to lose flexibility, power, and speed.

Even more important, our bodies are significantly more vulnerable. Over half the people in middle age have some form of chronic disease (asthma, emotional problems, sensory problems, etc.), although only a small minority are severely disabled by them. Excessive exertion immediately evokes severe fatigue and signs of physical strain. We sleep less well, suffer more from indigestion, and see doctors more often.

Men tend to worry more than women do about the loss of physical capabilities, and strive to maintain their bodie's performance. In general, their concerns are realistic; men do suffer more from physical impairment, and their occupational complications are more serious. Men suffer more from coronary heart diseases, manifest more visual and hearing problems, and have a death rate that is twice that of women and six times what it was during their twenties. Physical strength, coordination, reaction time, and such things as sensitivity to glare all are affected adversely by aging.

Since a man's occupational abilities can be seriously eroded by age, it becomes necessary for him to compensate by exploiting his decades of experience, by being more conscientious, and by doing jobs more carefully. Mid-life workers are the most stable, possess the lowest rates of unemployment, and hold the jobs with highest status, seniority and authority.

Women are more frequently concerned about the changes in their physical appearance, and in their sexual-reproductive functions (which are associated with attractive femininity). One of the most attention-getting areas is that of menopause.

Menopause, which once referred only to the time when menstruation stops, now covers the years just before and after. During the two to four years this normally takes, the uterus shrinks; the vagina decreases in size and is less able to expand; and the exterior tissue surrounding the vagina becomes less elastic. The result is pain and irritation in foreplay and intercourse. However, the clitoris—the central area of sexual responsiveness—is still highly reactive.

Most of the problems women experience are culture-created. Many women expect the menopausal period to be marked by symptoms of all kinds. In fact, however, only a few symptoms are actually connected with menopause: hot flushes, hot flashes, sweating and insomnia. Other symptoms are probably due to such factors as personality, marital difficulties, changes in the family structure, and cultural expectation. Thus, younger women are much more negative in their characterization of the menopausal period than are menopausal women. In our youth-worshipping, sex-saturated society, the loss of reproductive capacity is sometimes seen as the end of attractiveness, as a partial death. Once in the period, though, the menopausal woman discovers for herself how wrong the stereotypes can be. The anticipation is much worse than the actual experience.

Some claim that there is a male change of life, too, and call it the male climacteric. It refers to the idea that at middle age men have reached the top of their ladder and have no place to go but down; sometimes a writer pictures the age as one in which males flip out. It is suggested that because men undergo serious changes and disturbances at this time, they tend to do things like abandoning their wives for younger women, quitting their jobs to become beachcombers, and drinking to the point of becoming alcoholics.

The male climacteric, if it exists, is very different from the menopause. Men don't show a significant decline in the production of the male sex hormones, while women show a massive decline in the concentration of feminine sex hormones. Thus, the problems males face are basically social and occupational. Still, it is true that patterns of sexual responses do change in men, too.

In line with the general decline in vigor, there may be a limited decrease in sexual interest and ability. However, none of these changes necessarily impairs the ability to enjoy sexual relations. What husbands and wives must accept is that they are likely to show less initial sexual responsivity, less intense orgasms, and a quicker loss of excitation.

Some people speak of a midlife crisis as an almost universal phenomenon. In the middle years, we take stock of our lives; we evaluate our past behavior—and, if we find it lacking, we modify our lives. At this point, career advances are less likely; job opportunities are becoming fewer, and take longer to master; our past mistakes are becoming increasingly difficult to remedy; our energies are running out; and the competition of young adults is becoming increasingly difficult to meet.

Our past decisions were based on a picture of ourselves which might have failed to include much of what we now know we are. We have a last chance to change our lives before old age overtakes us. As our family obligations decrease, we must use the opportunity to balance our own lives and do the things we really want to do.

Why call it a crisis? Because so much is at stake and the pressures are so intense that the re-evaluation can't be conducted dispassionately. We are emotional; we become upset at the lost opportunities; and we agonize over the person we could have become. Our life may seem very wasted, sacrificed for nothing at all. Recriminations fill our minds, and we can almost mourn for the dead past.

However, the re-evaluations need not lead to drastic changes. A person may conclude that he is reasonably satisfied with his life. Still, in many cases, careers are changed; families are broken up by divorce; new starts are made. There is an increase in male suicide, heavy drinking, and depression. The re-evaluation is especially stressful if a person feels trapped and totally incapable of making his life what he now feels it should be.

On the other side of the fence, we find many who reject the notion of a universal storm-and-stressful midlife crisis. They are willing to talk only about a midlife transition, and claim that a "crisis" is seen only in people who have been emotionally disturbed for many years.

The transition is created by three basic factors: (1) the middle-aged person has more time and energy to devote to himself and his spouse; (2) the decline in biological capacities no longer can be ignored; and (3) awareness of death as a personal outcome is now impossible to deny. Thus, middle-aged people come to focus on the relatively limited number of years left for them to live. Understandably they ask questions about what to do with the rest of their years and whether they really want to spend them as they are now living. Because some people do change in crucial ways, their style of life may no longer be acceptable; because most people are pretty stable, they tend not to veer off in many radically different courses. Change and transition, yes; crisis, no.

To highlight the logic of their position, those who see midlife as a transition can point to two major events in middle age: the empty-nest syndrome and the reversal in male and female traits.

The empty-nest syndrome is supposed to involve depression, a sense of purposelessness, and a feeling that life has lost all meaning—because of the departure of children, and the resulting gaps in the life of the parents (especially the mother). In fact, this condition is rare; most parents feel better after their troublesome adolescents leave home; they find the peace and opportunities for self-development gratifying. The women who develop the empty-nest syndrome, therefore, turn out to be the ones who have built their whole life around their children. Having put all their eggs in one basket, life can lose its meaning when the kids depart until new goals and activities are found. In short, the syndrome appears in those whose marriages are unsatisfying and who have nothing but their children to fall back on. In contrast, those who value their new freedom and have satisfying ways to fill it, remain happy if not happier.

Earlier (p. 31) we said that the husband and wife ignore certain of their characteristics: the woman her independence and achievement orientation; the man his dependence and emotional sensitivity. Each subordinated these traits to the tasks that were assumed in marriage. The woman, as mother, tried to be warm and supportive and empathic; the man, as the traditional breadwinner, tried to be aggressive, dominant and cool. Now, with the kids gone, the two find it possible to re-activate their latent qualities. Men appreciate their feminine side more, and try to develop it; women similarly appreciate and develop their masculine side—becoming more assertive, dominant and independent. Some men, in particular, are shocked by the fact that their wives no longer are willing to compromise as they did in the past. They can't figure out where the soft, submissive helpmate disappeared to.

Clearly, some mutual adjustments must be made, and some conflict is natural. Nonetheless, the transition-caused adjustments can be made. The man can abandon his feelings of betrayal, and the woman can drop her bitterness about being blocked by her husband's attempt to run her life.

Again, such reversals don't constitute a crisis. They involve a continuously unfolding life sequence. At all times we are adopting and dropping roles, and behaving in ways compatible with our respective roles. The fact that we can't express all of our personality all of the time doesn't mean that we're disorganized and emotionally crippled; when an opportunity arises to develop a latent facet of our personality, we welcome it. All of us want to be whole human beings!

THE ELDERLY

Old age is something that is frequently feared in our society. The elderly are stereotyped as stupid, mindless, boring incompetents who are too cranky and unattractive to be around. This stereotype is a tragic and cruel characterization of the senior citizen.

To set the record straight, we must differentiate between aging and senility. Aging refers to the changes that typically occur in people as they move through the adult years. Senility refers to a relatively infrequent condition characterized by substantial mental and physical deterioration.

Most people in their 70's and 80's have aged, but are not senile. True, they have still more biological limitations: bones become more brittle and can get shorter; the kidneys filter blood less adequately; the capacity of the lungs decreases; nerves send up messages to the brain at a slower rate; hearts don't function as efficiently. Nonetheless, old age is not synonymous with illness.

Healthy old people can be vigorous, interesting, deeply involved in living, and mentally alert and resourceful. Unfortunately, the stereotype doesn't focus on them; it focuses on the sick, senile elderly person; it disregards the fact that the stereotype doesn't fit a large percentage of the elderly.

Our society therefore glosses over the needs of many elderly. Rather than seeing their difficulties as being due to actual deprivations and threats of deprivations, it tends to treat them as normal features of the pre-death period. It's as if we reason: people have to die of something; therefore, old people must get sicker and sicker until they die.

Biologically, the elderly are more vulnerable. The longer we live, the more opportunities there are for adversity and diseases to attack us. The older we are, the more likely a problem in some area of our life or body will affect other areas; the interdependence grows year after year. And, the older we are, the less resilience and compensatory power our bodies have. Thus, the elderly, if anything, need the best of support systems, because no aspect of their lives and bodies can be ignored.

The abilities of the elderly are typically well preserved until a year or more before death; then cognitive and intellectual performances drop sharply. Before that death drop, as it is called, speed is the most serious deficiency of the elderly. It takes them longer to get ready to act, and it takes longer to perform the act itself. Thus, the elderly are at a greater risk in any situation where fast action is required.

Memory loss increases as the years pass. In particular, it's harder for some older people to acquire new knowledge. The problem seems to be that the elderly don't organize new information as efficiently as they once did. Such inefficiencies can spill over into recall, as well; some elderly people have trouble remembering things they once knew. Instead of zeroing in on the to-be-remembered material, they passively wait for material to burst out of their memory systems. When taught to use successful strategies for learning and recall, and when given the time and confidence to use them, the elderly can improve their performance. Their minds aren't shot; the potential is there, and can be demonstrated.

Decision-making appears to be more difficult for the elderly.

Many were educated in schools that stressed rote memory rather than the analysis, organization and integration of information. Being ill-equipped to deal with new problems in creative ways, the elderly are more likely to experience frustration and failure. When that happens, the elderly erroneously conclude that they're too incapacitated to do things well—and the people around shake their heads as if agreeing that the stereotype is true.

To make matters worse, some of the elderly are beset by many urgent problems that preoccupy their minds. Their energy and attention can be so drained by these problems that learning and decision making abilities become seriously impaired. Equally bad, the elderly may become so cautious and overly meticulous that observers characterize them as indifferent, incompetent and out of it.

The situation is caused by poor early training, a fear of failure, a fear of ridicule, and an inability to proceed at a pace that is comfortable for the elderly person. Thus, the failures of the elderly are frequently due to society's unwillingness to provide reasonable conditions in which the elderly can use their brain power effectively.

Some years ago, a few theories claimed that old people must withdraw emotionally, psychologically and socially from the outside world. By withdrawing, they could more easily tear out their earthly roots, and by focusing inwardly, come to accept their forthcoming death. Society, in turn, could fill the places once occupied by the elderly with young fresh blood. Most important, it was suggested that the elderly are happier and more satisfied when such disengagement occurs; the process of withdrawal was treated as saying goodbye to this world.

The facts are otherwise. While turning inward and to the past does occur to some degree, the elderly are unhappy when disengagement occurs. When deprived of desired activities and social relationships, the elderly become despondent and apathetic—and perhaps even die before their biological time. True, the personality of the elderly person is important: the more introverted and socially uninvolved an individual has been, the less he is disturbed by disengagement. Still, it's rare to find an individual who wants to shut out the outside world completely.

Moreover, the elderly are best adjusted when they have somebody around in whom they can confide (remember the importance of chumships in the adolescent period?); this makes it easier to tolerate the socially forced disengagement. After all, young and even middle aged people frequently want to avoid old people; to them, age symbolizes ugliness, deterioration and death. Being around old people makes others think of these processes affecting them; and in our society, death isn't treated as an acceptable topic. Not even hospital staff members, who have much experience with death and dying, are comfortable enough to deal with them.

Disengagement theory does stress one important theme: older people do turn inward and seem to engage in a life review. The life review involves a final evaluation of the individual's experiences. However, many people see this as living in the past—a useless, time-filling, repetitive and boring replay.

The life review has many functional reasons. The older person's life is bound up mostly in the past; his present and future are limited. Just as we talk about the things we know well, so does the elderly person talk about the past, which he knows best. As he reviews his past, he can draw conclusions about the goodness and righteousness of his life style. To the degree that he finds his life good, he can accept death more easily.

In the past is where the elderly find their achievements. But, as they look around the present, they find that few have confidence in their abilities—and treat them as being in their second childhood. To bolster his confidence and to motivate himself to undertake an independent, self-reliant stance, the elderly person must reactivate his past accomplishments. He must constantly remind himself that he *can* do it—just like he once did other things. The past, in short, fills him with the confidence needed to take on the present (and even death).

In old age, people frequently move to different quarters or are institutionalized—leaving behind their memories, experiences and landmarks. That's not easy. The physical mementos are hard enough to discard; the psychological attachments are much more difficult to loosen. By recounting the experiences and attachments of the past ("I once lived in a house . . . I used to go to the grocery store on the corner . . . My best friend lived down the block and we used to . . ."), the elderly person becomes more objective about them. In time, he sorts out those things that are gone forever, and increasingly focuses on those things that he can carry around with him. The past has ended for the elderly person, but he himself has to determine the boundaries; it takes time to discover where the past ends.

Frequently, the various features of the past have disappeared. A neighborhood may have been torn down, a community may have changed its religious or ethnic character, family traditions may have been discarded by the new generation. Sometimes memories are all that is left of these non-existent features. By recounting events linked to these features, the elderly memorialize and perpetuate them. As long as the elderly are alive and talk about them, the elderly feel these features live on.

Finally, if we listen carefully to elderly people, we find that their recollections of the past aren't aimless. The events they repeatedly discuss are those that have great emotional significance for them. Just as we might play and replay records of songs that we especially love and which mean much to us, so the elderly replay the experiences that symbolize their past. Because their stories can be reactivated at will, the elderly feel less helpless and more competent.

Unfortunately, our society is oriented toward the present and the future. For most of us—until old age—the past is over and done with, water under the bridge, never to be encountered again. With that kind of attitude, the elderly are hard to take.

For the elderly to get fair treatment, the stereotype of the aging process has to be corrected. The elderly can play an active and productive role. The real question is: will we let them?
words to describe their experiences, we can benefit by not having

5 | LEARNING TO BE A PERSON

WE ARE IN THE COMPANY OF OTHER PERSONS all through our lives—and, to varying degrees, we frequently influence their actions. As parents, we raise children and try to mold their behavior properly. As work supervisors, we try to direct people to act for the good of the organization. And as individuals, we strive to influence our friends and loved ones to behave in ways we find personally satisfying.

Why do people behave the way they do? How can we prepare ourselves for what they might do? How can we influence them to act the way we want?

A learning theory describes how people develop habits, how they change, and—once changed—how they stay that way. Three widely accepted theories are classical conditioning, operant conditioning, and observational learning (modeling).

CLASSICAL CONDITIONING

Ivan Pavlov (1849-1936), the Russian physiologist, formulated the principles of classical conditioning—but people had sensed them for centuries. In the 1600's, for example, a play by de Vega told the story of a novitiate who was made to eat his meals on the floor when he misbehaved. The cats, of course, swarmed all over his food as he tried to eat. So one day the novitiate grabbed the cats, stuffed them into a sack, and began to train them. First he would cough—then he would whale the daylights out of them.

He kept repeating the sequence, coughing and whacking, until he got tired; then he let the shrieking cats loose. For good measure, he repeated the treatment a few more times. From then on, whenever he misbehaved and had to eat with the cats, he merely coughed—and away fled the cats. Then he could eat in peace.

This story contains the basic elements of Pavlov's theory: (1)

an experience (the whacking) which generates a specific reaction (the pain); (2) a neutral experience (the coughing) which, by itself, would not normally cause that reaction; and (3) a pairing of the two experiences, with a resulting transfer of causal power from the first experience to the second.

Pavlov recognized the importance of pairing experience only after working with dogs for a long time. What brought it to his attention was the fact that his dogs salivated when they saw him. Why should a dog's mouth fill with saliva just because Pavlov was around? Perhaps, he hypothesized, it was because he was the one who brought food to the dogs, and therefore brought out the same reaction that the food did. To test his theory, Pavlov decided to pair food with other things in a scientific way.

Pavlov paired food with such things as bells, lights and vibrations. After a period of time, the dogs would salivate to the formerly neutral stimulus. For example, Pavlov would repeatedly sound a bell and then present food to the dog. Upon seeing the food, the dog would naturally salivate. Over and over, Pavlov paired the two; every once in a while, he rang the bell without giving the dog food. On the first test without the food, the dog disregarded the bell and didn't salivate. But as the number of pairings of the bell and the food increased, the dog salivated more and more often at the sound of the bell when there was no food; the bell had taken over some of the causal power of food to make the dog salivate.

Pavlov called the neutral stimulus (in this case, the bell) a conditioned stimulus; he suggested that after the pairings, it became a signal. By reacting to the conditioned stimulus, the dog anticipated the subsequent event (being fed) and prepared his body for the food. That preparatory action (in this case, salivating) he labeled the conditioned response.

In contrast, an automatic natural experience is called an unconditioned response. Thus, the term "conditioned" refers to a feature associated with learning; the term "unconditioned" refers to features which are automatic and not dependent upon learning.

By paying attention to signals that telegraph oncoming events, we give our bodies and minds time to prepare appropriate responses. But classical conditioning involves more than signals.

Life often revolves around labels and words that are associated with emotional feelings. A word like "good" or "bad," when applied to people or products, can cause us to react to them emotionally—even though we've had no experience with the people or the products. When other people use such labels and words to describe their experiences, we can benefit by not having to find out everything for ourselves.

When advertising pairs a product with music we like or with other things we value, the product takes on a psychological signif- icance that fills a crucial vacuum for us. Thus, some people buy Marlboro cigarettes because the brand is paired with a machismo cowboy type whose strength and independence they crave. The fact that "different" brands of products typically aren't actually different is of little importance; what is important is that the pairing makes us feel differently about the products.

Unfortunately, since a natural stimulus can transfer some of its casual power to almost any other stimulus, pairing can produce harmful consequences. Suppose a girl is unknowingly allergic to roses (unconditioned stimulus), and reacts with an allergic attack (unconditioned response) when she sees or smells them. If her grandmother often brings roses when she visits, the girl might have an allergic reaction just by seeing her grandmother without the roses. Similarly, someone who has had an accident on a plane may become frightened by seeing (or merely thinking about) planes.

If a worker has a bad accident with a machine at work, he may react emotionally whenever he is near the machine even after the machine has been repaired and he knows that there is no further danger.

The classical conditioning linkage can be activated merely by thinking or using certain words. If someone says to himself: "I'm afraid" or "I can't do that," he makes it difficult for himself to act effectively. And if he uses ethnic slurs, like "He's a dirty kike" or "He's a dumb Polack," he can transfer hate and hostility to people he has never seen. The words evoke the emotional responses with which they were previously linked.

Generalization is a form of classical conditioning. When we generalize, we react in the same way to things that are somewhat similar but not identical. People dress differently, act differently, and are seen in different environments; by generalizing, we can ignore the inconsequential differences or changes. Ralph is still

Ralph, whether he is wearing a pin-striped suit or a bathing suit, and whether we see him at work or at church.

Generalization can also get us into trouble. We often take a liking or disliking to people before we really get to know them—because they remind us of other people we liked or disliked. Logic tells us each person should be treated on the basis of his own particular characteristics. But our brains—and our lives—operate in terms of similarities. Nothing is a perfect reproduction of anything else; things can only be pretty much the same.

Once a conditioned response has been built into the brain, that pattern never drops out—but it can be superseded by a newer, stronger association. When Jay was young, for example, he was taught that sex was sinful; consequently, anything relating to sex—words, acts—causes him to feel guilty or dirty. The only way he can now behave in a more natural fashion is by developing a new association (sex is good and moral)—one that is much stronger than the linkage drilled into him as a child. To develop that association and make it stronger than the old one, Jay may need expert help.

This means that all of us have to live down much of our early training. As adults, we have to behave in ways different from those we were taught as children. When the childish habits and associations aren't suppressed by stronger mature tendencies, we are unprepared to deal with the adult world.

OPERANT CONDITIONING

The fundamental notion in operant conditioning is that our behavior is influenced by the consequences. If an action is followed by a positive reward, we continue to behave that way. If an action is followed by a negative (painful, unwanted) event, then we stop behaving that way. Thus, we operate in a way that maximizes the positive rewards and minimizes the painful experiences.

In classical conditioning, the signal was the key that brought things together. In operant conditioning, the key is consequences; when we do something, what happens?

If I am pleasant to the person next to me on the bus, what happens? If the person responds in an amiable fashion, then my efforts seem worthwhile and I continue to reach out. But if the person gives me a cold stare, buries his head in the paper, and mumbles: "I don't talk to strangers," then I clam up.

Reinforcement refers to the nature of the outcomes. If the outcome is something I desire and will work for (money, food, love, attention), then it is a positive reinforcer. If the outcome is something I want to avoid and will work to escape (punishment, pain, criticism, rejection), then it is a negative reinforcer.

Many people think operant conditioning is the most precise and effective way to mold children and even adults. Its two basic features are the method of approximation and schedules of reinforcement.

THE METHOD OF APPROXIMATION   When we teach new behavior through operant conditioning, we first reward any response that is approximately like the one we desire. Then, as the approximate behavior becomes frequent, we can push for more perfect behavior by rewarding only the actions that are progressively more like the desired action.

For example, if I wanted to teach a child to swim, I would get him to move closer and closer to the water—praising him and rewarding him until he was at the edge of the pool. Then I would get him to step into the shallow water, and then into deeper sections—still continuing to praise and reward him at each step. Finally, I would move him through the paddling, floating and swimming patterns, directing him through reward and praise.

At no time would I try to accomplish the whole bit at once. I would try to ensure that at every step the child could succeed, and would not become frightened. I would let the child move ahead at his own pace. I would raise my standards gradually, according to the child's ability to meet higher standards.

We train people effectively if:

(1) We know what it takes to do the task—the specific skills required, and the sequence in which a person must master them.
(2) We have the patience to wait while the trainee gradually learns.
(3) We space our rewards in such a way that the trainee is willing to work for them.

Unfortunately, patience is an uncommon virtue in parents and trainers. After we learn to do something, we expect others (children included) to pick it up quickly. The common directive at work is: "Go with George and watch him. You'll pick it up right away."

This approach is very ineffective. Approximation requires that each successful step be rewarded as we move toward the ultimate goal. Rather than heap praise at the conclusion, we should parcel out praise at each sign of increased progress.

SCHEDULES OF REINFORCEMENT The pattern by which we reward performance is crucial. There are two dimensions to a reward schedule: (1) ratio versus interval, and (2) fixed versus variable. Ratio refers to the numbers of times that we must act before we get rewarded; interval refers to the length of time that must pass before we get rewarded. The first dimension question is: shall we reward a person because of what he does or because of how long he waits?

In the second dimension, fixed means unchanging; variable means that the standard changes.

Putting the two dimensions together, we have four basic schedules: fixed ratio, variable ratio, fixed interval, variable interval.

Fixed Ratio An example of fixed ratio is piecework; you have to put out a certain amount of work to get paid a certain amount. No work, no pay; a little work, a little pay. There is a direct relationship between activity and reward. Sweatshops exist, and workers are exploited because of the direct relationship between output and pay.

Variable Ratio A variable ratio has a changing standard. A good example is a slot machine; it may pay off after ten plays, or 20 plays, or 100 plays; we never know how many plays are required for the next payoff. People can't figure out when they are going to win; they keep saying: "Maybe it will happen next time" and continue feeding the machine.

Fixed Interval Salaried people are paid regularly, regardless of the amount of work they turn out. This results in a time-focused pattern. Some people on salary slack off after payday, and work harder just before payday. Similarly, in college, students may coast along during the semester—then in the last days before exams, cram day and night to get good grades. In contrast to the ratio schedules, interval schedules tend to discourage commitment and diligence. We don't work as hard, and often use as an excuse: "I've got plenty of time left; why do it now?"

Variable Interval People wait unreasonably long times for a bus in freezing weather. They keep dialing a telephone number for several minutes when the line is busy. When they're waiting for an important letter, they check their mailbox a number of times that day.

All these rewards come at variable intervals. Yet we continue to persist in areas where uncertainty is great, even though we never know when (or even if) the reward will come.

These four schedules show the ways we can influence people to behave as we want them to.

• If I want to get a certain amount of work out of a worker, I would put him on a fixed-ratio schedule.

• If I were a worker seeking security, I would want a fixed interval schedule—so I would know how much I would get, and when.

• If I, as a college teacher, wanted my students to study their lessons diligently, I would tell them their grades depended on a number of surprise quizzes I would give them—a variable interval schedule.

• If I were a sweatshop owner and wanted to extract the most work for the least money, I would tell my workers that their piece-rate pay each day would depend upon the orders I had received by the *end* of each day—a variable ratio schedule.

One of the most important applications of operant conditioning involves the use of programmed learning. The material to be learned is broken down into a sequence of small units that starts out quite easy, and gradually becomes more difficult. There are questions after each paragraph or two; the trainee must answer the questions correctly before going on to the next part.

If he makes an error, he knows it immediately—and must review the material until he gets the answer correct; this keeps him from getting totally lost. When he does answer a question correctly and moves on to the next part, he is encouraged by his success. Equally important, the student isn't embarrassed by his failures, doesn't get reprimanded by a teacher, and isn't made to feel inferior by getting a failing grade. Finally, each student can move ahead at his own pace. Bright students don't have to be held back, and weak students don't have to be sacrificed in order for the class to be kept on schedule.

OBSERVATIONAL LEARNING (MODELING)

This type of learning involves watching and imitating other people. For example, many people base their behavior on what they see on television and in the movies. Many adults have imitated the Russian roulette scene in *The Deerhunter;* so far, twenty-four persons have killed themselves. Some adolescents firebombed a bum on the street after seeing a similar scene in a movie. While re-enacting a scene from *Dirty Harry,* a 14-year old boy killed his 11-year old brother. A precocious adolescent robbed a supermarket after deactivating the electronic burglar alarm, as he had seen done on *Mission Impossible.*

By the age of five, a child watches television two to three hours a day; by ten, it is from four to six. It has been estimated that by the age of 16, an adolescent has watched 13,000 TV murders. Clearly, we need to know how TV violence affects our aggressive tendencies.

The basic feature of observational learning is that we don't need to do anything or receive a reward. We can acquire new knowledge and new behaviors simply by observing, without receiving any direct external reinforcement.

Children learn language skills by listening to parents and other people speaking. They learn family, social, and political customs through observation. In fact, if we had to depend upon rewarding and punishing—the method of approximation—most children would never acquire adult socialization. And what about teaching millions to drive cars?

Still, no one takes on all of the behaviors he observes. Most people know how to rob and kill, yet few people do these things. Three factors determine whether an observed act is actually performed.

ATTENTION   The observer must pay reasonable attention to the behavior that is being modeled. If he is bored or daydreams, he can't keep careful track of the behavior, and can't accurately repeat it.

RECORDING   The observation must be recorded in the memory system, and arranged into a pattern that's easily remembered. For this to happen, the behavior must be simple, specific and reasonably presented. If the behavior is presented too rapidly or is too complex, it will be necessary to learn each part of the behavior separately.

MOTIVATION   The observer must have a reason for carrying out the act at some later time. No one can become an expert tennis player merely by watching the greats. Everything happens fast, and the skills are complex; playing involves strategies, physical coordination, and wide experience. Only by continuously supervised practice can someone acquire the feel of the game.

But to pick up a gun and shoot a person requires no prior training; merely watching the act on television is sufficient. Still, we must have a reason for acting—for performing in real life the acts which we can do.

Having a reason can be reduced to the basic idea of expectations: (1) under what conditions can we expect certain acts to be rewarded? (2) under what conditions can we expect certain acts to make us feel good or bad?

In operant conditioning, the crucial factor is the consequences themselves. In observational learning, it is our mental picture of the consequences; we ourselves, rather than the external environment, control our own behavior.

How does the foregoing apply to aggression? To grow up requires that we learn when, how and against whom to be aggressive. We learn aggressive behavior from our parents and peers. They criticize us for our aggressive acts—but then they hurt us. When that happens we pick up the same aggressive techniques they used on us.

When a child sees his father act aggressively, his TV hero slaughter a tribe of Indians, or 007 blow the enemy to smithereens, he learns that violence is a "good" thing. What these scenes teach is that in order to be a hero and resolve problems by killing, only a "good" reason is required. Why should anyone be surprised that aggression has become a most difficult social problem? Who lacks a "good" reason?

The exposure to violence in real or reel life greatly affects us and our children. It teaches us aggressive ways of behaving; hardens us so that we are not upset when people are battered; encourages us to imitate the aggressive acts we view; and teaches us that aggression is not only a powerful way of solving our disagreements with others, but can often be the best way.

However, modeling covers *all* behaviors (achievement, sociability), not just aggression. Given the proper conditions, we can learn anything we can observe.

PUNISHMENT You may have concluded that punishment is not an effective way to train children. B. F. Skinner, a pioneering psychologist in operant conditioning, is absolutely opposed to punishment; he stresses the superior outcomes resulting from positive reinforcement. Besides upsetting people, punishment doesn't teach anyone what to do; it only focuses on what not to do.

It is ironic—but the more parents use violence to try to control their children, the more violence-prone their children become. The punishment suppresses the undesired behavior only temporarily.

We know most children won't raid the cookie jar when mommy is there, that drivers slow down when patrol cars are near, and that most students don't cheat when the teacher is present. But what happens when the punisher is not there? The lesson often learned is: don't get caught in the act. Thus, constant monitoring and surveillance are necessary.

Skinner contends that punishment is used because it makes the punisher feel good, not because it works. By punishing their children, parents let off steam and experience a feeling of power; they conclude that they're doing something about their children's misbehavior. Punishment becomes reinforcing for the parents instead of for the children.

However, punishment for children *can* be effective—under the following conditions:

The punishment is administered *before* the child gets into the objectionable habit. It is not wise to look the other way or be endlessly patient. Since the punishment temporarily suppresses the response, it can be used to buy time to actively strengthen another *approved* behavior.

The punishment promptly follows the improper act.

The punishment focuses on a specific act, and is not given in a spirit of revenge.

The punishment is consistently applied to every repetition of the act.

The child understands that the punishment is because the act is unacceptable, he knows what he should have done, and he knows what will happen if he repeats the act.

The punishment is used only for important transgressions, and is a minor technique in socializing the child. In this way the child suffers little from his parents' training, and does not learn to hate them.

6 | THE UNCONSCIOUS

OUR CONSCIOUS LIFE IS LIKE A STREAM: the stream seems to remain the same, but the water in it is constantly changing. And so it is with consciousness; we feel we are the same, but our thoughts and sensations are always changing.

The stream of our consciousness interacts with the preconscious (as Freud named it). The preconscious is similar to a reservoir: it stores many thousands of experiences which we aren't using at any given moment. Because so many pass through our mind, we must sidetrack most of our experiences; we can keep track of only the most important ones. Our consciousness is our working mind, and we can't allow it to be cluttered up.

The stream of the consciousness and the reservoir of the preconscious feed into the huge ocean of the unconscious. The unconscious contains the millions and millions of thoughts, experiences and emotions that have long been forgotten. Some of the most important of these can be brought back into our conscious mind by hypnosis and analysis.

While we think we are guided by our *immediate* experiences—by what is contained in our conscious minds—we are heavily influenced by the thousands of similar or related experiences that are lodged in our preconscious and unconscious. These impressions haven't been erased.

We go through life unconsciously being governed by what has served us well in the past. In this sense, we are unaware of why we behave the way we do. Our millions of feelings and ideas, though we can't remember many of them, have left their guiding mark on us. We are our experiences.

Freud, the mind-healer, saw emotionally sick people. They came to him because they had problems of living—problems at home, at work, or in social contacts. Some of them had incapacitating symptoms—for example, paralyzed legs—that their doctors had diagnosed as being physically healthy. Freud listened to his patients' complaints, collected a great deal of information about their experiences, and used such data as clues to the causes of their problems.

However, very soon Freud hit a stone wall: the data didn't enable him to solve a patient's problems. He needed to know much more; but how could he get more information out of his patients? After much experimentation, he resorted to a method he called free association. Patients were instructed to say whatever came to mind, especially those things that related to an experience or dream.

Suppose a patient described a dream as follows: "I saw a bear chasing me through the forest. The trees were small and I had no place to hide, and the bear was twenty feet tall. I ran as fast as I could but the bear roared at me, and I froze in my tracks."

Freud would ask the patient to take each idea (bear, forest, small trees, running fast) and say whatever came to mind. He traced these initial thoughts again and again until all the associations fell together like a jigsaw puzzle. Of course, Freud also had the background data on his patients—the kinds of people the patient met and the kinds of problems the patient faced—and combined this information with the associations to figure out the conflicting pressures on the patient.

Conflict, Freud found, is characteristic of everyday life. Take, for example, a worker named George. He hates his job and wants to quit, but can't because he needs the money. He is a semi-skilled worker and can't get a better job. He is the only worker in the family, and he has to keep working to meet the family obligations. His wife can't stand George, but divorce is out of the question because she can't support herself and the children.

In cases like this, we see conflict: the worker wants to quit his job but the money ties him to it; the wife wants to leave her husband but can't because of her desire to provide for her children.

Unfortunately, life often doesn't flow the way we would like it to. We sometimes have to choose between things that we hate— and, no matter what we choose, we feel cheated and miserable. To be constantly aware of the conflicting desires is just too hard. If we continuously thought about these conflicts, we would end up being totally frustrated and deeply depressed. Freud concluded that painful conflicts frequently force people to push things out of their mind and to keep them out of their mind. He called this tendency repression.

George has stewed in his conflict about his lousy job for a period of time, and has succeeded in repressing it. But deep inside, the conflict boils. George hasn't been able to resign himself to keeping the job, and he can't bring himself to take a chance and quit. George has to fight to keep the upsetting thoughts from pushing into his mind, and he expends energy doing it.

Just as we need physical energy to engage in tasks like working and playing, Freud found we needed psychological energy to accomplish mental tasks—especially repressing bothersome material. Thus, George depletes his supply of energy by fighting against the conflict. He might therefore come home dead tired every day, with little energy left over to do anything except plop himself down before the television. Every day is a hard day at work.

Suppose, however, that George can't suppress his bitter anger at how life is cheating him. The growing pressure might force him to find ways to release these feelings. George might drink too much—and, while he is a bit high, get some of the feelings out of his system. Or if the pressure becomes impossible to bear, George might develop a physical or psychiatric illness.

It is likely that George doesn't realize that his drinking and sickness are related to his hate for his job. In fact, if asked about his job when he is sober, George might even say: "It's not so bad—you know . . . a job's a job!"

But we can't solve our conflicts simply by blowing off steam every once in a while. We have to face our conflicts—and either commit ourselves to some solution, or resign ourselves to living with a lousy job or rotten spouse. The first step is confronting the conflict; that's where free association enters. But how can we get at something that's locked up in our unconscious?

Suppose George develops a psychiatric illness; suddenly, he finds his arm is paralyzed and he can't work. He goes to a doctor, and is told that there is nothing physically wrong with his arm. The doctor refers him to a psychiatrist (fortunately, the union has negotiated an ideal medical package). The psychiatrist, after getting all the facts George can give him, resorts to free association. He tells George: "Say whatever comes to mind. Don't censor anything, and don't try to look good. Say whatever is in your mind!"

George feels guilty about not being able to work, and is bored with lying around the house. Because he is suffering and wants to be helped, he wants to cooperate with the psychiatrist. Sooner or later, George will talk about important things that relate to his illness and its causes.

Think of how you try to recall a name that you've forgotten. You might say to yourself: When did I meet the person? Who was I with? What were we doing? What did we talk about? Who introduced us? In short, you would try to remember as many connections to the lost name as possible; you would try to close in on the name by surrounding it with all kinds of facts related to it.

The difference between trying to remember a name and George's treatment is basically this: George, without realizing it, can't think about his conflict. It's as if a wall surrounds it. The wall has to be broken down; the process can take a long time—in some cases, months. The conflict must be approached gradually. Only little by little does George come up with clues and connections that are closer and closer to the bothersome conflict.

Finally, George talks about the conflict and gets the feelings out of his system. Then the psychiatrist can help George deal with the conflict itself. Once the conflict is resolved, George knows how to live with his problems and can solve them. He no longer is forced to repress his feelings and resentment, and they don't have to cause drinking bouts or illness.

George has no control over this process. He is just like a person who smokes and develops lung cancer. We can't say that the smoker caused the cancer himself; the cancer was caused by a set of conditions, and similarly George's illness too is caused by a set of conditions. In neither case do we want to blame the victim or withhold treatment.

Is there really such a thing as the unconscious? Are people actually that ignorant about their own feelings and conflicts? In everyday life, many people have a feeling of control. They might be sarcastic and say: "I know all about myself; I do what I want when I want to do it. Don't give me that bull about hidden things inside me that dictate my actions. I'm my own boss and I know exactly what's on my mind."

Proof of the existence of the unconscious can be found in such phenomena as amnesia, infantile amnesia, slips of the tongue, and dreams.

AMNESIA   Some people have lost their memories. The lost memories can cover periods of a year or even twenty years. What causes amnesia?

Suppose Paul is late to work one morning. He rushes into his car and drives recklessly down the street. He fails to see a child run into the street, can't stop the car in time, and kills the child. There are witnesses, and Paul has no excuse for the homicide.

Paul may blot out the entire sequence; he can't remember the child running out and his car hitting the child—but he also can't remember getting into the car or driving away from his home.

Paul can't blot out just the accident—because thinking about other actions that morning can lead to the traumatic material he wants to forget. It's safer to blot out the whole situation.

Suppose George (our unhappy worker) is in really bad shape. His misery builds up, day after day, at work and at home. Finally, it reaches a point where he can't take it any more.

Suddenly, he finds himself in another city. He can't remember who he is, and he doesn't remember that he is married and has children. Without going to the police or to a psychiatrist, he tries to create a new life for himself. In one such memorable case, the person married, had a second set of children, and built a new career. It wasn't until he needed to be fingerprinted for an assignment, that it was discovered that he was a missing person. Even after seeing his first wife and their original home, all the material relating to this life remained completely blotted out.

Some people may feel he is playing a game and fooling everybody. But in most cases of this kind, experts who have studied these persons intensively for long periods say they are not pretending. Amnesia is for real.

INFANTILE AMNESIA   Can you remember what happened at your fourth birthday party? If you can, it is likely that you are merely repeating what others have told you about the party.

In general, few people can remember with any accuracy what happened the first four or five years of their lives. But through free association or hypnosis, adults have been able to recall such details of their childhood.

One of the most dramatic cases of infantile amnesia involved a woman whom the professionals called Bridey Murphy. Under hypnosis, she talked about her earlier life in Ireland in the 1800's. Her material was very detailed: she talked about specific people, stores, homes, and incidents. Reporters found that Bridey's stories were very accurate. The people had existed; the houses were still there; and some people even remembered the incidents of which she spoke.

Since she had never been in Ireland, and her stories took place a century earlier, some people claimed she had been reincarnated. But others looked for a more logical explanation. Finally, they discovered that when Bridey had been a child, an old neighbor had told her stories of his earlier life in that village in Ireland. Bridey was fascinated by these exciting stories and learned to repeat them almost word by word. But Bridey had forgotten about the neighbor and his story-telling. The stories were inside her, and later were released through hypnosis.

All of us retain many incidents that we cannot recall without the use of some special technique like free association or hypnosis. We know more than we think we know.

SLIPS OF THE TONGUE   Almost everybody has had slips of the tongue. Take, for example, the woman who hated her mother-in-law, and started a letter to her with *"Dead* mother." After writing the letter, she carefully reread it—yet didn't discover her error.

Or the professor who, at a good-bye party for a colleague he detested, said: "We all hate to see you go and wish you the *worst* of luck!"

Freud treated such slips as part of what he labeled the psychopathology of everyday life. These slips are frequently caused by an inner conflict. Consciously, we don't want to make such mistakes; they are very embarrassing, and make us look like idiots. However, when our feelings become too strong to contain, they can spill over into such overt expressions.

DREAMS   Laboratory experiments show that people dream every night. If our sleeping hours are regular, we dream about 20% of the time. In a normal period of eight hours of sleep, about 1½ hours will be spent dreaming. However, it is not unusual to find a person who says: "I never dream." It would be more correct for him to say "I don't *recall* dreaming."

Psychiatrists who use dreams to help understand their patients periodically encounter a patient who says he does not dream at all. Sometimes the patient is asked to sleep a few nights in a sleep laboratory, where he is wired to a monitor. When eye movements and brain activity indicate that the patient is dreaming, he is awakened and asked to report his dreams to a tape recorder. Night after night he finds he has been dreaming in spite of the fact that the next morning he can't recall one of them!

There is no physical location we can point to and say: "Here is where the unconscious is located." The best way to think about the unconscious is in a scientific way: people live and act as if they possessed something which we are calling the unconscious, a place that holds information that we can't reach or bring to mind.

Is all forgetting due to repression or amnesia? No. While the forgetting we described above is purposeful forgetting, there are mechanical failings as well.

All day long we are surrounded by sounds, sights and incidents. Our minds can't hold them all. We must ignore most of what goes on around us; to do that, our nervous system shuts out a large proportion of this clutter. This is mechanical forgetting—and it is a normal, necessary part of our lives.

To forget, then, is convenient and psychologically advantageous. But something that is hidden in our unconscious can still slip out and affect our behavior in crucial ways.

7 | PERSONALITY

EVERY DAY, WE INTERACT WITH MANY PEOPLE. Some of the interactions are intimate, personal and of long duration—such as among members of the family. Others focus on tasks that need to be performed—such as those that occur in the work group. Still others are brief and impersonal—such as with clerks at the grocery store.

In these interactions, each person must be able to picture what the other people are like, and to use these pictures to predict what effects his own actions will have on the others.

A person's personality includes characteristics and tendencies that enable others to predict his behavior. Personality is all the things we say and do to signal our moods and action patterns. When others learn these signals, they can anticipate our feelings and our actions—and how we might be affected by their actions.

Such anticipations help us avoid being surprised by others. Nothing threatens a relationship more than not knowing what a person will do next. We like to be able to take the behavior of others for granted, and know that we have successfully sized them up.

Personality includes all those activities which make us effective in our dealings with others, so that we can satisfy our important needs. We must be skilled in influencing people, in making them feel comfortable in our presence, and in enabling them to find pleasure in their relations with us.

Personality includes all the activities, people and possessions with which we associate ourselves. To identify to others the kind of a person we are, we wear certain kinds of clothes, drink a particular beer, and join certain groups.

If we are asked: "Who are you?", we are likely to list the associations around which we have built our identity. Years ago, the answers would have covered sex, occupation, political party, and religion. But today people tend to look at themselves more personally.

People now find it hard to answer the question: "Who am I supposed to be?" Advertising for beer, cigarettes and clothes tries to establish an identity for the user. A sparkling example is "Charlie," the perfume for women that became an overnight success. Women uneasy about their career orientation grabbed at the opportunity to identify with the beautiful, successful and socially skilled "Charlie" personality.

When we are given options—choices of books to read, movies to see, careers to aspire to—we reveal our nature through our choices. The strategies and tactics we choose are good indications of the kind of person we are. Do we want to win at any cost in work, at play, in love? What are we like in our leisure activities? Some people are very competitive, aggressive and willing to do almost anything to get ahead; others are passive, afraid to fight and compete openly, and resign themselves to the leftover crumbs. Some people plan their lives meticulously with one, five and ten-year goals; others let fate decide their life: "Whatever will be, will be."

Personality is revealed through the standards we set for ourselves—how we classify various acts. Some people consider theft and bribery to be legitimate; what they consider bad is being caught in the act. On the other hand, some people feel guilty if they take home a pencil from the office. Each of us judges our possible actions and chooses those we find morally and ethically acceptable.

Personality is somewhat like a house. A house is composed of many rooms, but is a single unit. Personality, similarly, has many parts and facets—but it is still a unitary thing. However, there is at least one critical difference: we can't study personality as a whole, but must choose which features to concentrate on.

Some scientists focus on our sensitivity to others and our need to manipulate people; they stress that personality is mask-like—the way we pretend to be to get our way. Others claim that we are what we've been trained to be. Both groups take an external perspective: figure out what a person gains by his actions and how he tries to achieve these gains.

A second perspective concentrates on the internal guidance system. It pictures people as if they were self-directed, independent creatures whose real self is locked away inside. These theorists

PERSONALITY / 61

claim that because people pretend, we can't go by what they do; we must unmask them and show what they're really like.

Following are descriptions of three basic approaches to the study of personality: a behaviorist's view (Skinner), a psychoanalyst's view (Freud), and a humanist's view (Rogers). Notice what they disregard as well as what they emphasize. Ask yourself, too, which one is talking about you (or anyone else you want to analyze).

A BEHAVIORIST VIEW

B. F. Skinner is one of the most important psychologists alive today. He, more than anyone else, has molded our contemporary views of the external perspective. Skinner started with the notion that interpretations are too dangerous to tolerate. He cites, for example, the times when even the most brilliant people believed in witches, or claimed that the planets had to revolve around the earth.

While ideas are fun to play with—who doesn't enjoy figuring out what makes other people tick?—ideas and conjectures have no place in science as data. The only accurate information we can collect about people is what they do. We can see what people do; we can measure what people do; and we can determine the consequences of their actions.

Should we care at all about people's inner thoughts? In literature and in everyday life, yes; in science, not unless we can observe and measure them. After all, what do we gain by knowing that a person has fantasies about robbing banks—so long as they remain fantasies? Everyone has some crazy thoughts at one time or another.

Skinner makes an even more important point. No one has ever entered someone's head. No one can directly control our thoughts and feelings; parents, teachers and peers can only attempt to control our behavior. If someone with power over us dislikes what we do, he can pressure us psychologically or physically into changing our behavior—but no one can pressure us into changing our inner thoughts and feelings. Therefore, Skinner says, we must define personality in terms of: what a person does in specific situations, the consequences he seeks to maximize, the extent to which these action tendencies spill over into similar situations, and the extent to which an individual continues to behave in the same way when the consequences occur infrequently.

Skinner uses learning principles to explain all kinds of behavior. To him, personality is only a convenient term for describing the behavior of a specific person. Once we have determined the situations a person confronts and his behavior in those situations, we have fully described his personality. We are what our social and physical environments have trained us to be.

But if that's the case, why do psychoanalysts consider it essential to study the internal processes as well? The behaviorists have a simple answer: most analysts start with a preconceived notion that personality is relatively permanent—something that doesn't change. Behaviorists reject this notion of personality being fixed and rigid. They say a person behaves in a consistent way only in the same situation; change the situation, and the person may behave in a different way. A person may be docile and submissive before his boss, and domineering and aggressive when out with the boys. An analyst would see a contradiction here, and try to reconcile both behaviors by digging deeper and coming up with the real person; a behaviorist would say that both are the real person. It is normal for different patterns of behavior to be used in different situations, and no contradiction exists that has to be explained away.

THE ANALYTIC VIEW

Freud developed the structural approach, which sees our personality as having three basic parts: the id, the ego, and the superego.

Our body needs many different kinds of nutrients, both physical and psychological. We need food and water, love, and the opportunity to release anger and aggression. When such needs become intense, the body signals what it needs. The body has a structure that monitors these conditions, reads the signals, and reports to an action-oriented part of the mind.

THE ID   The id is the structure that monitors our body, collects information about our bodily needs, and transforms that information into psychological experiences. For example, information about a low level of sugar is translated into the desire to eat.

But the operations of the id are always unconscious; we are only aware of its transformations—the impulses that enter our mind. Thus, the id is uneducable—its monitoring and transforming functions can't be modified by the mind. But when we start to develop defense mechanisms to cope with problems, the id's reports may be blocked or distorted.

THE EGO   The desires generated by the id are reported to the ego. The ego specializes in reality testing. Through experience, the ego learns what the real world is like, and keeps track of what can and can't be done safely; it specifies what is physically possible. When the id picks up a need and reports it to the ego, the ego offers a list of physically possible actions.

My ego tells me through experience that I can't jump from the second floor to the first if I want to get a candy bar. When I walk by a bakery and smell the delicious cakes, my ego tells me whether it is physically possible to break the window and get a cake.

But this brings up a new problem: everything that is physically possible may not be ethically desirable. We therefore need still another control system if we are to channel our behavior successfully.

THE SUPEREGO   While the id is reporting to the ego and the ego is trying to formulate decisions, the superego is monitoring their activities. The superego uses two standards to evaluate the id's report and the ego's possible solutions: (1) the conscience that we have internalized as children, and (2) the ego ideal—the kind of person we strive to be. The superego asks two questions about our thinking and contemplated action:

• Is it moral for me to have such thoughts and carry out such actions?

• If I carry out such actions, will I be true to my ideals?

The superego doesn't wait until we are engrossed in such thoughts and plans; it acts as soon as the id starts reporting to the ego. Parts of the ego and the superego operate on the unconscious level. When certain desires begin to move toward the conscious parts of the mind, the superego can censor them by causing the ego to apply defense mechanisms.

If no defenses are activated, the information moves through an unconscious layer of the mind and passes into the conscious mind. Now we can think about what can and may be done to satisfy our needs.

In other cases, ideas may move into our conscious mind and be prevented from being expressed. We might think: "I can't do that; what if people found out I did it?" or "I'm not that kind of person." The superego produces feelings of guilt, shame, and embarrassment. Guilt feelings are associated with violations of our conscience; they are produced when we want to do something we consider immoral. Shame and embarrassment are produced when we imagine what others will think of us if we were to do something bad and it became known.

There are three possibilities when defenses are activated: (1) the information can be completely blocked off—a person may remain unaware of inner feelings of anger and fury; (2) the information can be distorted—some obese people who feel hungry may actually have the need for companionship and love; or (3) the information can appear when our defenses are relaxed. When we are fatigued or when we dream, the real needs may penetrate into our minds.

But not everything that passes into consciousness is expressed in our behavior. We might allow ourselves to have all kinds of sexual or aggressive fantasies, yet not do anything about them. These desires are not blocked at the unconscious level, but are inhibited at the conscious level. Our feelings of guilt and shame prevent us from making the fantasies come true.

Those who have cruel and sadistic fantasies and do not feel guilty and ashamed are capable of carrying them out. Such persons can rape and kill and experience little or no guilt. Their behavior reflects a different (but abhorrent) code of ethics and set of ego ideals.

THE HUMANISTIC VIEW

Carl Rogers feels that parents and society impose uniformity and cultural traditions to such a degree that our uniqueness is seriously endangered. The logic of their views is easily rationalized: babies at birth are ignorant and innocent, and need to be protected if they are to live. Babies must be socialized; they must be trained to act and think properly and believe in the right things. Because parents and social institutions are sophisticated and wise, the babies of the world must follow the dictates of their parents.

Rogers, in rejecting such parental tyranny, uses a different kind of logic. Babies at birth already possess a guidance system that, in time, will enable them to behave in ways that are good for them and for society. The basic task of parents is to facilitate the development of that internal guidance system; in fact, one of the most crippling things parents can do is to attempt to substitute a list of rights and wrongs for the guidance system. Tragically, very few parents have the necessary confidence in their children, and a large percentage of children grow up with deformed personalities.

The internal guidance system initially indicates to a baby what is good and bad for him. For example, given sweet food, babies swallow; given bitter food, babies are likely to spit it out. As a child, too, the guidance system may register "good" to the boy when he pulls his sister's pigtails and when he empties all the drawers on the floor. This, in the eyes of self-righteous parents, requires drastic action; the "brat" has to be taught the difference between right and wrong, and it is considered legitimate to use both physical and psychological punishment to implant these moral lessons.

In pressuring kids, parents have one especially potent weapon: their love. Kids desperately need love, affection and respect—and are willing to exchange their independence (and their internal guidance system) to obtain these positive regards. When parents attack their child ("Bad, bad boy! If you do that again, I won't love you!") they force the child to disregard his internal guidance system.

The kid can't trust the judgment of his own guidance system; following it gets him into trouble and threatens to alienate his parents' love for him. So he must memorize his parents' list of what is "good" and "bad." Worse yet, a child's picture of himself is based on this list. If he behaves in "good" ways, he feels proud of himself; if he behaves in "bad" ways, he feels ashamed and anxious.

The result is that the child becomes blinded in two important ways: he no longer knows what he himself really wants and likes, and his personality includes only those things that are acceptable to his parents. For example, if parents hate music and criticize their child for liking music, then he might be pressured into believing he actually hates music, too.

The child is subjected to strings or conditions: only if he behaves in acceptable ways will his parents love him. The strings are standards against which the child evaluates his behavior; he feels proud of himself only when he abides by these conditions.

Here is how Rogers answers the question: How should parents raise their children?

First, never attack the preciousness of a child as a person. Parents are entitled to attack and control the behavior of their child (within reasonable limits), but they must never poke fun at or ridicule their child as a person.

Second, parents must make an attempt to see things from their child's point of view. To do that, a parent must be willing to put aside his knowledge and values and say: "What does that experience feel like to my child?"

For example, many adults have disputed the claim that drug experiences could be pleasant and good. Such adults, regarding drugs as illegal and immoral, can't accept the idea that marijuana can be enjoyable. To them, drugs are bad, they must produce bad experiences, and the people who use them must be evil.

The consequence of this attitude is that those adults lose any chance of influencing their adolescents. Users are turned off by such an attitude; they conclude that these adults are too ignorant to pay attention to, and they keep on using drugs.

The disagreement revolves around the importance of inner experiences. Young users attach primary significance to what they feel are pleasant inner experiences; the adults consider such inner experience to be irrelevant, and focus instead on law and order and legitimate behavior.

If the parents start out by accepting the inner experience as genuine, and then move on to an analysis of the costs and disadvantages of drug use, the results might be entirely different. Just as a child can be helped to understand that pulling pigtails is unacceptable because of its consequences, so can an adolescent be helped to understand that the positive feeling created by drugs should be avoided because of their consequences.

Third, parents must be capable of experiencing and displaying in healthy ways all of their emotions and the different facets of their experiences. If parents, on moralistic or prudish grounds, try to hide their true feelings or lie about their experiences, they will mold their children to behave in the same way.

Under these conditions, children can practice using their guidance system, learn to see things from other people's viewpoints, and gradually develop into individuals who do what's good for them and for society. "Doing what the Jones do" doesn't produce ideal human beings; "Doing what my parents do" doesn't produce ideal human beings either.

Nature provides each person with a unique set of potentials. No test exists which can discover all of the potentials. To develop our personal set of potentials, each of us must follow his own guidance system. When parents nurture that guidance system, they help guarantee that their children will develop the kind of personality that is best for them—and for society.

Finally, Rogers notes that we can't stop with child-rearing. He believes his democratic and individual-oriented approach should be followed in marriage, at school, at work, and wherever else we find people. There is no substitute for self-development. People must have the opportunity to be themselves and to become what nature intended them to be.

The essence of Rogers' person-centered theory is that whenever people interact, their relationship facilitates growth if:
• Each recognizes that the other is constantly changing, and all focus on working together on the basis of the current version of each person's personality;
• Communication among the people is honest and uncensored;
• Roles, especially when played in a static, unchanging way, are not used as a basis of a relationship (As a wife, you should . . . As a worker you have to . . .); and
• Each works at becoming more empathic in his perceptions.

Do any of these things apply to you or other people you know? Can they help you understand better why people act the way they do? If not, psychologists have created many other theories that can be tried on for fit. If the theories do help, then you will have demonstrated to yourself that theories are useful and practical.

But in any event, people will remain our most interesting and intriguing attraction. Keep your eye on them.

8 | DEFENSE MECHANISMS

THE BODY HAS WAYS OF DEFENDING ITSELF from invading organisms. And similarly the mind has defense mechanisms to protect itself against pressures and help maintain mental health and emotional equilibrium.

All people are subject to stress in one form or another. If we don't become skilled in handling these pressures, we suffer horribly and cannot relate well to others.

We live in a world where all kinds of things happen: people get robbed, raped and killed; accidents occur on the road, at work and at home; and all of us live under the shadow of nuclear destruction. If we worried constantly about all these possibilities, we would waste our energy and suffer acutely.

A father who is frustrated by his teenage son can become very upset just by thinking such unthinkable thoughts as: "I would like to kill him!" Some people have been hospitalized because such thoughts tore them apart. That's why we need to limit our actions and thoughts to those that are reasonable.

Freud saw defense mechanisms as maneuvers which the ego uses to keep the id and superego under control. They regulate our awareness of troublesome experiences and help us control what we do and say. They allow us to think or act in a certain way even though something tells us to think or act in another way.

For example, a wife might believe that sex is dirty, evil and disgusting; how successful can she be as a wife? Or a businessman might believe that it is totally wrong to compete against others; can he succeed in business? In such cases, some way must be found to function effectively in spite of these feelings. Defense mechanisms represent the different ways such problems can be handled.

While defense mechanisms are sometimes successful, in many cases they are like band-aids that are applied when major surgery is required. Successfully or not, we use them all the time. The fundamental ones are described in this chapter.

REPRESSION   Repression is the unconscious pushing out of the mind of intolerable thoughts and memories. Repression makes them disappear automatically into the unconscious.

The difference between repression and suppression is that the first is unconscious, while the second is conscious. If you know you're pushing something out of your mind, it is suppression; if you're unaware that you're doing it, it is repression.

It is sometimes absolutely essential to keep our minds clear of troubling thoughts. What would happen to a newscaster if all the bloopers he had ever made kept popping into his mind while he was reporting the news? Many of us can't afford to cripple ourselves by dwelling on the past. When we have important tasks to do, we have to focus on the job.

Still, we must be able to profit from experience. Shutting out thoughts of previous failures can prevent us from learning from them and functioning more effectively. For example, Freud found that women were having a terrible time in the Viennese society at the turn of the century. Morals of that time forbade women to show an interest in sex, let alone acknowledge having an orgasm. His office was filled with women who were repressing their sexual thoughts and desires.

In many ways, people who use repression extensively are immature. Growing up means becoming more capable of meeting our needs and solving our problems. When we shut out our experiences and feelings, it becomes more difficult to improve ourselves.

DENIAL   While suppression and repression can act to cleanse our minds, denial serves to purify the world. It blocks out unacceptable perceptions.

Take, for example, the novice parachutist who is scared stiff before his first jump. He may resort to denial to rid himself of terrifying perceptions. Using denial, his fears may be blocked out, he may smile and appear relaxed, and yet at the same time he may urinate and defecate in his pants.

More typical is Pollyannish denial, named after the sweet, pleasant girl of fiction. Some people can't stand to see the world as evil and threatening, so they use Pollyannish denial to block out their awareness of such characteristics.

These people minimize the problems of, say, unemployment. Their reaction: "Sure, a few people are out of jobs, and some might lose their homes. But it's not worth bothering about such exceptional cases. Most people are getting along just fine."

A denier always has excuses and explanations; his conclusion is predetermined. The world has to be the way he wants it to be; anything that is threatening to him simply does not exist.

People who use denial excessively are not just difficult to deal with; they are very sick. But even normal people find the world's problems too difficult to face all the time. Do any of us want to be reminded constantly of the people who die needlessly each day, or of the brutal hellholes of our prisons? For this reason, even very intelligent people and world leaders may fail to recognize imminent catastrophes. This may be one reason for the years that passed before any action was taken against Nazi Germany, in spite of its many aggressions.

In both repression and denial, troublesome material is kept out of the mind—at a very high cost. There are less costly protective devices that allow the material to enter the mind, but require that we do something to render it harmless. The material must be distorted or broken up into meaningless bits through projection, intellectualization, reaction formation, or undoing.

PROJECTION   In many important situations, it's generally not logical or wise to take another person's word for his motives; we must then guess at them. To understand others, we typically use ourselves as a model of human nature because we think we know why we act as we do.

When we see someone take some questionable action, we ask ourselves: What motive would I have if I were in *his* shoes? We assume that other people are pretty much like us, and that we can use our self-understanding to flesh out our understanding of others.

Sometimes these attributions produce accurate inferences; other times, they may result in disaster. Since people possess different amounts of understanding and self-acceptance, there are three types of attribution.

OBTUSE PROJECTION   Some people, particularly males, are insensitive. The stereotype of the male is that of a strong, courageous person who never shows emotion; crying is for women and sissies. He prefers to act rather than sit down and analyze himself.

The macho man tells it like it is. He might choose to "help" a friend by pointing out his faults, with explosive results. An insensitive person cannot picture others as being sensitive either. He believes that the unadorned truth is what counts and is what everybody wants. His limited self-understanding makes it hard to understand other people.

We expect our friends to make us feel better; even "constructive" criticism is hard for most people to take—especially when it comes across as an attack. We might accept someone who says: "Here is a better way of doing that task." But we get upset when someone says: "That's all wrong; you're not doing it the right way. Let me show you the intelligent way." When criticism is expressed this way, the effect is usually negative.

When his suggestions provoke a negative reaction, the obtuse person might be honestly surprised. He can't understand why everything went so badly when he was only telling the truth. This bull-in-the-china-shop approach can inflict all kinds of suffering upon others.

EMPATHIC PROJECTION   To empathize is to look at the world through another person's eyes—to try to understand his reactions to what is happening. It sounds easy, but it isn't.

If your adolescent son comes to you and says: "I've had it with school and I'm going to drop out." you might decide to humor him. You might say: "I know exactly how you feel. When I was your age, I wanted to do the same thing. But after I thought it over and talked to my friends, I decided to stay in school."

Is that empathy? In most cases, no. What you are assuming is that your son's feelings are just like yours. But he is a person in his own right; there is no reason to believe his feelings duplicate yours.

Empathy means ignoring your own attitudes—and *listening* to your son with a mind that is open to *his* feelings, so that you can understand what he's going through from his point of view.

Unfortunately, people are busy formulating responses instead of listening; they are waiting for a chance to interrupt and talk sense to the other person. No wonder the common complaint of adolescents is: "My parents don't understand me." Actually listening to what others say, at home or at work, is a rare event.

PATHOLOGICAL PROJECTION   Very few people are completely satisfied with the way they are; there is a gap between the "real me" (the person I actually am) and the "ideal me" (the person I would like to be). People are more or less aware of their limitations, and most of us try to live with them.

But sometimes a person finds a personal characteristic so disturbing that he can't live with it—unless he justifies it by attributing the characteristic to other people as well. This is pathological projection. Take the miser who hates to donate a penny. He may feel pangs of guilt, but he still can't give. So he draws up a list of millionaires with their stingy habits. He says: "Look—they aren't interested in helping others, either. In this world, it's everyone for himself. Why should I be a sucker and let others take advantage of me?" In this way he no longer sees himself as being stingy; he now justifies his behavior by calling it the smart and realistic thing to do.

Such an example appears innocuous. But suppose a person is so filled with hate that he claims everybody is out to cheat and harm him. He might conclude that the best defense is offense. He may sue people at the drop of a hat—or in extreme cases, even go for his gun so he'll "get them before they get me."

INTELLECTUALIZATION   When someone intellectualizes, he represses all signs of emotion. He acts like a robot, and does not display basic emotions such as joy and sorrow. To listen to such a person is like listening to a weird creature in a movie laboratory, a humanoid without feelings.

The intellectualizer can explain his behavior: "Why get emotionally upset about anything? Isn't it better to be calm and collected, to use your head? Nothing is solved by getting all worked up; think and work through your problem." It's true that, in many situations, it is necessary for a person to be calm and unemotional.

But intellectualization involves more than coolness in a specific situation. It refers to a general pattern where a person's whole life is conducted in this way: at home or at work, with friends or strangers, at social gatherings or a dangerous situation. He has banished feelings from his life.

For example, a surgeon has to keep his cool during an operation. But if he always treats his wife, children and everybody else in this way, he's got a problem because he is using intellectualization.

REACTION FORMATION   In reaction formation, a person publicly acts in the exact opposite of the way he would like to act.

Phil has an intense interest in Playboy centerfolds and x-rated movies. But he can't enjoy them fully. Every time he looks at them, his intense pleasure is smothered by a sense of guilt; he feels he is doing something "dirty." So he may assume a morally pure posture, proclaim that such "filth" corrupts the minds of people and turns them to sin, and become a censor of magazines and x-rated movies. Phil declares that he is subjecting himself to this terrible filth in order to save the public morals; his sacrifice is for the good of the people.

Note the beauty of the technique. He gains access to sexy materials under the umbrella of morality. However, if he realizes he is enjoying the material, then he faces another problem. He has to convince himself constantly that the material is terrible, he hates looking at it, and his only reason for doing so is to contribute to the welfare of others.

Aggression is another feeling that often is treated this way. Suppose Charles is filled with anger. His life has been miserable and he is furious about it. It seems only right for him to pay back the world for his suffering. Charles would like to lash out, but he feels overwhelming guilt whenever he thinks about hurting others.

Charles may turn to reaction formation. Perhaps he becomes a peacenik—one who sincerely believes all violence is evil and immoral. Peace becomes so important to him that anything and everything must be done to ensure peace; even violence is permissible in order to attain peace.

In the late 1960's we witnessed such a life style. Among the anti-war activists were some people who made bombs, attacked government offices, and splattered officials with rotten eggs—all in the name of non-violence.

This brings up the question: how can we tell when a person is doing something because he really wants to do it? In part, the answer is that people who are inflexible are using reaction formation. If Phil claims that no one but his group should see center-folds or even nudes in the museum, then we can assume that he is motivated by reaction formation.

UNDOING   Most of us at one time or another will disappoint and frustrate someone or fail to fulfill our obligation to others. We then feel guilty, and try to make up for the hurts we have caused others.

Say a boy forgot that he had a date with a girl. He might bring flowers or candy and apologize profusely for standing her up. In a sense, he is undoing the harm he inflicted on his girlfriend. But undoing, as a defense mechanism, is much broader. It involves psychological atonement, and refers to behavior intended to minimize the significance of previous acts.

The minimization in the above example makes sense because the boy tried to make his friend feel better and forget his thoughtless behavior.

But minimization can be a problem. Suppose a man robs a mom and pop grocery store. Feeling guilty, he then robs a bank. Still finding this hard to live with, he then commits murder.

This is the fundamental meaning of undoing: what I have done before is so unimportant in comparison with what I am doing now, you should forget the previous act. Why worry about a small robbery when I've done something much worse?

In addition to protective measures that act automatically without our awareness, there are also mechanisms that can be used both unconsciously and consciously.

COMPENSATION Many people have inadequacies and these can make us feel inferior. To control these feelings of inferiority, we can try to excel at something else.

If a high schooler does poorly in his school work, he might channel all his energies into sports, and become the top athlete in school. By excelling in sports, he (and others) can overlook his poor academic work.

RATIONALIZATION To rationalize is to makes excuses—by distorting facts or attributing motives that in reality aren't involved. Rationalization is frequently used to explain away defects, failures and misdeeds.

Rationalization helps us to justify our behavior and soften intense disappointments. A lazy worker, for example, might justify doing as little work as possible by saying: "My pay is so low it doesn't make sense to work harder." A manager who has just fired a fine employee because the manager saw him as a threat to his own job might say: "The economy is lousy, and we have no choice." Or a woman might marry someone for his money that she doesn't love, and insist: "He'll make a kind and devoted husband."

One form of rationalization is sour grapes. (In ancient Greece,

Aesop told of the fox who tried to reach the grapes. When he couldn't, the fox said: "The grapes were probably sour, anyway.") If a worker is passed over for promotion, he might try to save face by proclaiming: "The job is no good anyway. The hours are too long—it would kill my family life!" If a manager is released, he might try to preserve his self-esteem by alleging: "They're getting ready to play dirty, and they know I won't play that kind of a game. I'm glad it happened."

By itself, rationalization doesn't work well. When friends and family reject the excuses, other defenses have to be used. It's just too easy to see through such pseudo-logic.

DISPLACEMENT   When someone hurts us, we want to return the hurt. Frustration in particular often brings out this kind of hostility. The classic case of displacement is the boy who kicked the dog.

My boss chews me out in front of my co-worker; I'm furious and want to give him a piece of my mind—but I know he won't take any lip from his subordinates. I have to sit on my anger, and when I leave work I'm still boiling. When I get home and dinner isn't ready, I berate my wife. She lets it out by yelling at our son. He sees she is being unreasonable, but is afraid to scream back. So he ends up kicking the dog.

The anger (or any emotion) is shifted from one person or thing to another, because it is safer and more convenient to take it out on substitutes. Note the downward shift in power: If our attacker is more powerful than we are, we are likely to look for someone weaker to attack. Scapegoating and blaming the victim are good examples of displacement.

FANTASY   Life rarely goes the way we think it should. There is frequently a long delay between a desire and its satisfaction—or, worse, the desire may never be satisfied. Thus, the pressure of unsatisfied desires can burden us for long periods.

In situations like this, we resort to fantasy and daydreams. In our daydreams, we always get what we want right now; in our imagination, we are fully in control.

The most typical daydreams are those of the conquering hero and the suffering hero. The story line of the conquering hero daydream is: "I am overlooked and rejected. People don't recognize how brilliant, creative, and exceptional I am. I possess outstanding intellectual and executive abilities. A challenge appears and I demonstrate my superior abilities. The jerks that ignored me before now feel stupid. I beam with joy and bask in their adulation."

The story line of the suffering hero type is: "I am a terrible misfit, and I need sympathy. I am in terrible pain (or financial difficulties), and I need help. The problems I face are so overwhelming that I may get sick or even die! Now the people who didn't help me will feel awful because they acted so cruelly." Note that this type of dream focuses on guilt. Such daydreams are most effective when we picture ourselves dying, and the others as stewing in their remorse. Death is final, and the jerks that refused to extend aid will have to suffer forever.

But daydreams are useful and practical, too. If I have to make an important presentation in three weeks, I keep thinking about the presentation and how it might be received. I picture my presentation as fantastic, with everyone applauding wildly. Or I see myself as bombing out—because of a horrible case of stage fright. My fantasies prepare me for any kind of outcome.

Such fantasies are common and can be helpful, but there's a catch—we must concentrate more and more on the task as the time approaches. Our realistic preparations must crowd out the daydreams of what might happen.

In another way fantasies serve a purpose. Workers doing boring repetitious tasks (and even participants in a boring sex act) can introduce interest and excitement by adding imaginary events or people. If we turn on our imagination we can be as happy (or unhappy) as we want.

SUBLIMATION   Often, we do not get the affection and respect we think we are entitled to. Nor are we able to express our anger and hostility toward those who have frustrated and disappointed us. To sit on these feelings is hard. Over the years, the feelings will become more intense and harder to contain. The price we have to pay in tensions (and even physical disturbance) can be excessively high.

Under such conditions, we tend to seek out socially acceptable ways of releasing the tensions. Boxing, for example, is a socially acceptable way of clobbering people; the harder we hit, the more the onlookers love it and the better we feel.

Writing a love novel might serve as a substitute for a person incapable of establishing a love relationship. An executive unable to attain the power he wants in the business world, might get a comparable sense of accomplishment by throwing himself into the role of husband and father. A husband, coming back to work from a terrible weekend at home, might vent his pent-up aggressions in difficult and bitter labor negotiations.

In sublimation, the strong feelings are channeled through socially appropriate activities. If these qualifications are not met, then the feelings are being displaced and shifted.

As you can see, we have a wide assortment of defense mechanisms which we can use to deal with problems and stress. Each one involves both benefits and costs.

Everyone uses defense mechanisms; that's not bad. What is bad is to use them in a way that makes life miserable for ourselves and for others.

Know thyself. Know your defense mechanisms.

9 | STRESS

A PLANT MANAGER MIGHT DEFINE STRESS as the pressure on him to cut costs and increase productivity; an air traffic controller, as the urgent need to concentrate on his scope without losing his cool; an athlete, as the expectation to get in there and win; and a doctor, as the awesome responsibility for the life and health of his patients. Stress means different things to different people—including scientists.

Psychologists, psychiatrists, sociologists, biochemists and other scientists are interested in different aspects of stress, so each discipline studies stress through different methods. Consequently, there is little agreement among them.

Nevertheless, it is generally accepted that: (1) many kinds of events evoke stress, and (2) individuals react to stress in different ways.

One definition of stress is any environmental event or crisis which requires unusual responses or exceeds our tolerances. Imprisonment, combat, or physical injury are examples.

HOLMES

In a study of the effect of stress on health, Holmes and Rahe rated stressful events according to the degree of stress. These are listed in the chart on the next page with their change units.

The authors declare that of those people with over 300 Life Change Units in the past year, almost 80% will get sick in the near future, while of those people with less than 150 Life Change Units, only about 30% will get sick in the near future. Note, too, that the table treats some very desirable things as being stressful (getting married, getting a significant raise, and outstanding personal achievement). Many examples of meteoric achievement (to name three: Leon Spinks in boxing, John Belushi in movies, and Freddy Prince in television) show that beneficial changes can be dangerously stressful.

SOCIAL READJUSTMENT RATING SCALE (slightly modified)

	LIFE EVENT	MEAN VALUE
1.	Death of spouse	100
2.	Divorce	73
3.	Marital separation	65
4.	Jail term	63
5.	Death of close family member	63
6.	Personal injury or illness	53
7.	Marriage	50
8.	Fired at work	47
9.	Marital reconciliation	45
10.	Retirement	45
11.	Change in health of family member	44
12.	Pregnancy	40
13.	Sex difficulties	39
14.	Gain of new family member	39
15.	Business readjustment	39
16.	Change in financial state	38
17.	Death of close friend	37
18.	Change to different line of work	36
19.	Change in number of arguments with spouse	35
20.	Mortgage or loan for major purchase (home, etc.)	31
21.	Foreclosure of mortgage or loan	30
22.	Change in responsibilities at work	29
23.	Son or daughter leaving home	29
24.	Trouble with in-laws	29
25.	Outstanding personal achievement	28
26.	Wife begin or stop work	26
27.	Begin or end school	26
28.	Change in living conditions	25
29.	Revision of personal habits	24
30.	Trouble with boss	23
31.	Change in work hours or conditions	20
32.	Change in residence	20
33.	Change in schools	20
34.	Change in recreation	19
35.	Change in church activities	19
36.	Change in social activities	18
37.	Mortgage or loan for lesser purchase (car, TV, etc.)	17
38.	Change in sleeping habits	16
39.	Change in number of family get-togethers	15
40.	Change in eating habits	15
41.	Vacation	13
42.	Christmas	12
43.	Minor violations of the law	11

Some events that were found to foreshadow a mental breakdown were arguments with a spouse, marital separation, a new type of work, death of a family member, and serious illness in the family. In particular, Holmes found conflict with a spouse to be fifteen times as frequent among patients who become depressed.

People who become seriously depressed suffer from higher than normal life changes. Though the changes may cover a six-month period, there is an abrupt and significant peak three or four weeks before the breakdown.

The pattern of schizophrenics, the most serious of the mentally ill, is somewhat different from that of depressed people. First, the stressful events are concentrated in the three or four weeks before the breakdown. Second, different items are associated with their breakdowns: job changes, health changes, and changes in residence. Third, while the depressed person apparently suffers losses in the personal and family sphere, the schizophrenic seems to withdraw from people and becomes preoccupied with himself.

In a special study of sailors, Holmes found that the higher the life changes score, the greater the likelihood of subsequent illnesses. This study, like many others, shows that stress can help cause illness. Situations which threaten us, overwhelm us, or leave us feeling quite unsatisfied, tend to make us sick. A few studies even suggest that the more intense the pressure the sicker we are likely to become.

Holmes and his team also tried to determine whether injuries are associated with stress. They studied the University of Washington football team, and found that the risk of injury increased in direct proportion to the magnitude of the stress. Perhaps the stressed players found it harder to attain tip-top shape, concentrated less intensely on the subtle clues that give away the opponent's plays, reacted more slowly, and failed to compensate physically when knocked about by the opposing team.

HANS SELYE

A second way to define stress is in terms of the changes that occur within our bodies. When a worker gets into a heated argument with his supervisor, he might find that he is trembling, his heart is racing, his fists are clenched, and he is covered with perspiration. Hans Selye spent his professional life exploring the question of which bodily reactions to measure.

When Selye was a medical student, he unwittingly encountered the stress syndrome; he merely labeled it the syndrome of just being sick. What suggested the syndrome was the fact that all kinds of sick people appeared pretty much the same: they looked tired and felt sick, lost their strength and ambition, had no appetite, generally lost weight and preferred to lie down rather than be active.

Selye found that no one was interested in his sickness syndrome. Each doctor was interested only in his own specialty, and looked for diseases that fell into his area of expertise. Selye's professors ignored his syndrome and even made him feel foolish. Not surprisingly, Selye forgot about his syndrome.

His interest in this sickness syndrome was rekindled later when he subjected animals in the laboratory to various traumatic agents and conditions (heat, cold, surgical removal of various bodily organs). He discovered that all the animals reacted in a similar fashion regardless of the nature of the traumatic condition.

The adrenal cortex became enlarged; their thymus, spleen, lymph nodes and lymphatic structures shrank in size; and deep bleeding ulcers appeared in the stomachs and upper gastro-intestinal tracts.

Apparently, the stresses threatened the animals, and their bodies responded by mobilizing to fight off the threat. Most importantly, the adrenal glands released massive amounts of chemicals that increased body activity. As the traumatic conditions persisted over longer periods, this mobilization, instead of alleviating the effects of the harmful conditions, often caused the animal's body to break down and develop various diseases.

Selye drew three major conclusions from these findings: (1) *The physiological stress response doesn't depend upon the kind of stress to which we are exposed.* The physical damage is part of a general nonspecific stress reaction; almost every part of our body is involved in the response to stressors. The sickness syndrome represents a universal protective pattern that is activated whenever any stressors attack us.

The stress hormones pour out when we are faced with any demand; even great joy produces the same neurophysiological and biochemical reaction in our body that intense pain does. Both positive and negative life events can generate stress responses.

(2) *With prolonged or repeated exposure, the protective re-*

sponse progresses through three basic stages. These are the alarm phase, the resistance phase, and the exhaustion phase. These three phases are referred to as the general adaptation syndrome.

As soon as a stressor affects our body, the body's stress mechanism is mobilized. The stressor has a generalized effect upon the whole body. Chemicals are released into our bloodstream, and act as an alarm which arouses our body. Simultaneously, messages speed through our nervous system to coordinate bodily counteractions and activate our body's energy reserves.

Almost every major organ system is alerted. Adrenalin is released (which makes possible such amazing feats as lifting a 2,000 pound car off an accident victim); breathing is increased, as are heart rate and blood pressure; blood cholesterol level jumps up; the blood-clotting mechanisms are activated; and all senses become heightened.

The initial response to stress is very much like the reaction of a person who is confronted with a sudden and unexpected danger. Suppose you came home one day and found burglars stripping your home. The odds are that all the above changes (and more) would occur.

But our body cannot remain at a high level of arousal for a long period. So, during the alarm phase, the body seeks out and delegates the responsibility for dealing with the stressor to an organ or system that is capable of handling it. Then the alarm reactions disappear, and the person protects himself by intensifying his use of defense mechanisms or by attempting to eliminate the stressor. Typically, the person adheres rigidly to his pattern of dealing with the stressor; he tends not to re-evaluate his situation or find new ways to cope.

Resistance to the specific stressor is high, but two problems arise. If the stressor continues for a long time, then our resources are used up in fighting the stressor. And other parts of the body are weakened by being deprived of their needed resources. Thus our body's ability to fight against other stressors is seriously impaired, our resistance drops substantially, and physical and mental problems can arise.

Ideally, the alarm and beginning of the resistance phase both buy time for us to neutralize and get rid of the stressor. Nature never equipped us for a continuous fight.

If the stressor plagues us for too long a period, the organ or system that has been assigned to defend us against the stressor becomes worn out. New measures become necessary. Once again, the body must create a general arousal like that in the alarm phase. But by this time, the bodily resources have been depleted and the most effective defense has been exhausted. The organ or system has burned out.

Fortunately, only the most severe stresses lead to exhaustion and death. Most physical and mental stressors affect us for only limited periods, and provoke only the phases of alarm and resistance. These two phases may be experienced again and again.

(3) *The protective responses can provoke disease states which Selye called "disease of adaptation."* These diseases are the price we pay for having the protective mechanism. Consider, for example, the corticosteroid hormones that the adrenal cortex produces.

These corticosteroids can create tears in the walls of the arteries. These tears are frequently filled with cholesterol bundles called plaques. The plaques are a type of scar tissue, and produce hardening of the arteries.

Once the arteries harden, the heart gets supplied with less blood and oxygen, and various heart conditions can develop. The cholesterol plaque can become detached from the artery walls, travel to the heart, and block major arteries to the heart. Some heart muscle can die, or the person himself can die of a heart attack.

Ironically, the ability of the various parts of the body to respond efficiently is impaired by the protective mechanism itself. The diseases of adaptation are not the direct result of the stresses, but are consequences of our body's inability to generate appropriate reactions that will not be harmful.

Prolonged stress thus has significant physical and psychological consequences. They may operate at various levels and elicit various behaviors:

Mental: aggression, anxiety, fatigue, irritability, low self-esteem.

Behavior: excessive drinking and smoking, drug use, emotional outbursts, impaired speech, restlessness.

Perception: inability to make decisions and concentrate, forgetfulness, sensitivity to criticism.

Bodily effects: sweating, dryness of mouth, difficulty in breathing, increased heart rate and blood pressure.

Work behavior: poor productivity, absenteeism, job dissatisfaction.

Some examples of prolonged stress that show how these kinds of symptoms develop:

• In Sweden, some women employees in an insurance company were required to work overtime for a two-month period. Because of their housework responsibilities, most chose to work the extra hours on the weekend.

Investigators noted that the women found it very difficult to relax at *any* time. Their bodies were most hyped up in the evening after work. The hyped-up state got worse and worse. They found it difficult to unwind at any time, and they became very irritable and showed typical stress symptoms.

• In 1979, a small plane hit an airliner above San Diego and 144 people were killed. The bodies were torn apart and spread over the entire area. Even the hardened policemen and firemen were shaken by the sight.

It became difficult for them to push the scenes out of their minds. Many suffered from nightmares, insomnia, headaches, gastro-intestinal problems, and memory loss. A few even had problems going back to work.

These effects were so devastating that 25 psychologists in the San Diego area volunteered free counseling for all city employees who had witnessed the carnage. About 100 employees, many of them veteran police officers, took the counseling. They continued to find it difficult to dismiss the terrible scenes from their minds. They were also ashamed of their inability to deal with the experiences.

• Zimbardo, a psychologist, cites the following incident. A healthy woman demanded admittance to a Baltimore hospital because she was scared stiff and feared imminent death.

She explained she had been one of three baby girls on whom a midwife had put a death curse—that they would die before the ages of 16, 21, and 23, respectively. The first had died just before 16 in a car accident, and the second in a nightclub brawl just before 21. Now the third woman feared for her life.

The very next morning in the hospital, this woman was found dead—just two days before her 23rd birthday. The curse had stressed her to death.

• The health status of men and women differs significantly. We know that men, on the average, die eight years younger than women. Also, at certain ages, men are:

Four times more likely to die of coronary heart disease.

Four times more likely to die in an accident.

Five times more likely to die from alcohol-related diseases.

Five times more likely to be murdered.

Seven times more likely to kill themselves.

Men suffer more frequently from the diseases of adaptation. Why? One possible answer is that women are genetically more physically competent. But given the radical changes in disease patterns in this century, genetics can't be the main factor.

Instead, it seems more likely that the different roles of men and women are the causes of these differences. In the past, the man was the breadwinner; he made the major decisions; he was exposed to the unhealthy work environment; etc.

Today, more women are working and being confronted with these kinds of pressures. Women are experiencing job, career, and organizational stressors as never before. As we might expect, the difference in stress disease is narrowing. Coronary heart diseases, peptic ulcers, and disease-predisposing behavior (for example, smoking) are increasing among women. Worse yet, our society is ambivalent about women's new role in the workplace; sex discrimination is still a stressful burden that many women have to bear.

Now that we have a working definition of stress and a way to measure it, we can tackle this question: Is any stress good for us? Our answer is a twofold one.

First, remember that stress is created by change. If we are to develop and rise to our level of competence, then we must subject ourselves to new challenges. As such, stress is a normal part of living. A reasonable amount of change—and stress—is crucial to a good, happy life. Change is what makes life interesting. In fact, some executives even suggest that when things get too monotonous for them, they create emergencies to enliven conditions. Some doctors won't practice preventive medicine because it's too dull for them; they like the excitement of emergencies and the tension of life-death risks.

Second, when our bodies are alerted, we frequently are in better shape to succeed at tasks or to grapple with difficult or threatening situations.

So our problem isn't to avoid all alarms. Our problem is to match our mobilizations to the circumstances we face, and to find ways to solve problems before prolonged stress saps our physical and psychological systems. Just as we try to match jobs and skills, so must we match our resources to our life events.

Selye says that good stress motivates us to become more successful and competent human beings; bad stress (long-term stress of increasingly higher levels) can cripple or kill us.

10 | EMOTIONAL ILLNESS

BY ITSELF, HAVING PROBLEMS DOESN'T MAKE A PERSON SICK. All people have problems. Whether a person remains emotionally healthy or sick depends on his coping skills, resources and vulnerabilities.

Coping skills emerge and develop through the childhood and adolescent years. Different people possess these skills to various degrees; these skills determine how we try to solve our problems and how successful we are.

Our ability to apply the skills is affected by our available resources: the kind of job we have, the social support provided by family and friends, etc. For example, a wealthy woman whose husband dies can spend a great deal of time with her children; she can hire babysitters and get away from the children when the pressure becomes intense; and she has no problem paying for anything, including babysitters. In contrast, a poor widow will have to work or resort to public aid, and she will have a limited opportunity to mother her children in a tension-free atmosphere.

Adults in contemporary American society have five basic vulnerabilities, according to Wolberg: dependency needs, strong feelings of resentment, feelings of external control, an insecure self-image, and detachment needs.

These vulnerabilities can make us so emotionally upset that we find it almost impossible to solve our problems, especially when adequate resources are unavailable.

DEPENDENCY NEEDS Decision making is becoming increasingly risky. Thus, many people try to find and become attached to someone who is decisive and powerful. Wolberg draws an analogy to a tired swimmer who is worried about his ability to sustain himself; he searches for someone or something upon which to lean.

However, it is not only difficult to find a satisfactory person upon whom to lean; our society also places a high value on self-reliance and self-sufficiency. Consequently, dependent people are often exploited by those who appear to be more powerful; and they feel ashamed and trapped by being forced to exchange self-respect for security.

RESENTMENT   Dependency breeds anger and resentment. Few people are willing to dedicate their lives to someone else's personal development. Most people disappoint, frustrate and reject a leaner—either because they are taking care of number one, or because they are doing what they think is in the best interests of the relationship. The leaner feels guilt and shame ("Why don't I try to stand on my own two feet?") and hostility ("Boy, are people callous and cruel!"). Thus, a person may find himself straining to control strong feelings of fury and resentment that can become almost intolerable.

FEELINGS OF CONTROL   Our society is becoming more and more difficult to navigate. While our American norms insist that any intelligent and capable person can figure out how to be successful, many people consider this to be unrealistic.

Battles loom on all sides: discrimination versus reverse discrimination, E.R.A. versus traditional roles, trickle down versus trickle up economics, unemployment versus inflation—and the list continues. In effect, the little guy seems to be caught in a terrifying crossfire. Many people feel that they are not in charge of their own lives, and that it is not possible for them to achieve important goals (jobs, security, love, acceptance, etc.). Such failures are hard to swallow, and a heavy burden of guilt and frustration weighs them down.

SELF-IMAGE   When we fail to meet what we consider our legitimate obligations, we lose respect for ourselves; our self-image focuses on feelings of incompetence, inferiority and inadequacy. Others can intensify these feelings by challenging our attempts to shift the blame. If we say: "I can't get a job because of the economy," an unsympathetic listener might retort: "But other people get jobs in this economy; what's wrong with you?" It is always possible for someone to point a finger and claim that the true problem is us.

DETACHMENT   One way to minimize feelings of guilt and resentment is to limit our attachment to people and goals. If a person can harden himself to the attacks that others make on him, and if he can avoid becoming emotionally attached to others, then there is little danger that others can aggravate him.

One type of detachment is dropping out completely and turning inward to self-controlled pleasures. Drugs, for example, serve that purpose relatively easily; by taking a chemical and giving himself a high, a person avoids having to depend on others.

At the other extreme is the super salesman who uses people— then discards them after they have served his purpose. One night stands, following the big bucks in the job market, etc.—these are alienated, exploitive patterns of detachment. To get ahead, this type of person avoids weighing himself down with a burden of loyalty, devotion and emotional attachment. If he doesn't love someone, then nobody can hurt him; if he doesn't let the company he works for become part of him, then he never has to worry about its future.

Problems that involve such basic features of human existence can't be ignored. The solutions below are maladaptive—but even unhealthy solutions are still solutions. Emotional illness is a way of handling problems that overwhelm us.

NEUROSIS

Neurotic behavior is self-defeating. Its goal is to minimize feelings of anxiety, guilt, hostility, or inferiority. At the heart of a neurosis lie tendencies to feel inadequate, to perceive everyday responsibilities as threatening, and to resolve threatening situations through various cover-ups and self-protective maneuvering.

A neurotic person is so concerned about failure, inadequacy and rejection that he has adopted a protective life style that prevents personal development and makes social relationships difficult. The most important of these protective life styles are described below.

HYPOCHONDRIASIS   A hypochondriac is a person who unjustifiably complains of physical problems such as backaches, headaches and stomach pains. Although doctors are unable to find any physical basis for the pains, hypochondriacs are well aware of the fallibility of doctors; they won't accept a diagnosis they don't like, and shop around until they find a doctor who will treat their complaints.

The hypochondriac needs to feel sick. He isn't malingering; he isn't consciously pretending to be sick. Rather, the physical complaints serve as an escape mechanism. People who develop this disorder tend to have few social skills, and believe that our society is filled with cruel people. Presumably, they were hurt in earlier social relationships.

Feeling sick serves two purposes for a hypochondriac. When confronted with a difficult situation, he develops pains to get himself out of the situation. His theme is: I'm suffering too much to be subjected to such stress.

In addition, the hypochondriac needs some social contacts. If he is lucky enough to find a doctor who will take his symptoms seriously and spend time talking to him, he is satisfied.

Hypochondriacs tend to be lonely, unhappy people. Their lives revolve around their symptoms and their bitterness toward unresponsive doctors.

HYSTERIA   Like hypochondriacs, the hysteric has physical problems that have no organic basis. But unlike hypochondriacs, hysterics frequently aren't concerned about their physical problems; they don't seek out doctors. Their problems are things like psychological blindness, psychological paralysis, and other restricted sensory and bodily defects.

A specific stressful situation often triggers the disorder. For example, a professional pianist may have an unsuccessful career—and hates his wife. He might suddenly develop a paralyzed hand. This permits him to stop playing (no more failure); forces his wife to go to work (revenge); and gets him into physical therapy (physical contacts with other women).

Moreover, the symptoms cause others to feel guilty, and the hysteric becomes the center of attention. Such secondary benefits make it difficult for the hysteric to abandon this coping technique.

DISSOCIATION   We can minimize stress by running away psychologically, escaping physically, or splitting our mental life.

We can run away psychologically by developing amnesia. All of a sudden, our mind goes blank—wiping out the situation (and the problem) because we can't remember it.

In addition, we may also flee the scene physically. All of a sudden, we find ourselves halfway across the continent—with no idea of how we got there.

Or we might develop a set of different personalities within one body. The books *Three Faces of Eve* and *Sybil* are true cases of multiple personalities. While such cases are rare (perhaps two hundred on record), they are fascinating to study. Through different personalities, a person can satisfy many repressed needs and avoid painful situations. When the conscious personality is turned off, the person can do all kinds of things without forcing the conscious personality to face responsibility. In fact, the conscious personality doesn't even know what the other personalities are doing.

It is difficult to convince people that someone suffering from multiple personalities isn't faking. This skepticism makes life complicated for him.

DEPRESSION   The loss of important things—a relative or friend, a promotion, an organization—can cause depression. Depression has two basic features: feelings of inadequacy and abandonment, and an acute need for reassurance.

Depressed people need others. But they are incapable of obtaining social support. Sometimes it is because of inadequate social skills; sometimes there are only a few people in their lives. Take the wife who gave up her friends and social activities to build her life around her husband. With the death of her husband, she is likely to find life devoid of satisfaction, and thus become depressed.

Unfortunately, a depressed person often tries to use self-depreciation as a way of soliciting support: "I'm no good; I'm guilty of hurting others and deserve such punishment." People around her may soon get annoyed by such depressing talk. The more grudging the support that is given, the more she pressures others to furnish more. They get still more annoyed, the support dries up even more, and suicide becomes a distinct possibility.

OBSESSIONS AND COMPULSIONS   Unwanted thoughts (obsessions) or actions (compulsions) plague some people. An obsessive mother might constantly think about an accident happening to her children if they are playing outside. A compulsive hand-washer might wash his hands two hundred times a day.

In both cases the person feels an alien force controls his or her mind and body. There is no way to end these behaviors. In extreme cases, the obsessions and compulsions so completely occupy the waking hours that there is no time to think or do anything else. Such a person has to be hospitalized.

PHOBIAS   A phobia is an irrational fear of an object or situation which evokes a panic-reaction. A person with a fear of darkness, for example, may go to pieces in a dark room: his heart races, he trembles, sweat pours off him, and he might even scream in fright. But when a light is turned on, he calms down and appears normal.

Fears of high places, enclosed places, open street areas, and crowds are found with some frequency. The victim is aware of the object or situation that elicits the panic-reaction—so he might find it possible to avoid the frightening events. But in extreme cases, the fears may force him to become a recluse.

PSYCHOSIS

Neurotic people usually recognize that they are sick, are capable of fulfilling basic everyday obligations, and usually don't need to be hospitalized. In contrast, psychotics are less likely to recognize their illness, have a very limited ability to meet basic obligations, and frequently must be hospitalized (or at least medicated with powerful tranquilizers) for long periods.

The two basic psychotic conditions are schizophrenia and manic-depressive psychosis. The first is a thought disorder; the second, a mood disorder.

SCHIZOPHRENIA   The schizophrenic is a person whose thinking, feelings and activities strike us as bizarre.

One type of schizophrenic might make up words, string words together in a meaningless fashion (strong, long, dong, tong, wong, kong), and keep mixing together real events and mental fantasies.

Another might suffer from delusions. He might believe the FBI and KGB are out to get him, or that he is the Messiah and can save mankind.

Another type focuses on a crucial breakdown of motor behavior. Such a schizophrenic might stand in one place, fail to swallow saliva until it putrifies in his mouth, and oppose any attempt to move him. Or the breakdown may take the opposite form; he paces up and down, shouts and waves his arms, and stays on the go until physically or chemically restrained.

MANIC-DEPRESSION   The most striking symptoms of a manic-depressive are the changes in emotional tone that range from severe depression to ecstatic euphoria.

A victim of psychotic depression feels his case is hopeless. He often believes he has committed a totally unforgivable act. Such a patient might even believe that he is the one who is causing the whole world to suffer.

By proclaiming that he is the world's worst sinner or most venal criminal, the depressed person ascribes to himself importance and special status. He refuses to be consoled, and can deeply resent any attempt to dismiss his charges against himself. The depression can be so deep that the person won't talk, ignores the world around him and must be fed intravenously. He doesn't undertake even the most basic life-sustaining activities.

The manic patient shows the opposite pattern. He is on the go 22 hours a day; he overflows with energy, plans and activities; he wants to organize the world to achieve spectacular results; he is constantly trying to do things with, for and to people. If not protected, such a person can kill himself by his own activity. He can even become very aggressive and assaultive when people balk at cooperating and helping him fulfill his goals. The pressure to do something is relentless. He isn't enjoying himself, and can actually burst into tears in the middle of his frenetic actions.

PERSONALITY DISORDERS

Personality disorders are reflected in the way a person manipulates other people. The passive-aggressive personality tends to be superficially compliant and submissive—but he doesn't carry out what he agreed to do. He won't openly insist on having his way—but under the smokescreen of compliance, he manipulates people or situations until he gets his own way.

The explosive personality behaves the opposite way. He projects an aura of potential violence, and intimidates others into submitting to his demands. While he may actually become violent, his stance and reputation are usually enough to cause people to knuckle under. He is loud, bullies people, and takes pride in making others look cowardly. He has few social skills; his fists, muscles and mouth are his persuaders.

Thus, the neuroses, psychoses and character disorders are the major types of emotional illnesses. While their symptom patterns differ, they have in common the fact that each is an inadequate way of coping with personal and social problems.

There is no substitute for confronting and resolving problems.

11 | ORGANIZATIONAL ROLE THEORY

MOST OF US THINK THAT THE COMPANIES we work for revolve about people—and that, therefore, we are indispensable. But that view is not shared by most organizations. Organizations constitute impersonal bureaucracies. They avoid excessive dependence upon specific people. They focus on the jobs that need to be done, and on the rules and regulations needed to get the jobs done.

Most organizations emphasize a division of labor—the deskilling of jobs. With jobs fragmented and simplified, turnover and absenteeism are less of a problem. Also, wages are lower for less skilled workers. Thus we can view an organization as a set of interrelated activities performed by people in order to achieve specific results.

Organizations have been called role systems. To understand what that implies, consider the theater. In a theater, a role refers to the behavior of a character—not to the person who plays the part. Whatever role an actor plays—a doctor, a parent, a thief—his words and actions are dictated by the script; regardless of whether the actor or his understudy plays the part, the results are supposed to be the same.

Nothing in the personal lives of the actors is permitted to interfere with the role-dictated behavior; the show must go on. If each actor feels and acts his part and forgets about himself as a person, the play can be a success.

The director's job is to police the behavior of the actors, ensuring that they produce the behavior required by the part. He focuses on the play (his product); the people who produce the product are like raw material in a factory: the actors are relatively unimportant as people.

In an organization, the activities associated with each job are called a role. These activities are performed under the guidance of a person or system which has the power to reward or punish. They are standardized; anyone who carries out the tasks is expected to perform them in the same way. The organization stresses standardization because it wants a stable and predictable production of goods and services.

This requires that each worker do his assigned share of the work and cooperate with other workers. To ensure that tasks are done properly and on time, organizations write job descriptions and work rules, and appoint overseers to control the behavior of workers. The organization assumes that pressure must be used to guide behavior.

The overseers, like the director of a play, concentrate on the activities needed to produce the product—rather than on the people who perform the activities. The organization hopes to guarantee that (1) workers will be paid only for doing their jobs, so that neither time nor money will be wasted, and (2) the organization will not be dependent on specific people.

If this is accomplished, the organization can perpetuate itself simply by having the roles carried on by other people.

Organizations are very impersonal. They care little about who performs their activities. They are concerned only with getting the work done that is needed to produce their product. Organizations don't want to become dependent upon specific workers. People don't really count—they are expendable; the health and success of the organization depend on the activities being done. It is not surprising, therefore, that managers of production lines are delighted to have robots which can perform certain activities as effectively as people.

Management puts its faith in the role system. But faith isn't enough. Job descriptions and work rules are theoretical descriptions of how things are supposed to work—but what is more important is what actually goes on. Often, workers find it impossible to follow the theoretical descriptions.

There are many examples of the inadequacy of organizational role systems. It is a common practice for workers in Britain to call attention to their grievances by working to rule. The British Railway trains come in late—if they run. The Postal Workers park their trucks only in approved zones, and never leave packages unless a member of the family is home. The result is that these governmental systems are paralyzed because the workers merely follow the prescribed rules.

Organizations are too complex to be run by rules alone. The work itself may be different from the job description. The way the job has to be performed is important, too. If we have hostile co-workers, the job is going to be harder to do. The overseer's job is to make people behave in ways that make the work easier and more pleasant for everyone; unfortunately, that doesn't happen often. If the work rules are insufficient or inappropriate and overseers are ineffective, how can we learn to do the job the way it's supposed to be done?

Each person in an organization is associated directly with many other people, because he depends on other workers to get his own job done. The people whose behavior affects one another are called a role-set.

The role-set of a foreman in a plant includes the workers under his supervision, the other foremen with whom he must work, and his superintendent. He is fundamentally rewarded or criticized according to the performance of his workers.

Generally, all members of a role-set develop expectations about how the others should do their jobs. These cover both the way the job should be performed, and the attitude the worker should show; they are the standards against which our behavior is evaluated.

It takes time to learn these expectations—and often, they are not clearly communicated. Many workers are forced to rely upon trial and error, and the praise or criticism of co-workers, to learn what is expected of them. Where expectations are not clearly spelled out, workers get into trouble because of the way they do things.

ROLE CONFLICT   Another source of problems arises when a worker is caught between contradictory pressures that push him to behave in different ways at the same time; to comply with one demand makes it impossible to comply with the others. The contradictory demands may be made by different superiors, or even by the same supervisor. Different expectations may be held by the worker and his superior, or even by the worker and his family.

A supervisor may instruct a foreman to fill orders immediately—but prohibit him from adding extra help or overtime work. A manager may even be pushed into illegal actions, such as a pay-off, even when such actions affront his conscience. Finally, members of the role-set may have different ideas about how to spend their time, how much work to put out, or how to act at work.

Role conflicts subject workers to excessive psychological, physiological and social strains. The result is that they trust their co-workers less, communicate less with them, and may develop various illnesses. The effectiveness of the organization suffers, too. Organizations depend on agreement about who should do what and when. When this condition is violated—for example, when powerful supervisors are involved in the conflict—a subordinate can be turned and twisted. Whatever enjoyment he got from his job is now eroded by the unpleasant battle surrounding him.

Both flexible people and introverted people suffer greatly when subjected to role conflict. Introverted people are likely to be less socially involved; they tend to work at their jobs and ignore the people around them. They are independent and self-sufficient. It's hard for them to fight for clarification of their responsibilities. However, their feelings are deep, and the strains they feel can be very intense.

Flexible people try to accommodate everyone. It's hard for them to say no. As a result, they put themselves out to achieve everything demanded of them. Contradictory demands pile up higher and higher, and the person becomes overloaded. Worse yet, the flexible person blames himself when things go wrong.

ROLE AMBIGUITY   Role ambiguity generally refers to uncertainty about how we fit into the system and what we are supposed to do. These uncertainties include the basis on which we are evaluated, the standards to be met in order to be rated excellent, the consequences for failure to do the job, and our future in the organization.

When work objectives are poorly defined, expectations can't be predicted, and, in the absence of important information, it's hard to make extensive use of our personal abilities. Because we can't see how to apply our abilities, we can't make a maximum contribution to the company.

Thus, both the organization and the worker suffer from role ambiguity. The organization misuses its human resources. A worker, seeing little opportunity for advancement, may either leave or resign himself to staying and keeping his nose clean.

Role conflict and role ambiguity cause much dissatisfaction, and loss of pride and morale. Some industry leaders and consultants are now recommending such approaches as MBO (management by objectives), quality circles, and other forms of employee participation to reduce these destructive reactions. But these kinds of programs are still not common today.

12 | THE JOB WITH A FUTURE

FOR DECADES, SOCIAL SCIENTISTS HAVE TRIED—and failed—to define the ideal job. There is no one job that is perfect for everyone, because people are unique.

Still, a large percentage of workers rate some job features as more desirable than others—for example, good pay and freedom from close supervision. In that sense, the scientists are right: there is such a thing as a good job.

However, it makes more sense to talk about human nature, rather than the "good job" described in the research studies. Therefore, we shall characterize the ideal job from the point of view of people and their role in the changing world of the 1980's and 1990's.

When examined from this perspective, a number of points stand out:

We are creatures of habit.

We seek status and self-actualization.

We are cooperative.

We are adaptive.

We are responsible.

We differ widely in talent, interests and goals.

We are learning creatures.

We go through all kinds of change as we pass through our life cycles.

True, no one job can be everybody's ideal job. But, just as we must all drink and eat to maintain our physical health, so we must have certain kinds of experiences to be well-adjusted psychologically and socially.

WE ARE CREATURES OF HABIT   Every time we face a novel situation, our brains and bodies become vigilant. These mobilizations use up energy and arouse us psychologically so long as we are uncertain about what to do. Once we have figured out how to handle the situation, we relax. Thus, were we to face new situations all day long at work, our bodies and minds would be under a tremendous amount of stress. Moreover, we would find our resources exhausted in short order.

To avoid such a drain, we resort to routine, habitual ways of doing things. Frequently, management exploits that need by setting up standard operating procedures. Routine avoids new problems and too frequent mental and physical mobilization. Once a job has become habitual, a worker can daydream or concentrate on all kinds of other things.

However, the price we pay for going to the other extreme—from too much variety to too much routine—can be high. Our nervous systems are not constructed for sameness either; we need opportunities to use our brains in new situations. When we do the same things over and over in the same ways, we put our minds and bodies in strait jackets. Evidence even suggests that sameness can inhibit the development of our brains, just as lack of exercise can cause our muscles to degenerate.

Efficiency experts have found that more work is produced when people are given the opportunity to vary their work methods. Kerr found that when jobs are too routine and repetitive, accidents are more frequent. Klein, a social psychologist, suggests that because the workplace has become excessively routinized, many people are forced to seek novelty by taking risks in everyday life: driving too fast, using drugs, and engaging in such emotionally exhausting diversions as one-night stands.

We all need both routine and challenge on the job. The proportion of the two and the kinds we prefer depend on our talents and personality.

WE SEEK STATUS AND SELF-EVALUATION   The typical characteristics by which people are ranked include occupation, schooling and earnings. People who are ranked high are pictured as being more valuable, important, successful and good. People who are ranked low tend to be treated as inferior human beings who deserve little consideration.

For example, some people claim that only the wealthy and successful deserve the best medical care. Their justification for such discriminatory treatment is that special rewards are essential to encourage ambition and workaholism. If, in the process of providing special rewards, some people are hurt, then the cost is held to be a reasonable one. In short, wealth and position in life—not the fact that one is a human being with needs—are given as a justification for medical care.

Workers observe the same attitude in their community and workplace. They recognize that jobs and salary levels dictate their social value. Studs Terkel, in his book *Working,* tells of a well-educated steelworker who discussed literature in social groups. His views were highly respected—until someone asked him what kind of work he did. When the guests learned he was a steelworker, the conversation would suddenly die down, and people would edge away. The people didn't seem to understand, or want to believe, that a steelworker could be well versed in literature and have opinions worthy of discussion.

The saddest part of this is that people tend to view themselves as others view them. Thus, the lower the rank of a worker, the more he needs proof that he's not an inferior, brute-like creature.

Of course, all of us can't be chief executive officers. Still, we need opportunities to make contributions—suggestions, quality circles, participation in decisions, or other input to the decision-makers.

The important thing is that workers should be able to have others view them as sufficiently intelligent and knowledgeable to have ideas worthy of consideration. When others view us as stupid, it's very difficult to view ourselves otherwise; basically, our self-concept is a mirror image of the way other people treat us. Because we spend so much time in the workplace, and society ascribes such great importance to our job levels, we must be treated on the job as worthwhile people. The philosophic underpinning of future collective bargaining requests may well be: "They used to want more pay; now they want more say."

WE ARE COOPERATIVE   The business world revolves around competition. Managers believe that when people are challenged by others, they will produce more. Companies offer promotions, raises and bonuses as rewards for outstanding work; workers can get ahead only by being better than others.

This competition among co-workers can hurt social relationships. As human beings we need social relationships—yet only by suppressing our social tendencies can we develop a "winning is the only thing" attitude. Fallding suggests that competitive feelings create social tensions and animosities. Competition causes us to perceive our fellow workers as near-enemies; when we socialize with them, we find it necessary to drown our resentment in alcohol. The liquor at executive lunches and the six-packs at blue-collar socializing are essential for smooth relating.

We need opportunities to socialize with fellow workers; work stations and noise levels should not prevent such interaction. We need opportunities to work together to achieve common goals rather than have to focus on taking care of number one. And we need to feel that promotions, raises, and bonuses can be attained without depriving others of the opportunity to achieve them.

Not all workers are equally concerned about these factors. What we require is an opportunity to select the extent to which we are involved in competitive and cooperative relations; we need both. Different proportions can be given different workers; this has been demonstrated in a number of Scandinavian workplaces. The problem lies not in our technologies, but in management stereotypes. The best evidence of this is the experiment at the Gaines Plant (p. 182).

WE ARE ADAPTIVE   Very few people use their abilities and talents to the fullest degree; many never even discover all the things they can do. This is partly due to the fact that we aren't given opportunities to face different problems. Only at the management levels are promising candidates moved around and given all kinds of challenges; the typical worker, by contrast, is assigned a specific task, and is expected to contribute by becoming more and more proficient at that job.

However, all people need new challenges—whether they are blue-collar workers, clerks, or executives. Unfortunately, promotions don't come that often, and not everybody can get promoted. How then can such needs be met?

The range of challenges can be broadened by job rotation, enrichment training programs, and special teams. At Volvo, for example, an absentee pool was created—people volunteered to serve in the pool to fill daily vacancies. This gave them the opportunity to engage in, and become skilled at, a large variety of tasks.

People don't have to be chained to one specific job for long periods of time. When workers seek variety and an opportunity to learn and apply their abilities, they should be provided such opportunities within the organizational structure.

RESPONSIBILITY As we move through childhood and adolescence, we are held to higher and higher standards—especially as we pass into adolescence and early adulthood. People expect us to recognize our obligations; failure to meet them is punished, while success rewarded. Thus we learn to take responsibility, and we know we will be evaluated on the basis of our actions.

Often, however, the workplace does not permit such responsibility. Supervisors typically look over a worker's shoulder, and his work is checked and re-checked as part of quality control. Companies have even installed TV systems so their workers can be observed constantly. Such close supervision is strongly resented, and external quality control is, at best, merely tolerated. The reason is simple; this kind of treatment suggests that the worker can't be trusted; that he can't be changed through training; that he's too immature to regulate his own behavior; and that he could cause too much damage if he were responsible for his own results.

Perhaps management feels that by preventing workers from functioning as mature human beings, it can solidify its hierarchy of authority. Also, many supervisors have grown up in the authoritarian "tell them what to do" tradition, and feel unneeded unless they boss their subordinates.

Under these circumstances, many errors occur; absenteeism and turnover are serious problems; and complaints are heard on all sides. Job enrichment studies demonstrate that such treatment is unnecessary. And in the case of Motorola, defects were greatly reduced—from 180 defects to 4 per 100 TVs—when management's approach was changed.

Robert Ford described what happened when management at Indiana Bell Telephone gave employees more responsibility. Previously, their new directories had been hard to get ready by deadline dates, and had an unacceptable number of errors in them. In addition, many of the employees quit, and those who stayed were unhappy.

To remedy the problem, the company analyzed job assignments.

It discovered that the task as a whole had been broken down into 21 steps—and that no one person was responsible for any complete unit of work.

The job assignments were changed drastically; some workers were assigned a specific directory, and were held responsible for any mistakes in it.

As a result, the number of mistakes dropped sharply—in some cases there were none—and workers, now having realized their potential for responsibility, moved rapidly up the ladder.

We all need to feel trusted—but not everyone is equally self-confident and blessed with self-esteem. Some workers are more comfortable when others check their work; others greatly resent such supervision, perceiving the checking to signify incompetence. Overall, however, once workers are sufficiently well-trained, some capacity for responsibility has to be present and needs to be used.

Psychologists stress our need to feel in control of our lives. They believe that work conditions affect our motivation to exercise our skills, our belief in our capacity to achieve, and our success in problem solving. To achieve that level, we must have opportunities at work to make judgments, to develop our own solutions, and to apply them successfully.

One computer company was having a terrible time meeting deadlines set by customers. On the advice of consultants, the executives set up a new system. Each Monday, members of the staff bid for the company's new projects, and were assigned the projects on the basis of the shortest completion date and fewest number of hours needed. In a short period of time, projects began getting completed on time, the staff became more involved in self-improvement and workers were eager to bid on the more challenging tasks. Each worker considered it a matter of pride to meet his personally set deadlines. Thus, by increasing the staff's responsibility—rather than trying to manage them better—the company solved the problem.

When management insists upon running a company, subordinates have little opportunity to assume responsibility. When managers are willing to focus on goals and help subordinates attain them, then workers in the company can successfully assume and meet responsibility.

INDIVIDUAL DIFFERENCES   Each of us is a unique person. We all differ in regard to the abilities we possess, the strength of the needs we must meet, and the personality traits we develop. While businesses can't cater to the whims and preferences of each worker, it's equally true that a rigid disregard of individual differences isn't logical. Some people aren't interested in promotions or responsibility; others can't wait to be promoted and be given more responsibility. Some prefer sameness, wanting to do the same job day in and day out; others suffer because of the sameness of their tasks.

Robert Kahn, an organizational psychologist, recommended work modules so that workers could sign up for different tasks at different times. For example, a clerk could choose to work part of the time on filing, part of the time on typing, and part of the time on the phone. No one would be forced to opt for variety; those who sought change would be treated as a separate work group.

LEARNING CREATURES   The brain is capable of collecting, organizing and interrelating information. While we have accepted the fact that our senses must be used or they will deteriorate, we haven't applied this principle to the brain. We assume that our brains remain effective whether or not we use them.

However, recent psychological and physiological studies suggest otherwise. For example, children who watch TV programs in a second language don't become skilled in that language unless they actually practice using it. The brain not only must be fed new information, but also must apply it. This makes us more experienced, and upgrades the powers of our brain.

When people watch TV for hours they are too passive to master anything complicated. Without direct involvement, little is learned. At work, too, we need more than variety; we need an opportunity to learn new facts and techniques and to apply them to problems. The Quality Circle and the Scanlon Plan (see p.189) are relatively simple brain-stimulating techniques. Ideally, workers need career lines which provide increasingly complex tasks to master and new types of information to integrate.

But our population is increasing, as is the number of the electronically controlled factories. Our economy may no longer be able to provide jobs for everyone—and, from management's point of view, career lines for people are less crucial today. Therefore, we can expect management to oppose any significant change in organizational structure; it's much simpler to install newer and more sophisticated machinery.

LIFE CYCLE   Workers can't count on being able to hold the same job for decades; many social scientists are predicting that the typical worker will be forced to change jobs periodically. Retraining and retreading apparently are here to stay; workers will have to continue learning new information and skills. Furthermore, as more and more women enter the workplace, postpone marriage, and have children during work and career periods, companies will have to provide pregnancy leaves and child-care opportunities. And more husband-wife job opportunities will have to be provided. Some universities are offering classes on company premises; some companies are paying tuition for courses and degrees; and a few are providing educational leaves.

Of increasing importance today is effective career counseling. Until now, the emphasis has been on retirement and outplacement counseling. Career counseling of the future will have to be geared to the changing needs of workers and professionals. In particular, workplaces will have to help workers to prepare for imminent changes in job opportunities (as they do in Europe).

How will workers take to a changing life style? Their reactions will probably include anxiety, uncertainty, and a realistic fear of being exploited. Our society tends to blame workers when they are unemployed; their psychological health and economic welfare will depend upon their willingness to plan for such changes.

Older workers might be hurt most by changes; unemployment in some industries without unions is destroying seniority. Some companies have gone bankrupt, then reopened under new management and used various techniques to circumvent the accrued rights of the workers.

A union is a reflection of its industry; the current, weakened position of the auto companies has weakened the position of the union. Workers will have to re-fight the battles of the past and prepare themselves to meet a constantly changing industrial workplace. Security will lie in the ability of unions to keep pace with technological advances, and in the ability of workers to keep up with changing needs for skills.

SOCIOLOGY

13 | WHAT IS SOCIOLOGY?

THE MOST POPULAR VIEW OF SOCIOLOGY is that it is the study of people: sociologists ask people how they feel about this or that topic such as abortion, or a political candidate, or how the government is working. This does describe what some sociologists do some of the time—but overall, it is not an accurate description.

For instance, the polltakers who supply newspapers and television with data on voters' attitudes usually are not sociologists, even though both polltakers and sociologists use questionnaire surveys. The major difference is that a sociologist designs political research to answer questions about human behavior in general, while a polltaker has a more practical interest: who is going to win the election?

Some people take all this to mean that the sociologist's activities are not practical or are just academic. On the contrary, sociologists believe that the results of sociological research and thinking about human behavior can be of great use to a variety of people. Finding out how people interact in conversations, for instance, or what the rules of conversation seem to be, can help make your own interactions with others more effective. Knowledge about how social groups in organizations operate can help your own groups get their work done better or be more enjoyable.

Sociologists do not usually provide specific answers to practical questions, but they do give us the information we need to ask better questions—ones that will have the most useful answers because they can be based on good evidence.

It is too bad that somehow sociology has been defined as the study of people, because several others fields that are quite different could be defined the same way: psychology, history, anthropology, economics. We could even put newspaper reporters and novelists in the same category, since they have a general interest in people.

A DEFINITION

Three factors set sociology apart. Sociology has (1) a *general* interest in (2) the *patterns* of (3) human *social* behavior.

Sociology's interest in people and their behaviors is general in a special sense. Unlike news reporters, sociologists are interested in all human behavior—not just what people do that makes news. The person who robs the bank is of interest to the sociologist but so is the guy who goes to work every day and does things with his family on the weekends. Unlike economists, who are interested only in human behavior that has to do with the flow of money and goods, sociologists take *every* piece of human behavior—from attending church to joking among buddies to discussions at a union meeting—as equally interesting and valuable to understand. The term "general interest" does not mean that sociologists do not make specific statements—they do. The interest is general because sociologists are interested in being as specific as possible in understanding all that can be known about people and their behaviors, wherever they may occur.

Second, sociology focuses on patterns in human behavior—the regular, the routine, the more or less predictable parts of human life. Most of our behavior is patterned in this sense. Even if some stranger stops us on the street and asks for a match, there is a pattern that most of us will follow in reacting to this request. The pattern changes depending on how we evaluate what the stranger really wants, what time of day it is, whether we are in a hurry or not, and so on. The fact that this example sounds familiar to you indicates that there is a set of patterns involved in how we think and act when strangers ask for matches in different situations.

Most of the time, sociologists focus on patterns that are broader than this—such as the patterns involved in living in a family or being in a work crew. But whether they study the operation of the U.S. Congress or the patterns of pedestrian traffic on sidewalks, they try to understand what the patterns are, how they got there in the first place, what keeps them going, and what effects they have on people's lives.

Third, sociologists do not study people in the sense of trying to find out what makes them tick. Instead, sociologists are interested in behavior that is social—the kind that takes place between two or more people. Patterns are a result of people acting together in one way or another (think of the stranger asking for a match, or several friends having a bull session). Even when we are sitting on the bank of a stream all alone, fishing and thinking, much of our behavior is still social. We think through the language we learned from other people, and what we think about is largely due to social experiences we have had. We think about work or what we will do when we go on our next vacation or how to solve family problems. Whatever our thoughts, many of them will concern what we have done or would like to do with other people, how they would react if we did certain things, what makes them act the way they do toward us, and so on and on. Our thoughts are social thoughts for the most part—and they are possible only because of a social tool: language.

We are tied into a social world in many other ways. Take our fisherman again. He probably got his fishing equipment from a store, which bought it from a manufacturer, who paid workers to make it out of materials that were purchased from a supplier whose employees delivered it to the manufacturer in trucks that were made by other workers under a contract made between their union and the company. The lone fisherman is doing his fishing as a result of having linked into a vast network of social activities by thousands of people.

SOCIAL RELATIONSHIPS

Now we can define a key concept of sociology: social relationships. The man who asks for a match on the streetcorner is entering a social relationship with the person he asks—one that will undoubtedly be extremely brief, unless the two strangers find some good reason for continuing to have social contact with each other. The friends joking about their boss on a lunch break are in a more complicated social relationship; it will last longer than the brief encounter between strangers, and depend on much more than a single interest. The social relationship between a husband and wife has even more bits of sociological glue to hold the relationship together—such as a marriage certificate, love and affection, obligations to children, and so on.

Social relationships are ties between people, based on mutual obligations and expectations, and on some shared agreements about the relationship itself. For instance, you would ask for a match (or prefer to be asked for a match yourself) differently if you were on a crowded city street at noon on a weekday than if you were on the same street at 3:00 a.m. There are right and wrong ways to ask for a match, especially if you do not want to be taken for a mugger or a rapist; the sex of the person who asks and of the one who is asked is also an important factor.

The way one asks for a match is guided by social rules; following or not following these rules determines what kind of ties (if any) will develop. The asker must ask in a certain way—for instance, by showing that he has a cigarette to light; this reassures the other person that the request is legitimate. He must follow rules about not touching the other person, and keeping a comfortable distance between them. The relationship can be decided by the person who is asked; if he refuses to answer, the relationship will end, unless, of course, the asker has something on his mind besides a match, like robbery.

We expect that anyone asking for a match from a stranger knows he is taking the risk of being turned down or ignored; one of his obligations is to accept that without protest. Ordinary rules of politeness do not extend to just anyone who stops us on the street.

In other words, the various rules about a stranger asking for a match are shared rules that everybody knows without thinking about them. If they are violated, someone will get upset.

Most social relationships that sociologists study are more enduring and more complicated than the one we have just described. For one thing, the expectations that govern social relationships are not based on common sense, but instead develop within the relationship over time. Every married couple, for instance, works out the details of their own relationship throughout the time they are together. Social relationships are patterned on regular social contacts, and change into new patterns as time goes by.

There are three basic types of social relationships: (1) relationships between individuals; (2) relationships between an individual and a social group; and (3) relationships between groups or institutions.

We have already looked at some relationships between individuals: the married couple, the friends in a group, the strangers on the street. A sociologist who investigates how patients feel about their doctors' ways of handling their complaints is looking at one part of the social relationship between doctors and patients. The sociologist who joins an automobile assembly line to see how friendship groups might arise is also trying to look at social relationships between individuals. One sociologist has even hung around certain public restrooms to find out about the social relationships between men who meet there regularly for homosexual encounters (he found out that what went on in their brief social relationships had a lot to do with their marital status, their occupations, and their religious beliefs).

Social relationships can also be formed between individuals and groups. Husbands, for example are related not only to their wives, but also to the family as a group. The family may expect the husband to provide certain things—money, emotional support, protection, etc. Another example is the worker's relationship to his or her company or union, both of which are complex groupings of other people. As an employee, the worker is in a formal social relationship with the company as a whole, not just to an immediate boss or supervisor or even to the head of the company. If the work contract is not fulfilled by the worker, the result may be the severing of his relationship with the company rather than with just some of its employees. The sociologist who studies workers' attitudes toward management is looking at a social relationship between individuals and groups; so is the sociologist interested in how the religious prescriptions handed down by different churches affect the behaviors and beliefs of individual churchgoers.

Finally, social groupings have social relationships of their own. These are the most complex social relationships of all because they are made up of other social relationships linked together. For instance, when Congress passes a minimum wage law, the law is the relationship between the government and private employers and workers. Many employers are huge corporations made up of networks of social relationships formed by separate companies, separate divisions (production. sales, distribution), separate work groups, and so on. Unions are patterns of smaller social relationships (locals) or even whole industries (steel, automobile, trucking). All the characteristics of social relationships apply here, just as they do when a stranger asks for a match on a streetcorner.

MICRO/MACRO

Sociological work is divided into two types: micro, in which the sociologist is interested in small-scale social relationships such as families or work groups; and macro, in which the focus is on the large-scale social relationships between whole groupings or patterns of relationships.

Micro-sociologists often get involved in intensive observations of interactions among people, and have face-to-face interviews with them; for example, they join work crews, or visit school classrooms to watch how social relationships form between the teacher and students. Macro-sociologists must rely on statistical studies that use large numbers of questionnaires or standard interviews; for example, they may study how relationships between large corporations and television networks affect the content of TV programs. Often, the macro-sociologist supplements questionnaire data by analyzing statistical trends found in government reports, the Census, foundation reports, business records, and so on.

DEBUNKING

What are sociologists after when they do their work? Peter Berger points out that they have a debunking viewpoint. A debunker is never satisfied with the way things appear to be or with the official explanations that people may have. It is not that sociologists think people are lying; it is more that they do not always take official statements as fully accurate descriptions of all there is to know. Sociologists are always aware that there is more than meets the eye. For instance, they find it interesting that Americans rely on official police statistics of the extent of crime. The fact that we get our information on how much crime there is from the people we pay to reduce it suggests that there could be a tendency for officials to interpret their records in a way most favorable to them.

It is one thing to have suspicions, but another thing to find out whether they are true. Various sociologists have tried to determine how much we can trust data on crime. These sociologists often work at the micro level, actually going out and observing what police do and how arrests are made. Jerome Skolnick, for example, rode around with police in two different cities for long periods and observed police behavior. He suspected that one of the most important factors in crime rates statistics (not crime rates) was the arresting officer—the person who decides whether a crime becomes a statistic in the first place. Skolnick is not the only sociologist who has found that many crimes reported *to* the police never get reported *by* the police—so these crimes do not become part of the official statistics.

Often, crimes that are considered by police to be too troublesome to solve are placed in some other category (for example, filed as "suspicious circumstances") where they are no longer crimes the police are responsible for. In other cases, persons arrested for a crime may actually be convicted of some lesser charge as a result of a deal between the defense lawyer and the district attorney. In any event, the official crime rate does not have a clear connection with the actual crime rate. In fact, it could be argued that nobody really knows what the crime rate actually is.

Sociologists are careful to point out that this situation is not necessarily, or entirely, the fault of the police. Arrest rates and solved crimes are criteria for promotions and pay increases among police detectives. Thus, they have a tremendous incentive for eliminating nuisance reports (such as crimes with totally unknown offenders who probably cannot be found) from the categories for which thcy are responsible. The police work in an almost impossible bureaucratic setting, and the public makes unrealistic demands on them; therefore, the numbers game they play to solve some of their work problems may be as reasonable a solution as those used by factory workers operating under an unrealistic piecework incentive system with very high minimum production standards. The point here is that the reason why official crime rates are inaccurate is not obvious until we peel back some of the sociological layers.

Sociologists try to debunk the misconceptions that grow up around any social relationship. In this way, sociology helps us figure out how to deal with problems that face us as citizens or as members of one or another social group. For instance, sociologists have shown fairly clearly that police effectiveness in solving crime is not dependent on pay scales alone. Therefore, we must attack the problem of crime in another way. Are the demands we make on police to solve crimes realistic? Should promotions and pay increases be based on the prevention of crime (instead of on arrest and clearance rates)? Crime prevention is not a major activity of many police. because society and the police bureaucracy do not value it enough to reward the police for doing it. Instead, we focus on arrest and clearance rates, while at the same time supporting a court system that many police feel makes their own efforts useless.

SOCIOLOGICAL IMAGINATION

Another sociologist, C. Wright Mills, said that sociologists (and other people) could benefit by using what he called the sociological imagination. People who use the sociological imagination, according to Mills, are able to see the connection between their own personal concerns and larger social issues. For example, if someone is unemployed and focuses only on that fact, he has a personal trouble to worry about. But if he is able to place that personal concern in the larger context of unemployment as a social issue, there is a good chance that he will have a better understanding of the problem and the ability to be more realistic about it.

If the unemployed person can see that he fits into a larger picture explainable by general economic conditions, he is less likely to blame himself or fate. Such a perspective can at least provide more meaning to our lives, even if our problems remain unsolved.

Sociologists, then, study social relationships from a critical standpoint that debunks myths and helps each individual to locate himself in the larger social picture. Sociology makes an attempt to understand social life; this can lead, through use of the sociological imagination, to better lives.

14 | METHODS

SOCIOLOGISTS HAVE SEVERAL TECHNIQUES TO CHOOSE FROM; their choice depends on what they are interested in and which methods best fit the questions they want to answer. For instance, sociologists interested in the attitudes of criminals toward their victims would have a hard time handing out questionnaires. On the other hand, these sociologists could interview convicts in a state prison; if they had the right contacts. they could even observe actual criminals and talk to them about their activities. One sociologist, Ned Polsky, has done exactly that—observing pool hustlers, illegal drug users and sellers, and other criminals.

Sometimes a sociologist is interested in exploring a whole new area of human activity that has not been described in detail before (like Polsky's interest in criminal behavior). When this is the case, the method chosen is often like the one that anthropologists use to study a primitive tribe that no one knows anything about: they go to the scene of the activities and find out what is going on by living with and observing the natives. This method is called participant observation; the researcher not only observes, but also gets a feel for the activities by participating in them.

PARTICIPANT OBSERVER

There are many well-known participant observation studies that have enlightened us about the social world of factory workers, streetcorner groups, neighborhood gangs, police detectives, restaurant workers, and so on. One of these, a study of how machine operators handled the monotony of their work, is a good example of how participant observation works.

Donald Roy, an industrial sociologist, got himself hired as a machine operator in a plant that produced plastic raincoats. Roy and three other workers operated punch presses that cut plastic sheets for raincoats. Since the cutting room was walled off from the rest of the plant, and supervisory personnel rarely visited it, Roy found himself in a small society.

After a few monotonous hours of punching out simple shapes in plastic sheets of the same color, Roy began to dream about the time he could change the colors of the sheets (after several thousand punches). He tried to make some sense out of things that the other workers were doing. At first, nothing seemed to be happening—except that once in a while they would get involved in horseplay of one kind or another. Soon, however, Roy saw that there was a definite pattern to these occasional spurts of activity.

Once he started paying more attention to the patterns, Roy discovered that the other men had organized the day into little periods when certain predictable behaviors would occur—and that these relieved the monotony. There was banana time, when one of the men would steal a banana from another's lunchbox and eat it after which they would have an argument. Later in the day, there was window time; one of the men would insult another, and the insulted man would open a window and let cold air blow in on the first man's workplace. Over a two-month period, Roy counted seven different times that occurred repeatedly day after day. It became clear that they represented a set of ways the men had worked out informally to manage the extreme monotony of the job.

Since the study was done over three decades ago, when there was little information about how informal social behavior affects work satisfaction, it added to our general knowledge about the operation of industrial workplaces. Obviously, none of the details described by Roy in his study would have been noted if he had simply passed out questionnaires, or even interviewed workers on a one-time basis. Participant observation allowed him to flesh out the human side of the work situation.

Another kind of sociological research involves observation of real-life situations—but without participation by the observer. William Foote Whyte observed the behavior of waitresses, cooks, and other workers in restaurants. He noted that newer waitresses would break down and cry when they became overloaded with customers during rush hours, and this shifted part of their workload to the older, more experienced waitresses. He also found that part of the problem was that younger waitresses let customers control the situation. The older women were not just being efficient by setting up the tables and dropping off the menus as soon as customers arrived; they were getting control over the whole process, scheduling the service to fit their own interests and work demands.

Whyte also observed that the cooks, who were men, disliked taking orders directly from the waitresses—who were not only lower in status within the restaurant, but were women as well. A tall barrier was placed between the cooks and the waitresses, and the waitresses put the customers' orders on spindles that the cooks could take whenever they felt like it. This helped to symbolize the cooks' higher social status in the restaurant, gave them control over their work pace, and made the orders from the waitresses indirect.

QUESTIONNAIRES

Much sociological research is carried out through surveys. These are questionnaires or interviews given to samples of people that are considered representative of some larger population. For instance, a sociologist may want to make a statement that is true for the entire voting population of the United States. Obviously, it is not economically feasible to ask every voter to answer a questionnaire; the cost of mailing a questionnaire would be astronomical. This is where sampling comes in.

A random sample is a miniature version of the population, but with all of its characteristics. For instance, if 25% of the whole population earns less than $15,000 annually, the random sample will have the same percentage. If there are 52% women in the population, the random sample will contain that percentage of women as well. The same goes for other sociological characteristics of the population and the sample. The crucial importance of a random sample is that, statistically, it is a perfectly legitimate basis for making general statements about the whole population, since it represents it in miniature. This is the logic used on election night when the TV networks predict—usually quite accurately—who will win and where the strongest and weakest votes will be.

Questionnaires can be sent to members of the sample, or interviewers may contact them to get their attitudes. In developing a questionnaire or interview schedule, the sociologist must be very careful about how he words questions—so that certain answers are not built into the question. For instance, a question such as "Why don't you like your work?" is not good, since it assumes that whoever answers must dislike his work. A better version would be, "How do you feel about your work?" This could be answered in the person's own words—or, if the sociologist is reasonably sure what the different possible answers might be, several alternatives could be listed and the respondent could check off the most appropriate one (for example, "I like my work very much" or "I am dissatisfied with my work," and so on). Where questionnaires are not returned, the social characteristics of those not returning must be investigated to see if they are a special group.

Another thing the researcher has to watch out for is the socially desirable answer. In studies of job satisfaction, for instance, it is very common for most people to say that they are satisfied or very satisfied with their jobs. While it would be nice to believe that this is actually true, there is some reason to doubt it. Various studies have shown that some of these same people will indicate that they do not like their jobs if you ask the question in a different way (for example, "If you had the chance, would you transfer to another job?"). After all, it is probably difficult for most of us to write down that we dislike our jobs when answering an impersonal questionnaire. We may wonder who is going to use this information, why we were chosen to be in the study, whether the management will see our answers, and so on. For these and other reasons, many of us simply state the most desirable or socially acceptable response, because it is safer and does not convey information we might feel is personally sensitive.

This does not mean that sociologists can never gather accurate information. It does mean that a great deal of attention must be paid to a number of matters if the research is to be a valid reflection of what the sample and population think. First, all ethical sociologists make certain that none of the information from a questionnaire is ever identified with the particular person who gave the answers. Also, it is not considered ethical to share research information with others (for example, management or union leaders) who could identify who gave which answers. In addition, as we have mentioned, great care must be taken to ensure that the questions are asked in a way that does not force certain answers.

TRIANGULATION

Another safeguard against inaccuracy is the use of triangulation, which is the use of more than one kind of research technique to obtain answers to the same question. For instance, a study of job satisfaction in a large industry would depend not only on answers to questionnaire items, but also on a check of company absentee rates, grievances filed, formal complaints made about working conditions, and so on. By using more than one way of evaluating workers' satisfaction, the sociologist is able to be more certain about his conclusions. The picture that one technique gives is pitted against the picture that another one offers. The deficiencies of any single method are to some extent cancelled out by the advantages of another technique.

It is generally a good rule to use triangulation whenever possible, no matter what technique is the major source of information. Even participant observers may interview some of the people they are studying, and they certainly will use both official and unofficial documents. Sometimes, however, a sociologist may find it necessary to depend on the limited information available from only one or two techniques. This happens most often when the people or the places being studied have characteristics that make other techniques difficult to use.

PLANNING A RESEARCH

One of the authors of this book, for example, is studying how people who have a specific disease that is continuous and sometimes disabling, can cope with the daily problems the disease causes for them. Since only some of the people being studied are disabled, they are not conveniently located for the sociologist in a hospital or other institution where they might be observed, interviewed or given questionnaires. Except for certain demands associated with their illness, most lead fairly normal lives. Since the research topic is how they cope with the disease, the obvious major technique would be some kind of observation. As it is unlikely that the people involved would like to have a sociologist come and live with them for a while—and this would not really be workable, anyway—observation of their daily lives is out of the question. Also, since people with this particular disease have never been studied before by sociologists, there is not even a sensible way of constructing a questionnaire before we find out something about them and the illness in the first place.

Given all these problems, the author decided to begin simply with open-ended conversations to bring out the most basic information about the disease, how it works, how it is experienced and coped with, and so on. The exploratory interview is a common beginning technique in this kind of research: merely exploring a topic for the first time to see what it might be all about. This becomes the basis for more research on the subject—providing enough preliminary information so that other techniques, like the questionnaire, can be used. Exploratory research should permit the development of hypotheses about how various things are related to one another. For instance, one hypothesis might state that coping with this disease will be more successful if the afflicted person has strong ties with family and friends. Hypotheses state what the sociologist thinks might be generally true, on the basis of what he discovered in the exploratory research.

The hypotheses discovered through the exploratory study then become the basis for an initial theory; this is a group of educated guesses related to one another. These can now be tested systematically in the verification stage. which determines whether the hypotheses are valid. It is often necessary to do several verification studies, usually with different samples, in order to have confidence in the results. Each of these studies may lead to even more hypotheses to be tested in subsequent studies.

SIMULATION

Some sociologists simulate a situation in order to study it. Haney, Banks and Zimbardo made a study of prisoners and guards in a simulated prison. Twenty-two college students were paid $15 a day for up to two weeks in a realistic prison set up in the basement of the university. The "prisoners" were even "arrested" by the city police and brought to the "jail."

Some guards were apathetic; others followed the rules in disciplining prisoners and some even went beyond the rules. The prisoners were oppressed and affected; the experiment had to be concluded on the sixth day because of danger to the subjects. Four were released earlier (some on the second day) because of extreme emotional depression, crying, rage, and acute anxiety. Another was released with a psychosomatic rash. This prison simulation gives us some idea of how prison in general can influence the behaviors of prisoners and guards.

Simulations may be developed to study the causes of specific real-life events. In a famous tragedy in the 60's, a girl named Kitty Genovese was raped and killed in New York City while 38 people heard or looked on from nearby apartments. Some of the people saw her stabbed repeatedly and heard her screams, but did nothing.

Later, simulation studies of bystander apathy were done to see why this might have happened. In one study, people in a waiting room heard what seemed to be a heavy filing cabinet fall on a secretary in the next office. It took longer for anyone to help the secretary when there were other people in the waiting room than when the subjects were alone. Researchers believe that being in a group somehow relieves each individual of his sense of personal responsibility, and makes everyone less likely to help.

Other simulations have shown that big cities, with their masses of people, are more likely to have certain crimes. In 1952, a car was left on a thoroughfare in New York City; another was left in a similar location in the small town of Palo Alto, California. In the New York location, a well-dressed family removed the radio and battery from the car in the first ten minutes—and within 64 hours, the car was vandalized 24 separate times. In Palo Alto, there was only one event in the same 64 hours: someone closed the car's hood so rain wouldn't get onto the motor.

The progress of research from exploratory studies to more tightly organized research using a variety of techniques is the essence of science—whether it is a natural science like physics or chemistry, or a social science like psychology or sociology. This is how science accumulates knowledge, always building on what went before. In itself, a single piece of research may seem to focus on only a small and apparently insignificant part of the world— but it can be a link in an important chain of activity that increases our scientific understanding.

15 | CULTURE AND SOCIALIZATION

SOMETIMES WE SAY, "THAT PERSON HAS CULTURE"—meaning he or she is well-read or highly educated and appreciates opera or ballet or the symphony. In the same way, the cultural events section of a newspaper reports where we might go to see some of these things, usually at a pretty high price. But when sociologists speak of culture, they mean something quite different.

For sociologists, a society's culture refers to the accumulated beliefs, knowledge, values, norms and ideas that are shared by its members and passed on to future generations. Opera or classical music and fine art are included in the idea of culture, but they make up only a small part of it. Culture includes the way we dress, the ideas we believe in, the way we hold our knives and forks, our fascination with *Star Wars,* and thousands of other things.

BELIEFS

Beliefs are ideas that we are convinced are true; cultural beliefs are those that members of a society share in common. Most Americans, for instance, put a high value on science and believe that science produces true facts about the world. We are so convinced about the beliefs of our culture that we are often shocked when we run into beliefs that operate in other cultures.

For example, in some traditional island cultures of the South Pacific a complicated set of beliefs centers on the idea of *mana,* a kind of superhuman force. If a man plants a crop, he must be sure to have in his possession certain stones that contain *mana;* if if he uses them properly, the crop will be successful—but if he does not, the crop will fail. The island farmer treats this belief the same way we treat our belief in science—it is just true; it is the way the world works.

If we were to come along and tell him that he should sprinkle manure around his plants to insure a successful crop, he might easily think that we were absolutely crazy. On the other hand,

American farmers probably would not take too well to the idea of using magical stones before they planted their fields.

Our belief in science and their belief in *mana* are both perfectly good beliefs in their own cultures. The island farmer might be better off knowing about fertilizing techniques, but these would not make sense in his society's culture.

Social scientists believe that other cultures should not be judged by comparing them with our own culture; that is ethnocentrism. Each culture should be evaluated in terms of its own logic, not in terms of some other culture's logic. Ethnocentrism lies behind a lot of prejudice and discrimination against other people, and has no place in social science. Cultural relativism, on the other hand, views other people and their cultures as being what they are— nothing more or less. Cultures create different worlds for different sets of people to live in. These worlds are very sensible to the society's members—so sensible, in fact, that it is hard for them to imagine any other way of thinking or doing things. The people of Columbus's time believed the earth was flat, so they organized their activities as if this were actually true. For them, the world *was* flat; the fact that the earth was round made no difference to them, since they did not know this and did not treat the world as being anything but flat. No one ever tried to sail around the world because they "knew" they would fall off the edge.

The people of Columbus's time lived in a different world from ours, partly because their beliefs made it that way. When Columbus went to the other side and came back, he set the stage for the creation of a different world—one a little more like our own. Cultures do change—but when they do, the world seems to change along with it.

In our culture, we know that various diseases are caused by microbes. As far as the people of some other societies are concerned, there are no such things as microbes—but there are such things as witches. A society's beliefs may not be "true"—but they can have very real consequences. Our own history includes a time when the colonists believed in witchcraft; people were accused of being witches, and were tortured and killed—often for having "caused" someone to become ill.

Beliefs create worlds that are quite real for those who live in them; the question of which culture is "better" or "worse" than another becomes irrelevant. The fact is that different cultures exist and function, no matter how unreasonable or crazy they may seem to an outsider.

Each society has certain basic needs to satisfy—including a need for food and shelter, a need for essential things to get done (like raising children and learning necessary tasks). Culture is the society's set of ways for doing these things. That set includes the society's beliefs about the way the world works.

VALUES

Another part of society is called the culture's system of values. These are our ideals—what we think are good, desirable, worthwhile. In American culture, some of the more important values are freedom, democracy, and equality of opportunity. Values like these are what most people think ought to prevail—not necessarily what actually does exist. For instance, there never has been total equality of opportunity in American society, even though it has long been a dominant value. Nearly thirty years after the Supreme Court decision that mandated an end to segregated schools, many school systems in America remain segregated.

Even though values may be very important to us, we rarely view any of them as absolute and without exception. For example, we all place a high value on individual freedom—but none of us would insist on it in every case. No one wants people to have the freedom to drive on whichever side of the road they please, or to do anything they want to do. And even though we all believe in preservation of life, very few people in our society would say that there is never a reason for taking another human life.

SUBCULTURE/COUNTERCULTURE

A subculture is a group that shares most of the overall culture's values and beliefs—but retains some different values of its own. The Amish societies in Pennsylvania and parts of the Midwest are American subcultures. Like other Americans, they believe in hard work, value human life, and so on—but they do not believe that the government can tell them to send their children to school. They also believe that they should dress and live as people did before the turn of the twentieth century—without electricity, automobiles, and other modern equipment. The Amish are honest, hardworking people who share in some parts of American culture, but the fact that they have developed and maintained a somewhat separate way of life makes them a subculture.

When a group has all the characteristics of a subculture, but actively defies the values and beliefs of the surrounding culture, it is called a counterculture; its ways run counter to those of most people in the society. The Hell's Angels actively and systematically deny the major values of American culture, such as respect for life and property, and working for a living. Still, they are not a separate culture entirely; they share in many of this society's social patterns and cultural beliefs, while denying or defying others.

If values are only ideals, and do not always reflect reality, of what use are they? Because values are shared, they bind us together as a society. Cultural values are much like religious beliefs: those who share the belief not only have something to believe in, but also feel a sense of comradeship with others who believe the same thing.

NORMS

Another important element of culture is the social norm. These are rules for behavior under various circumstances. In the famous Western Electric study, researchers discovered a norm that a work group had developed to protect its interests against management. They had set a work norm—what they considered a fair day's work. The men feared that management would raise the minimum production used to figure the piecerate incentive wage; this meant that everybody in the group would have to work harder just to meet the minimum. When a man worked too hard, other members would hit him on the arm as a reminder that he was threatening the group's interests. This was a message to the man that things could get uncomfortable for him if he continued his deviant actions—and, therefore, was enforcement of a social norm that helped hold the group together.

There are three types of norms. The first is the formal norm, which is a set of written expectations. Laws are formal norms. When we stop for a stop sign or file a Federal income tax return, we are following formal norms. Union contracts are formal norms that spell out specific expectations and obligations such as wage rates, working conditions, penalties for rule violations, and so on.

The consequences of not following formal norms are called sanctions. Not every violation of a norm results in punishment or sanction; people have been known to go through stop signs and not get caught, contracts sometimes are broken without sanctions being applied, and so forth. But the possibility of sanctions being applied is enough to make norms work fairly well.

Informal norms are unwritten agreements. Every family and every group of workers has its own informal norms that everybody knows exist. These norms develop out of the social relationships within particular sets of people. The people may not have meetings to develop the norms—but somehow the norms are obvious to everyone involved, partly because most of them agree that they are right under the circumstances. Similarly, sanctions are developed for different situations; the worker who thinks that hitting a co-worker on the arm is a perfectly appropriate way to keep a rate-buster in line does not go home and hit his wife on the arm if she violates an informal family norm (such as forgetting to put the car in the garage).

TAKEN-FOR-GRANTED NORMS

The third kind of norm is the kind that is taken for granted. These not only are unwritten, but are so obvious that usually we think of them as simply being common sense. Like other norms, they help bind people to one another and they involve sanctions; unlike other norms, they are very hard to think of as norms.

Suppose you're walking down a sidewalk and you see four strangers ahead of you talking together. You walk past them without speaking, and you keep at least a certain distance from them as you go by. Even if what they are talking about is interesting, you do not stop and listen; you try to walk around, not through the group. If you must walk between the group's members to get by, you excuse yourself or hold your body in a certain way as you go through—to let them know you are only trying to pass through, not to enter into the conversation.

Several taken-for-granted norms are at work here—norms about the proper distance between you and the conversational group, norms about ways to pass or walk through the group. Somehow, we know that there is a certain distance to keep between the group and ourselves, and that if we have to step into their territory we need to excuse ourselves through words or actions. And we somehow understand that there are possible sanctions for violating these unstated norms. When someone takes snapshots on the street, other people will usually walk out into traffic to avoid walking through the space between the photographer and his subject. Such taken-for-granted norms make life more or less orderly and predictable for us, even in our relations with total strangers.

Norms have a very strong influence on people, especially in group situations. Solomon Asch, in a classic laboratory study, showed that norms can make people say things that they would never say otherwise. Asch had a group of college students choose which of three lines matched another line in length. All the members of the group—except one unsuspecting victim in each group— were plants who were instructed to give wrong answers, even when lines were obviously not the same length. One-third of the victims followed their own judgment and made the correct match-ups. But two-thirds of the victims gave in to the influence of the majority, and went along with what was obviously the wrong choice.

SOCIALIZATION

The members of a society learn the things they need to know about their culture through the process of socialization. From birth onward, they are taught directly or indirectly about their culture; they become so familiar with it that it becomes second nature to think and act the way the culture says is proper. We are all being socialized and resocialized all the time as our society and culture undergo changes that, in one way or another, require that we change as well.

The most basic (and, in many ways, the most important) part of the socialization process happens in infancy and childhood. This is when we acquire the basic tools that let us start functioning in society as full-fledged members, and prepare us to be socialized even further as we move into the complex adult world. In this early stage, a lot of the socialization is unintended and indirect; people without any special training at all can bring a baby into the world and prepare it to understand basic cultural information. The key to all this is language.

Babies are born without language, and without knowing how to pick it up. Language must be learned in socialization, or it will not be learned at all. In a baby's first year, it utters various sounds; eventually, the infant says something like mama or dada—and, in our culture, this is taken to be the baby's first word. In societies that use languages other than English, this same process will lead to the baby's first word being the French or Italian or Swahili (or whatever) word for mother or father. When this happy event takes place, the parents pick up the baby, make a big fuss, and eventually convey to the infant that saying that word is a good way to get attention. This sets the stage for further refinements; now that the baby can say the word, the next step is to get him to use it correctly.

All of the infant's first words are learned like this. Later, it is not too hard to teach the child more words without all the fuss and excitement after each one is said. The infant now understands that everything has a name—and runs around asking "What's this? What's that?" This is followed by the learning of more abstract terms such as "happiness," "love," "dirty," "bad," "good." The process continues through childhood and beyond.

Alongside this language learning, the child develops a sense that he has a separate self, distinct from the rest of the world. He starts to get the idea when he pulls his own toes or ears or hair and feels the pain. But it is his name that lets him make the leap from feeling all mixed up with the world to feeling that he is a separate physical thing. His name is the basis for the development of his identity—his sense of being a unique person who is known and treated in a certain way by other people.

ROLE LEARNING

The child continues his development by playing games—pretending to be mommy or daddy or a police officer or a storekeeper. At first, it is hard for the child to do this with other kids, because he can hold onto only one pretend role at a time; it is just too much to pretend to be a storekeeper and try to figure out how to treat customers at the same time.

The child has not yet grasped the idea of taking other people's behaviors and feelings into account. Language lets the child think and act like a storekeeper—but it does not yet enable him to make sense of what storekeepers do in their social activities with other people. This is why it is common to see two children playing separately beside each other—both playing storekeeper, without a thought for playing store with each other. Since the child cannot take other people into account while playing, he cannot do this when not playing—so children at this stage are often viewed by adults as being entirely selfish.

In order for the child to participate in social activities the way adults do, he must somehow learn to take other people's behaviors and feelings into account. G. H. Mead called this ability role-taking; it lets a person evaluate his intended actions by considering how they would affect other people. On a baseball team, for example, each player has to anticipate how his own behavior will fit in with that of his teammates.

The ability to take the roles of others—to put yourself in their position and look back at yourself—also allows a person to get a clear sense of having a social self that is different from everyone else. This makes it possible for a person to feel true guilt or shame, since he can sense how other people feel about his behavior. Charles Cooley called this the "looking-glass self," in which we go through a three-step process of interpretation. First, we imagine how we appear to the other person. Second, we imagine how that other person judges us and our actions. And finally, we add up the first two impressions and feel a certain way about ourselves. This all depends on language—which allows us to think, to learn the elements of our culture, and to develop ourselves and be truly social in our behavior with others.

Socialization is never really completed. We continue learning about our society and our culture, we learn to fit in, we learn new skills and jobs, we grow older and learn how to be middle-aged and old, and we prepare to die. We need to be able to take the roles of others and see ourselves from other people's viewpoints; otherwise, we would be unable to adjust our behavior to fit into the social world that just keeps on going, whether we are ready or not.

16 | SOCIAL INTERACTION

PSYCHOLOGISTS FOCUS THEIR ATTENTION ON PEOPLE as individuals; sociologists concentrate on the relationships between people. Social interaction is the basic process in which these relationships are formed, maintained, and changed. No organization or group could exist unless its members were in interaction with each other.

Social interaction is so much a normal part of our lives that it is difficult to step back and analyze it objectively. That's why our understanding of social interaction can be aided by going to another society where social interaction is different from ours. When we see something unfamiliar happening between people, we can say to ourselves, "Hey, we don't do that back home." The contrast lets us see more clearly how our own society works.

Each society has its own rules on how much space there should be between people who are talking to each other. North Americans who get into conversation with people in South American countries experience an uncomfortable feeling of being pushed or hemmed in—because the rules in South America call for more closeness than we are used to in the United States. Here, a conversation between strangers should be carried on at a distance of at least two to three feet. Closer distances are reserved for close friends and relatives; when the distance narrows to eighteen inches or less, Americans are definitely in the zone of intimate conversation.

You would probably never even think of the subject of distance until a stranger on a Latin American streetcorner spoke to you with less than eighteen inches between your faces; the shock and discomfort would make you realize, for the first time, that people stand farther apart in their interactions back home. In our society, it is considered somewhat strange to flirt at a distance of five feet—and equally strange to carry on formal business at a distance much less than that.

The rules of personal space have some very practical implications. For example, people sometimes offend their superiors not so much by what they say as by their disregard for the superior's personal space. In our society, people in higher positions generally have the right to a larger amount of personal space than do those in lower positions. This is not something that people in higher positions necessarily demand or even are conscious of—but the rule has become such a taken-for-granted part of our culture in this society, the reaction may be almost automatic: the superior feels uncomfortable and offended. Any of us might have the same feeling if our own personal space were invaded by someone from another society, even though that person had no intention of offending anyone.

Just because we think of our own rules of interaction as "normal," that doesn't make these rules natural for all human beings. Social interaction operates under different rules among different sets of people. When a Latin American talks to a North American, both have a problem of space: the Latin keeps trying to close the distance between them, while the North American keeps trying to expand it.

Unfortunately, visiting a foreign country is an expensive way to find a contrast for our own forms of social interaction. A more feasible way is to draw a parallel between social interaction and something that has similar characteristics.

Sociologist Erving Goffman. taking a cue from Shakespeare. sees the world as a stage. Goffman's parallel is that when we engage in social interaction, we are like actors putting on a play in a theater—except that the audience is the people we are interacting with.

If we are actors, our behaviors toward others are performances. Much of what we express to our audiences is planned to present ourselves in a certain way—just as a stage actor tries to express his character in a particular way. For example, if we are trying to convince someone of our sincerity, we will not act as if we have something to hide.

Our behavior creates an impression even when we don't intend it to be viewed that way. When an actor gives a bad performance, his performance still tells us something—even if only that he is a bad actor. Someone giving a speech for the first time may unintentionally give a performance that tells the audience he is nervous and unsure of himself. By viewing ourselves as actors giving performances, we can think more clearly about the consequences of our behavior.

Like actors, we need the support of the right props and settings to make our performances believable. It would be difficult for the audience of a Western movie (supposedly set in the 1880's) to find the movie credible if the actors dressed in modern clothes and drove automobiles. No matter how good the actors are, the audience needs to see authentic-looking Western clothes, horses, six-guns, and scenery before the movie would make sense as a Western.

When we look for a job, we dress in a way that makes us look right for that particular job. If you're applying for a job on an assembly line, a three-piece suit is not the best prop for convincing the company that you are the person for that job. On the other hand, wearing denims on an interview for an office job will cause others to question your ability and interest. Clothing is a prop that is part of the message you convey in social interaction; it can support—or hinder—the image of yourself that you are trying to project.

Similar considerations apply to the places where our social interactions happen. When we see a play or a movie, the physical setting helps to make the performances believable. This is why marriage proposals seldom take place in supermarkets, and why weddings and funerals rarely do; the setting of a supermarket simply will not support these kinds of social activities.

When a boss talks to a worker in the boss's office, the boss has an added advantage—because the stage setting of the office is an expression of the boss's power and authority. Having the same conversation in a less-formal setting—such as in a local bar— would reduce this power advantage.

People whose jobs require them to work in settings that belong to other people—such as repairmen who fix office equipment in other people's offices—have problems that stem from their lack of control over the setting. It is much easier for the owner of the machine to gripe at the repairman here than if the machine had to be brought into the shop. In the shop, the machine owner could be told to come back next Tuesday, and would not be able to observe the actual repair work; in the customer's office, the repair job is open to anyone's view—and, therefore, to anyone's criticism and interference. This is why some repairmen compensate by making a great display of their props—the complicated tools of their trade that are signs of their expertise.

Goffman's parallel between life and the theater does not maintain that we are constantly trying to con other people with our performances; sometimes we do—but most of the time, we are not even thinking about our performances.

17 | SOCIAL ORGANIZATION

MUCH OF HUMAN BEHAVIOR falls into fairly clear-cut social patterns—regularities in the ways we act toward and with one another. Even the briefest meetings between people show easily observable patterns. Two strangers headed toward each other in a narrow hallway will manage to pass without touching, without looking directly into each other's eyes, without talking—because they are cooperating in a simple and very common social pattern.

In a more complicated pattern, a group of friends may find one of them is emerging as their leader—even though he makes no effort, and there is no formal vote on his leadership. It simply happens that the members of the group develop a general expectation that this person will offer advice, make important decisions, and perhaps lend money. Somehow, the members agree on all this; the result is a pattern in which the group revolves around the leader.

The most complex social patterns of all are the interrelationships within large organizations such as the U.S. government or General Motors. Smaller patterns (such as work groups) combine with others to form larger ones (such as business organizations, unions, or entire societies).

Social organization is the network of social patterns within a group or society. The AFL-CIO is a part of social organization; so are families, groups of friends, and bowling clubs. Some of these social patterns interwine with other social patterns. For example, you are a member of your family; you are a member of your work group; and you are a member of your union. They are linked by the fact that you belong to all three at the same time.

Social psychologist Stanley Milgram devised an ingenious study to show how closely people are linked to others through social organization. He gave several people in Omaha the name of a woman (the wife of a divinity student) in a small town in Massachusetts, and asked each of them to get a letter to this woman by sending it to someone they knew personally. The friend then had to do the same thing—sending the letter onward to a friend—and so on until the letter finally reached the woman in Massachusetts. In other words, the task was for someone to make contact with a total stranger thousands of miles away using only a chain of personally acquainted people. This kind of chain is what social organization is all about—the relationships that link people together in a variety of settings.

It took an average of five links for each of the people in Omaha to reach the woman in Massachusetts by mail. If you wanted to get a message of some sort (an idea, for example, or a fund-raising appeal) to someone you did not know personally, Milgram's study indicates that such a chain of acquaintances will lead eventually to the person you want to reach.

We can easily identify some of the positions we occupy in the social structure. We are sons or daughters, employees, parents, best friends, and so on. These positions identify our relationships to people in other positions. To be a son implies there are positions called "mother" and "father"; to be an employee implies that there is an employer somewhere in the social structure that has to do with your work. These relationships between positions in social structures are the basic units of analysis in sociology.

A social role is a collection of social norms that apply to a specific social position. Some roles are very formal—that of a shop foreman, for example. Many of the norms that make up the foreman's role are formally stated in company rules; however, there are also some informal elements in the role. For instance, the rules may say that the foreman must report people who take more than the allotted time for breaks. Informally, however, the workers know that the foreman won't report them for taking an extra five minutes.

Since most of us occupy several different positions in different social structures at the same time, the norms of our various roles may conflict with each other. It is common for one person to be a union steward, a worker, a spouse, and a friend to other workers. The norms defining these roles come from a variety of sources; sometimes they can be contradictory and confusing when a person tries to live up to the norms of several roles at once.

For example, if a weak grievance originates from a worker who is the steward's friend, the norms of the friendship may conflict with the norms for judging the merits of the grievance. If the steward chooses to do his friend a favor by presenting the weak grievance, he follows the friendship norms and breaks the grievance norms. If he rejects the grievance and displeases his friend, he follows the grievance norms and breaks the friendship norms.

Often, the role conflict is a no-win situation. But there are ways of arriving at a reasonable resolution of the problem.

A role is defined by the norms applied to it by other people. The foreman's role, for example, consists of norms sent by management and workers. Taken together, the positions that apply norms to another position are called role sets; the individual positions are called role senders.

Role senders frequently create role conflicts for others without realizing what they are doing; simply pointing this out to them may reduce or eliminate pressure from those sources. For example, the friend with a weak grievance may drop it when he hears about the problem he is creating for the steward; a wife may not realize her demands are contradicting the demands of her husband's other roles.

Sometimes role conflicts can be eased by shifting the conflict to the role senders. For instance, a worker whose supervisor asks him to do something that contradicts union policy may initiate a grievance. What was once a personal role conflict then becomes a conflict between union representatives and management representatives—the two role senders that generated the original conflict with their contradictory norms.

Sometimes it is possible to avoid role conflict simply by insulating your behavior from the role sender who would disapprove of it. If a steward is handling a grievance that he feels is without merit, he can meet privately with the foreman and tell him so. This allows him to preserve his credibility with the foreman without generating heat from the grievant (though it subverts union representation).

Another solution to role conflict is to eliminate one or more of the role senders—or, at least, reduce the amount of pressure they can apply. It is fairly common for new foremen to place limits on their friendships with former fellow-workers, in order to avoid the conflict between the informal norms of the work group and the formal responsibilities of the foreman.

Although it sometimes creates role conflicts, social organization enables us to get through life without having to make a decision at every step. Many decisions are made for us by patterns of norms and roles. This does not mean that social organization determines our behavior in some absolute way. People can always decide to change their social structures. The fact that we do not do this very often on a large scale testifies to the effectiveness of social organization in greasing the wheels of day-to-day activities.

18 | SOCIAL CLASS AND STRATIFICATION

MOST OF US INTUITIVELY RATE OTHER PEOPLE according to some kind of social scale. We see somebody as being our kind of person—meaning equal in status—or else above us or below us on the scale. This ranking is reflected in the way we behave toward each other. Like animals with their pecking order, humans have their own ranking system: we are just a little more subtle about it than animals are.

In society, people can be categorized into levels based on power or possessions or some other way in which they differ from each other. The basis for the ranking may not be the same in every society, but it always is something that a particular society holds in high regard. The more important something is in that society, the higher are ranked the people who have it.

Stratification is a word borrowed from geologists. Just as the earth's crust is composed of different kinds of rocks layered on top each other, a society is composed of different kinds of people layered from the very bottom to the upper crust. Stratification systems reflect the inequality of the people in a society.

In China from 200 B.C. to 1900 A.D., for example, there was a ranking system with five levels:

Royal family
Scholarly bureaucracy
Landed gentry
Peasantry
Outcasts

Even though the Soviet Union professes to be a classless society, it has evolved as many as eleven distinct classes: ruling elite; notables (scientists, artists, State heroes); superior intelligentsia; general intelligentsia; white-collar workers; aristocracy of workers; well-to-do peasants; average workers; disadvantaged workers of low skill; average peasants; forced labor. It is virtually impossible for people in the bottom six classes to move into the top five classes; only the exceptional worker can earn the hero award through outstanding productivity and get into the notable class—and even then this would amount to prestige without power.

We in America claim to have an egalitarian society—and we are more so than most; some of our people even deny that we have a class system at all. Most Americans see themselves as being middle class. People in the lower class regard their classification as repugnant—but concede that people in the classes above them have better jobs, higher incomes, finer homes, and behave differently.

People in different social classes tend to think and act differently. For example, workers feel jealous of and antagonistic toward supervisors; the same is true of followers and leaders. In *The Hidden Injuries Of Class,* Sennett and Cobb tell how one worker views the injustices of social class:

If I believe that the man I call "Sir" and who calls me by my first name started with an equal fund of powers, do not our differences, do not all the signs of courtesy and attention given to him but denied me, do not his very feelings of being different in "taste" and understanding from me, show that somehow he has developed his insides more than mine? How else can I explain inequalities? The institutions may be structured so that he wins and I lose, but this is my life, this is 30 to 40 years of being alive that I am talking about . . . I see this man, who I know is no better than I, being treated better than others—even I treat him that way.

And then the authors comment: "It is in this way that a system of unequal classes is actually reinforced by the ideas of equality and charity formulated in the past."

Stratification in the United States is based on socioeconomic status (SES). The major elements of SES are occupation, income and education; all three factors are strongly related to each other, and occupation is the best overall indicator of social class.

A five-tier system—an upper class, two middle classes, and two lower classes—is the most common stratification in Europe and America. In "Jonestown," a midwest rural community, W. L. Warner found five classes: upper class, 2.7%; upper-middle, 12%; lower-middle, 32.2%; upper-lower, 41%; and lower-lower, 12.1%.

However, in "Yankee City" (actually Newburyport, Massachusetts), Warner found that there were six distinct social classes:

1. Upper-upper class 1.4%   The "old" rich; the aristocrats
2. Lower-upper class 1.6%   The "new" rich
3. Upper-middle class 10%   Professionals; substantial business-
                            men; civic leaders
4. Lower-middle class 28%   Small businessmen; white-collar
                            workers; a few skilled workers
5. Upper-lower class 33%   Respected but poor hard-working
                            people
6. Lower-lower class 25%   Often on relief, they are not respected
                            or considered moral by the other
                            classes

In a southern town, sociologists found nine clear-cut classes—with the upper, middle, and lower class each having three subdivisions.

Many of our newer communities have been built with homes in a certain price range; the prices of the homes determine what class of people will live in them. Families in $200,000 homes may be all upper-middle class; those in $100,000 homes, all lower-middle class; and those in $50,000 homes, all upper-lower class. Therefore, the location and price of a person's home are surface indicators of his social class; other surface indicators are the way he dresses and the type of car he drives.

The listing on the next page shows how people rank various occupations according to prestige; the study was verified by almost identical results of the same test 16 years later.

Although there is more class mobility in America than in other countries, relatively few people rise to the upper class. Some factory workers have sons who become doctors, and some people start businesses which make them rich. But if a few are getting to the top, most of the others are staying pretty close to where they started.

Most of us in the United States are living better than we were one or two generations ago—but this doesn't mean people have moved to higher social classes. Everybody is moving up some—but the relative rankings stay very much the same.

On the other hand, job opportunities in the lower classes have been shrinking, and those in the higher classes have been expanding. There has been a tremendous shift of farm people to other kinds

PRESTIGE RATING OF OCCUPATIONS

U.S. Supreme Court Justice	96
Physician	93
State governor	93
Cabinet member in the Federal Government	92
Diplomat in the U.S. Foreign Service	92
Mayor of a large city	90
Scientist	89
College professor	89
Banker	88
Minister	87
Chemist	86
Lawyer	86
Dentist	86
Architect	86
Nuclear physicist	86
Member of board of directors, large corporation	86
Psychologist	85
Civil engineer	84
Artist whose pictures are exhibited	83
Sociologist	83
Accountant for a large business	81
Musician in a symphony orchestra	81
Author of novels	80
Building contractor	79
Public School teacher	78
Railroad engineer	76
Official of International labor union	75
Electrician	73
Farm owner and operator	76
Newspaper columnist	74
Trained machinist	73
Welfare worker for city government	73
Undertaker	72
Manager of a small store in a city	69
Insurance agent	68
Bookkeeper	68
Policeman	67
Railroad conductor	67
Mail carrier	66
Carpenter	65
Automobile repairman	63
Plumber	63
Garage mechanic	62
Officer of local union	62
Machine operator in a factory	60
Barber	59
Clerk in a store	58
Truck driver	54
Coal miner	49
Taxi driver	49
Dockworker	47
Bartender	44
Janitor	44
Garbage collector	35
Street sweeper	34
Shoe shiner	33

of work, as farms have become more mechanized and efficient. Manufacturing has contracted, too. Public service, business, clerical and professional occupations have expanded. Look at what is happening now, for example, in the huge computer industry, composed of all white-collar employees.

In fact, the line dividing the blue-collar worker from the white-collar worker has become blurred. Many of the white-collar jobs require little skill, with workers sometimes being on a production line with low pay.

And the proportion of people in higher education has doubled. Education is now America's largest industry, with a quarter of our people enrolled in, or teaching and administering, schools of all kinds. People with degrees are eligible for top jobs. Education is, of course, a primary determinant of occupational skills, social status, personal development and opportunity for upward mobility.

So we do have mobility caused by the shifting of lower class jobs (farm and factory) to higher class jobs (electronics, computers and government). The individuals themselves (except for those who get degrees) are not more mobile; the upper structure is now more open.

And coming in at the bottom of the occupational and economic ladder are the groups who are newest to the nation. The waves of Irish and Italians and European Jews ceased with immigration changes in 1924; more recently, Blacks and now Hispanics have been starting at the base of the ladder.

People in the lower ranks of the system generally have less access to health care, own less insurance, and get sick more than members of the upper levels. They are more likely to suffer from mental illness and family breakdown, though this is less likely to be brought to the attention of the authorities. Along with wealth, education, and other benefits, the higher classes enjoy many of the things that make life easier to handle.

Cutting across social class stratification are other kinds of stratification—such as age, sex, and race or ethnic background. These are also systems of inequality, and they are often related to social class stratification.

Until recently, for example, women have not even been considered by social scientists in studies of social class. Women are working more in the occupational system than before, but they are still mainly in so-called women's jobs, especially in lower-level clerical and sales positions. Women in the male-dominated university faculties often find themselves in part-time positions or in ones off the regular career track, despite the fact that their educational and skill qualifications are equivalent to those of the men. Similarly, a black man with the same education as a white man is likely to have a lower-level occupation than the white man. And when a person reaches the age of 70, he may be forced to leave an occupation altogether.

All societies have such systems of stratification; and throughout history, many people have tried to devise ways to eliminate them. Social scientists and philosophers have tried to understand why they seem to be necessary to human society, but results of these efforts have not been very impressive.

19|LEADERSHIP

IF SOMEONE GIVES YOU AN ORDER and you automatically do it—he has authority over you. Supervisors have authority over workers; sergeants, over privates; teachers, over students.

Leadership is not to be confused with authority. If you are given an order and you do not know whether or not to follow it, you are probably dealing with leadership. Leadership is personal and informal; authority is impersonal and formal.

For centuries, leadership was thought of as a matter of inheritance. Leaders were born, not made—and, of course, the aristocrats were the born leaders.

Later, leaders were thought to have certain traits—mainly physical. Military leaders were believed to need imposing physiques—until Napoleon disproved that notion. Political leaders were thought to need common sense and a forthright approach to problems—until Hitler demonstrated otherwise.

A distinction between a gifted speaker and an effective leader is this quote: "When Cicero had finished speaking, the people said: *How well he spoke* . . . but when Demosthenes had finished speaking, the people said: *Let us march!*"

The danger of this example is that it pictures a leader simply as a person who can move a large gathering to do what he wants. But for every spectacular example of a leader moving a crowd, there are thousands of less-visible acts of leadership.

For example, one member of the group can supply needed information; another can foster harmony among the members; another can get the group to act; and another can bring in people who can shed light on a problem.

The ability of a person to influence others is the core of leadership. There is no one ideal leadership style; the key to effective leadership apparently is an ability to adapt one's style to the situation.

There is often little difference between leaders and followers. Some persons learn to be good leaders by being good followers first. Many leaders simply have more enthusiasm and work harder than others do. Or they are more sociable and have better verbal skills.

Leadership is concerned both with accomplishing the group's task and with meeting the interpersonal needs of its members. Often the leader is so concerned with the task that he has no time for—or is insensitive to—the feelings of the group. Sometimes the task leader is assisted by a social leader who focuses on group feelings and social behavior. If the social aspect is not taken care of, it may interfere with decisions of the group, the group may split up, and the task itself may not get done.

A leader who is able to get high productivity or other action out of a group may generate respect among the members—but he may also arouse their hostility. During the early years of his leadership, he must be aware of and accept this antagonism and hostility if he is to continue as leader.

For example, a union leader may find that a member whom he was able to get reinstated is now sniping at him rather than singing his praises. While he is obligated to the union leader, the worker is also angry at himself for being placed in such a position of indebtedness. It is similar to borrowing money from a friend; you are grateful for getting the money—but so long as you owe him the money, you dislike seeing him because it reminds you of your weakness.

Some leaders protect themselves by working through lieutenants. They delegate the more unpleasant tasks to their staff, who then bear the brunt of the members' animosity. The leader can occasionally buy a little popularity by using his prerogative to give mercy.

The leader is the person with the most influence in the group. He is likely to give suggestions and directions that are most acceptable to the members, to intervene the most in group discussions, to initiate and receive more communications with more members, to give and have more opinions, to do the most to increase the group's morale, to give approval and disapproval to others' actions, and to represent the group to outside groups.

Leaders tend to be a little more intelligent and verbally fluent than others, and to have more self-confidence and self-esteem.

They need to know how their followers feel on specific issues, and these feelings should guide their behavior.

Different groups have different goals—and therefore need different kinds of leadership. In the work group, the steward will almost always be the leader—supported by a respected older worker or a young firebrand. When the workers adjourn to a tavern after work, the steward may be just another member; one or two others will take over, because jokes and pranks and drinking are the activities of the recreational group. When the company's bowling club meets, the leader may be the best bowler—or he could be an ebullient fellow with only fair bowling ability who acts as the spark plug.

Just who the leader is at any particular time depends on who can best help the group satisfy its current objectives. So, leadership may be the role—the function that needs to be accomplished—rather than the person.

In 1938, a landmark study showed the effects that three different leadership styles had on groups of boys working on crafts projects. (1) Using an autocratic style, a leader told the boys exactly what to do; (2) using a democratic style, a leader helped the boys to decide what they wanted to do; (3) using a *laissez faire* style, a leader gave the boys complete freedom to do whatever they wanted, with no guidance from him.

The boys under autocratic leadership turned out the highest quantity of work—but there was much hostility and aggression within the group and discontent toward the leader; there was also scapegoating, and some left the group. The boys under democratic leadership produced somewhat less work—but it had strong originality, and the members of the group had good feelings. The boys under hands-off leadership did the least and poorest work. All of the boys (except one who had an autocratic military father) favored the democratic style of leadership.

Several studies have shown that telling a group of people what to do is not as effective as having the members of the group discuss the problem and come to their own conclusions. This is why group discussions are the key to the success of Alcoholics Anonymous, mental health groups, Weight Watchers, and convict rehabilitation.

If changes are imposed on a group from above, they may be

resented and sabotaged. (Sabotage is a word derived from the workplace: Belgians would throw a wooden shoe (sabot) into the machinery to halt production.) This is why, for example, a company in serious financial trouble cannot just tell everyone to bear down harder to get out an unusual order. If the workers discuss the problem and the alternatives, they are more likely to put in the extra work that is required.

Power, which is part of leadership, is the ability to influence others. There are different kinds of power. You can have reward power, as a boss can give a raise. You can have legitimate power, as an organization can give you formal authority over your subordinates. You can have expert power, as doctors and lawyers have over their clients. You can have referent power, when your followers want to identify with you. Or you can have charismatic power, which makes your followers devoted to you.

20 | GANDHI: A LEADERSHIP PORTRAIT

GANDHI WAS HARDLY THE PHYSICAL IDEAL OF A LEADER. He was a skinny, old, toothless man wrapped in a dhoti, and held no office whatsoever. Yet he led the huge country of India into independence—and did it peaceably.

He was born of a good Hindu family, and married at the age of 13. For a few years, he was engrossed in his carnal pleasures. Then, at 18, he left his wife and small son in India and he went to England to become a lawyer.

He dressed in the latest formal English fashion, but cut a sorry figure—puny and unathletic. He was afraid to speak—even when he had his speech written out.

Gandhi was sent to South Africa to help on a legal case. His first day there, he insisted on riding on a first-class train; he was repeatedly thrown off because he was colored. (Then, as now, the Indians were above the Blacks in South Africa, but well below the Whites.) During that long cold night at a small railway station, he reflected on the fact that his hardship was a symptom of the disease of color prejudice—and that he should redress the wrongs of this prejudice. By the next morning, he had evolved from a private citizen to a political actor.

After having been an ineffectual person in London, Gandhi now found himself to be a man of superior talents. He had discovered an abused group that he could fight for with a clear conscience, and which would grant him respect and recognize his power.

Because he had a cause and no longer felt unworthy, he lost his shyness and inarticulateness. He became a highly vocal advocate of Indian rights in South Africa.

He found that the Indians were divided into many factions with diverse interests. He shaped a political strategy: the Indians—who did not have the right to vote—must unite and dramatize their plight through demonstrations, confrontations, and passive resistance. This was the philosophy that Martin Luther King was later to adopt in America. Money was raised, propaganda issued, and the government influenced. He organized a great march; he was arrested three times, posted bond and resumed the march. Concessions were won from the government.

He had come to South Africa as a lawyer in a bitter case between two Indian families. He arranged for the dispute to be arbitrated, thus avoiding the cost and delay of going to court. When his client won the award, he arranged for the losing party to spread the payments over many years.

In getting the two parties to arbitrate, and then persuading his client to allow the loser to pay in installments so he would not be ruined, Gandhi was practicing his philosophy that "the true function of a lawyer was to unite parties riven asunder. All my life through, the very insistence on truth has taught me the beauty of compromise." This non-violent solution became the model for many of his subsequent actions.

In his youth in England, Gandhi had tried to be like the English in order to be a man; he was unable to, so he reverted back to his mother's Hinduism, a workable identity. Gandhi's mother, like many Hindu women, used to fast herself in order to punish others for transgressions; when displeased with some member of the family, she would deprive herself of food. Gandhi took this practice and used it as a political tool against the English or his own followers, as the occasion demanded. The fast was Gandhi's singular contribution to political practice.

His family joined him in South Africa. By age 30, he had completely foresworn all sexual activity. He learned to live on fruits and nuts and water; he slept on the floor, he dressed in coarse cloth; his possessions could be carried in his hand. He searched for the truth to guide him in religious, philosophic and social life.

He would not accept a legal case in which witnesses needed to be coached or the truth could not be told. He fought the system, never the individual; he was forgiving of the individual. He was gentle and courteous, even when dealing with opponents. He was modest and unassuming, almost timid, yet with an indomitable spirit.

When he returned to India in 1918 at the age of 48, his reputation and tactics were well established. His first major effort involved the unrest in the textile industry in the city of Ahmedabal.

The workers went on strike for a 35% increase in wages. The strike lasted 21 days. Gandhi issued sixteen leaflets to explain the philosophy of non-violence and the need to protect the workers' interests while safeguarding the employers' interests.

Four days before the strike ended, Gandhi went on the first of what was to become 17 fasts to the death. Subsequently, an arbitrator granted the workers' request for a 35% increase.

Gandhi attached great importance to symbolic acts, and newspaper coverage ensured these acts were widely reported. He was an optimist who was confident the Indian people would follow him and have faith in token acts of truth. He said: "Believe me that a man devoid of courage and manhood can never be a passive resister."

In 1930, Gandhi made eleven demands of the British, one being that the tax on salt be eliminated. He and 78 followers walked 200 miles to the sea, where civil disobedience was to begin. He picked up a few grains of salt from the beach; this simple gesture told India what it must do after this long period of tension and indecisiveness. Gandhi was arrested and the civil disobedience spread to non-payment of taxes and boycott of foreign clothing. Eight months later he was released from jail, and he and the viceroy negotiated a truce between the Indians and the British.

Gandhi viewed himself as the most humble of the humble, and had taken on himself the abuse directed toward all Indians in South Africa. He claimed that all men were brothers, and would not admit that anyone was as low as he. He escaped from personal shame by asserting the autonomy and dignity of the lowly.

He ensured that Nehru would be the leader of the Indian Congress Party; he sought no office. In 1948, he was assassinated by a Hindu extremist.

21 | CONCEPTS OF SOCIOLOGY

CULTURE IS THE DISTINCTIVE WAY OF LIFE OF A GROUP OF PEOPLE. It includes knowledge, art, tools, morals, laws, customs—and the beliefs and ways of thinking that we take for granted, but which to an outsider might be very strange. Human society cannot exist without culture; culture exists only within a society.

BELIEFS are views which people accept as true. Most beliefs are handed down from teachers, families and friends, because no one can experience so many beliefs himself. In America, most people have a belief in God—although we have many religions and sects and even non-believers.

VALUES are views about what is desirable. Values are preferences about the way things should be. In this country we value such concepts as freedom, democracy, equality.

NORMS are agreements about what is expected. Norms define what is required or acceptable behavior in certain situations. Beliefs and values and norms are all interwoven; as beliefs and values change, so do our norms.

DEVIANT BEHAVIOR is behavior that varies significantly from the social norm. It might be a scab during a strike, or a rate buster on a production line.

SANCTIONS form the system that stabilizes the norms. There are both positive and negative sanctions; they take the form of reward or punishment—e.g., praise or spanking for children.

MORES are the important ideal norms of society. They are the special norms which society regards as necessary for its well-being, such as the Ten Commandments.

CONVENTIONS are rigid rules governing certain social interactions, such as the ethical behavior of doctors.

FOLKWAYS are the traditional ways of doing things that are not questioned—such as religious and marriage ceremonies.

LAWS are formal norms made by those who hold political power; they are enforced by the state.

INSTITUTION is an accepted way of behaving. It is a basic system of organized behavior to enable man to cope with his environment. Such institutions as the family, the economy, politics, education, and religion serve a broad purpose in an enduring way.

SYMBOL is a representation of something else. A cross is a symbol of Christianity; a dove is a symbol of peace. Language is a system of symbols with words representing ideas and feelings and objects.

SUB-CULTURE is a culture within a culture. It is a distinctive group that has some norms that set it apart from the total society.

COUNTERCULTURE is a sub-culture that is opposed to the dominant culture—such as hippies and communal living.

ACCULTERATION is one people's taking on elements from the culture of another. A dramatic example is Japan following World War II, when western culture was impressed on its traditional culture.

PRIMARY GROUP is a small group whose members maintain intimate, cooperative, face-to-face relationships with each other. The family is the best example, but street gangs and friendship groups are others.

SECONDARY GROUPS are larger, and its members have more formal and impersonal relations with each other. Religious denominations, trade unions, and political parties are examples.

PEER GROUPS are composed of individuals who are social equals; they could be classmates, street-gang members, etc.

MEMBERSHIP GROUPS are those to which we actually and consciously belong—family, clique, racial, political.

REFERENCE GROUPS are those to which we consciously or unconsciously aspire. A youth may be a member of a school gang whose behavior is at odds with the members of his school class. But his behavior is modeled after the gang to which he aspires.

SOCIALIZATION is the process by which new members learn the norms, beliefs, attitudes and values of society. It enables the child to evolve from an organism to a person.

RITES OF PASSAGE are rituals which mark the passage of a person to another status. Ceremonies mark a person joining an organization or retiring. Mourning marks a person dying.

Marriage is an important rite of passage in most societies. Western society requires and encourages the ceremony at many levels: legal (with a marriage license); religious (by a priest, minister or rabbi); social (eating and dancing); and folk (throwing rice, tying on cans, "buying" the bride).

ROLE is the behavior expected of one who occupies a particular status. A role is composed of the actions he is supposed to take, the statements he is expected to make, and the general impression he ought to convey.

ROLE CONFLICT is the dilemma a person faces when he has to behave in different ways at the same time—such as when a foreman finds it difficult to censure a worker because he is also his friend.

ROLE DISTANCE enables a person to avoid the strictures of the role by separating himself from the role.

SOCIETY is a group of people whose relationships are organized and structured by a culture.

NUCLEAR FAMILY is composed of the parents and children (and occasionally a close relative).

EXTENDED FAMILY includes the grandparents and other relatives. It is more common in small towns or rural areas, with certain nationalities, and in many primitive societies.

STATUS is a position in a particular pattern of social behavior. An individual is socially assigned to a status; when he puts the rights and duties of that status into effect, he is performing a role.

ASCRIBED STATUS is what you are born into and cannot change—your age, sex, color, race, and even class (when you are young).

ACHIEVED STATUS is something you earn—a college degree or a superior position.

GEMEINSCHAFT/GESELLSCHAFT is a comparison of folk society and urban society. Gemeinschaft is the communal society where everybody knows everybody else; it is a close relationship like a family. Gesellschaft is the city society, composed of all the secondary relationships, enabling diversity, change, and individual dualism; acquaintances are casual and people are loosely bound together.

ETHNIC GROUPS are racial or religious groups whom others regard as different from the majority.

ETHNOCENTRISM, a coined word from ethos (race) and centric (centered), is the tendency to use one's way of life as the standard for judging others. It is a dislike for a culture and goals different from one's own. It is a belief that one's own race, culture and society are superior to all others. It even applies to various groups within the society—religious, social, etc.

POWER is the capacity to get your own way regardless of the opposition of others. Authority is power that is accepted by those subjected to it.

PURE OR IDEAL TYPE is a sociological construction to explain behavior or happenings or events. By constructing an ideal type (say, a perfect priest), the sociologist can then explain how all other priests deviate from the pure priest. This enables us to visualize and understand reality.

PROTESTANT ETHIC was a concept developed by Max Weber: that hard work and saving money are worthy goals for all people to strive for.

SCAPEGOATING is the blaming of someone or something else for the cause of your trouble. Germany's blaming the Jews in the 1930's for the country's misfortunes is a prominent example.

ANOMIE (or anomy) is a word that Emile Durkheim employed to explain the rootlessness and detachment that many workers felt because they no longer had close primary relationship with their employer and co-workers.

CULTURAL LAG happens when a change occurs in one part of the culture but another part of the culture bound to this part does not change with it. Sometimes it is a technological change and the behavior of the people does not change to accommodate the technology. For example, stables were located away from houses because of the smell; but when automobiles replaced horses, people built garages where the stables used to be—instead of next to the houses.

SOCIOLOGY OF WORK

22 | THE WORK ETHIC

WHEN YOU MEET PEOPLE FOR THE FIRST TIME, the question most often asked is: "What kind of work do you do?" Your occupation is the best indicator of your social class. It has a strong influence on where you live, with whom you associate, and even, in a marked way, what your children will become. Freud said that work is the most important factor of self-esteem; it is the central activity which gives meaning to someone's life.

If you are apathetic at work, you may be apathetic at home; if you are frustrated at work, you may be frustrated at home; if your work gives you great satisfaction, this feeling will carry over when you get home. People who give a lot of orders at work do the same thing at home. People with socially isolated jobs tend not to integrate in community life. Leisure cannot fully compensate for a dissatisfying work situation.

The ancient Greeks considered work to be a curse. Homer said the gods hated mankind, and out of spite condemned men to toil. Slaves provided the necessities of life; Aristotle said: "Without the necessaries, life as well as good life is impossible."

The Hebrews thought of work as painful drudgery. They accepted work as a penalty through which men could atone for the sins of their ancestors and attain dignity.

Early Catholics built on this; they attempted to give work a new value as a means to a worthy end. St. Thomas Aquinas considered work to be a necessity of nature.

The Protestant Reformation advanced a new way for men to look at their lives. Luther in Germany and Calvin in Switzerland preached that man could have salvation by dedicating himself to a calling. Luther said that each variety of labor had equal spiritual dignity. Calvin, in speaking for the need to work for money to finance fresh ventures, heralded modern business. Religious philosophy now endorsed the new economics.

Adam Smith articulated this new spirit when he said that the wealth of a nation consisted of the quality of labor which it produced—and that any act that helped make raw material into something useful was productive.

A century later, Marx said that labor was the source of all productivity and that it expressed the humanity of man. He predicted the withering way of people working for other people in the future; he foresaw people spending time on work that fulfilled them—work that *they* wanted to do.

The Puritans brought this work ethic to America. They stressed individual achievement, hard work, scholarship, honesty, thrift, and social responsibility. When the churchmen emphasized these qualities on Sunday, they were establishing norms that would nurture a capitalistic economy during the rest of the week.

In 1633, Puritans inscribed into the law of Massachusetts: "No person, householder or other, should spend his time idly or unprofitable, under pain of such punishment as the court shall think meet to inflict." Jamestown, Virginia similarly had a rule: he who does not work shall not eat.

In the following century, Benjamin Franklin endorsed the virtues of industry in *Poor Richard's Almanack*. Some of them:

He that hath a trade hath an estate.

At the working man's house, hunger looks in, but dares not enter.

Industry pays debts, while despair increaseth them.

Sloth makes all things difficult, industry most easy.

Early to bed and early to rise, makes a man healthy, wealthy, and wise.

The work ethic—which is also called the Protestant ethic, the Puritan ethic or the character ethic—is a belief that work itself is important, and that doing a good job is essential.

People who have a strong work ethic generally acquired it from their parents in early childhood or adolescence. When parents establish discipline, delegate work, and encourage responsibility—and accompany this discipline with love and explanation—their children generally become self-reliant, responsible and well-behaved. But when supervision is authoritarian without explanation, the children are often withdrawn and dependent.

The most important aspect of work is not having a job. No

matter how unsatisfying a job may be, it is much more stressful to be unemployed.

Unemployed workers feel unwanted by society. Such feelings are much stronger among high-status workers, who are not accustomed to layoffs (as factory workers are).

When unemployed workers get jobs again, they feel more useful and regain their self-esteem—but they retain some cynicism about society. The unemployment experience leaves lasting changes in their concepts of self, society, family and friends.

Unemployment means loss of income, so people can't meet their obligations. It means a deterioration of the family fabric. It means the indignity of getting money through unemployment benefits or relief. It means the further indignity of having to ask for work.

But beyond this, the routine of life is destroyed. The bonds with work groups and friends are broken. Unemployed people are not meeting the work ethic that has been so strongly instilled in them.

Sociologist M. Harvey Brenner found that a one percent increase in the national unemployment rate was associated with increases of 4.1% in the suicide rate, 3.4% in admissions to state mental hospitals, 4% in prison admissions, and 5.7% in homicides.

These are powerful reasons for a governmental policy that supports full employment. We need jobs. Our economic, social and psychological health are dependent upon jobs.

23 | DIVISION OF LABOR: ADAM SMITH

A BOOK PUBLISHED IN 1776 BECAME THE BIBLE OF CAPITALISM, in the same way that Charles Darwin's *On the Origin of Species* in 1859 became the bible of evolution.

The book was *Wealth of Nations*. Its author was Adam Smith, a Scottish professor of moral philosophy. He observed social facts and searched for their significance, instead of drawing conclusions from abstract principles. The book became the foundation of economic thought of the modern world of capitalism, which was slowly breaking away from mercantilism and earlier feudalism.

Adam Smith's theory was based on three general assumptions: self-interest is the prime psychological drive in man; all these strivings add up to a social good; and economic progress can be best attained by leaving the process alone (what we term *laissez faire,* or "hands off" policy). The book was to serve the rising capitalistic class well, and give dignity to their greed and predatory impulses.

While the steam engine was being put to practical use as early as 1698, the inventions of James Watt (patented in 1769 and 1782) made the industrial revolution possible—by providing a dependable, large-scale source of power for machinery.

The opening paragraph of *Wealth of Nations* anticipated the coming emphasis of breaking work up into small specialized functions:

The greatest improvement in the productive powers of labour, and the greater part of the skill, dexterity and judgment with which it is any where directed, or applied, seem to have been the effects of the division of labour.

Smith then gives the famous example of the manufacture of pins:

To take an example, therefore, from a trifling manufacture; but one in which the division of labour has been very often taken notice of, the trade of the pin-maker; a workman not educated to this business (which the division of labour has rendered a distinct trade), nor acquainted with the use of the machinery employed in it (to the invention of which the same division of labour has probably given occasion), could scarce, perhaps, with his utmost industry, make one pin in a day, and certainly could not make twenty. But in the way in which this business is now carried on, not only the whole work is a peculiar trade, but it is divided into a number of branches, of which the greater part are likewise peculiar trades. One man draws out the wire, another straights it, a third cuts it, a fourth points it, a fifth grinds it at the top for receiving the head; to make the head requires two or three distinct operations; to put it on, is a peculiar business, to whiten the pins is another; it is even a trade by itself to put them into the paper; and the important business of making a pin is, in this manner, divided into about eighteen distinct operations, which, in some manufactories, are all performed by distinct hands, though in others the same man will sometimes perform two or three of them. I have seen a small manufactory of this kind where ten men only were employed, and where some of them consequently performed two or three distinct operations. But though they were very poor, and therefore but indifferently accommodated with the necessary machinery, they could, when they exerted themselves, make among them about twelve pounds of pins of a middling size. Those ten persons, therefore, could make among them upwards of forty-eight thousand pins in a day.

Smith explains that division of labor increases production by increasing the dexterity of every workman for a particular function; saving the time ordinarily lost going from one kind of work to another; and using machines which allow one man to do the work of many.

But, as we know, the division of labor has also created problems. It destroyed the all-around skills that took years to learn; every step in the production process has been reduced to simple labor, divorced from any special knowledge and training. Now it requires only limited skills; women and children, working for low pay, could be trained easily to do some of the less-difficult, less-skilled steps.

Before the eighteenth century, there were a few places where large numbers of people worked together: in 1371, a weaving factory in Amiens employed 120 workers; in 1450, a printer in

Nuremburg employed 120 people; and in the early 1500's, Jack of Newburg had a weaving factory with 200 looms and employed 600 workers.

But the usual method of production was through crafts in each trade, with the master craftsmen often formed into guilds. An apprentice learned his trade by helping in the workshop and being taught in turn; he lived with the master. When he had completed his trade, he would be hired by another craftsman, or possibly set up his own master-craftsmanship. In the late 1200's, Paris had 128 guilds with 5,000 masters, who employed 6,000 or 7,000 journeymen. England had a similar system of guilds, although nine out of ten males of the time were peasants.

It is interesting, two hundred years later, to reflect on his insight concerning the future development of our nation:

But though North America is not yet as rich as England, it is much more thriving, and advancing with much greater rapidity to the further acquisition of riches.

. . Every colonist gets more land than he can possibly cultivate. He has no rent, and scarce any taxes to pay. No landlord shares with him in its produce, and the share of the sovereign is commonly a trifle. He has every motive to render as great as possible a produce, which is thus almost entirely his own.

But it is his views of the owner and worker that are most interesting to us:

What are the common wages of labour, depends every where upon the contract usually made between those two parties, whose interests are by no means the same. The workmen desire to get as much, the masters to give as little as possible. The former are disposed to combine in order to raise, the latter in order to lower the wages of labour.

It is not, however, difficult to forsee which of the two parties must, upon all ordinary occasions, have the advantage in the dispute, and force the other into a compliance with their terms. The masters, being fewer in number, can combine much more easily; and the law, besides, authorises, or at least does not prohibit their combinations, while it prohibits those of the workmen. We have no acts of parliament against combining to lower a price of work; but many against combining to raise it. In all such disputes the master can hold out much longer . . .

We rarely hear, it has been said, of the combination of masters, though frequently of those of workmen. But whoever imagines, upon this account, that masters rarely combine, is as ignorant of the world as of the subject. Masters are always and every where in a sort of tacit, but constant and uniform combination, not to raise the wages of labour above their actual rate. To violate this combination is every where a most unpopular action, and a sort of reproach to a master among his neighbors and equals. We seldom, indeed, hear of this combination, because it is the usual, and one may say, the natural state of things which nobody ever hears of. Masters too sometimes enter into particular combinations to sink the wages even below this rate. These are always conducted with the utmost silence and secrecy, till the moment of execution, and when the workmen yield, as they sometimes do, without resistance, though severely felt by them, they are never heard of by other people. Such combinations, however, are frequently resisted by a contrary defensive combination of the workmen; who sometimes too, without any provocation of this kind, combine on their own accord to raise the price of their labour . . .

In the early years of industrialization, there was a great deal of sub-contracting. Skilled spinners, for example, arranged for their own help—often their children, and sometimes their acquaintances—and did the work at home or in some other place away from the factory.

But the factory owners found that off-premises sub-contracting gave them problems with the uniformity and quality of the product, and prevented them from increasing production. They had to have all of the production in the factory and under their direct control. From 1825 onward, the factory system was in full swing in the United States and several European countries.

England made trade union activity illegal by the Combination Act of 1799. The spread of industry based on the steam engine, and the activity of the workers, as described in *Wealth of Nations,* enabled the trade unions to become strong enough to convince legislators of the need for restraining legislation.

24 | SCIENTIFIC MANAGEMENT: TAYLORISM

AN AMERICAN FORMULATED A SYSTEM OF SHOP MANAGEMENT which later would become known as scientific management. Frederick Winslow Taylor (1856-1915), born of a well-to-do Philadelphia Quaker family, served a four-year apprenticeship as a pattern maker and machinist. He started as a laborer at the Midvale Steel Works (later, Bethlehem Steel), and soon was made a boss of the lathe department. With the complete support of management, he fought a three-year struggle with the machinists.

He told the machinists that they were turning out only a third as much work as they were capable of. He showed them how they could easily increase their output. When the workers refused to duplicate his speed, he laid them off. When this did not work, he tried another tack.

He selected some unskilled laborers and offered to teach them how to run a lathe if they would promise to do a fair day's work. But after being trained, the workers then sided with the machinists and refused to work any faster, so Taylor cut their rate in half. Then ingenious accidents started to occur, and machines would break down. Even though he could not show that it was the workers' fault, Taylor fined each man part of the cost of repairing his machine. After three years, he finally broke the spirit of the men.

When the men asked Taylor what he would do if he were in their shoes, he said:

. . . he would fight against turning out more work just as they were doing, because under the piece-work system they would be allowed to earn no more wages than they had been earning, and yet they would be made to work harder.

After a workman has had the price per piece of the work he is doing lowered two or three times as a result of his having worked harder and increased his output, he is likely to lose sight of his employer's side of the case and become imbued with a grim determination to have no more cuts if soldiering can prevent it.

These experiences led Taylor to confess:

It's a horrid life for any man to live not being able to look any workman in the face without seeing hostility there, and a feeling that every man around is your virtual enemy.

Taylor's definition of a fair day's work was as much work as a worker could do at a pace sustainable throughout his working life without injury to his health. In practice, he tended to set an extreme pace that few could maintain, and then only under strain. His economic philosophy was typical of the times: ". . all employees should bear in mind that each shop exists first, last, and all times, for the purpose of paying dividends to its owners."

His classic experiment was with a gang of 75 men who carried 92-pound pigs of iron. They each handled 12½ long tons a day, but he thought they should handle 47 or 48. Taylor selected a strong Pennsylvania Dutchman, who was close with his money and building a house, and asked him if he wanted to make $1.85 a day (the current rate was $1.15). The man was told when to rest and when to lift, and he succeeded in carrying 47½ tons.

But what is not generally told is that only one man in eight was capable of doing this amount, and Taylor even said he had to be ". . a man of the type of an ox" and ". . so stupid that he was unfitted to do most kinds of laboring work, even." Yet this tactic enabled Taylor to reduce the work force from 500 to 140, increase each man's earnings 60%, and save Bethlehem $75,000 a year.

From these early experiences were to come Taylor's three rules for choosing and directing workers: (1) select the best men for the job; (2) instruct them in the most efficient way to do the job; and (3) give higher wages to the best workers as an incentive.

The principles of Taylor's theory of scientific management are:

1. The managers assume . . the burden of gathering together all the traditional skills which in the past has been possessed by the workmen and then classifying, tabulating, and reducing this knowledge to rules, laws, and formulae . .

2. All possible brain work should be removed from the shop and centered in the planning and layout department . . [since no worker has the time or money to develop the science of doing work]. Furthermore, if any worker were to find a new or quicker way of doing the

work, or if he were to develop a new method, you can see at once it becomes to his interest to keep that development to himself, not to teach the other workers the quicker method. It is to his interests to to do what workmen have done in all times, to keep their trade secrets for themselves and their friends.

3. Perhaps the most prominent single element in modern management is the task idea. The work of every workman is planned out by the management at least one day in advance, and each man receives in most cases complete written instructions, describing in detail the task which he is to accomplish, as well as the means to be used in doing the work.

Taylor separated mental work from manual work—the production area from the area for design, planning, calculation, and record-keeping. Each activity in production has its parallel activity in the management center—devised, tested, laid out, assigned, checked, inspected, and recorded until completion.

So the term "Taylorism" is an anathema to all workers—and even to some employers. It represents the workers' lack of control over the way they do their work, and management's dictating of the precise manner in which work is to be performed by each worker. It has also meant the destruction of craftsmanship.

Frank Gilbreth later added method to Taylor's system—combining motion study with time study. Every motion of the body was broken down into elementary components of discrete movements. This has evolved to the world-wide recognition of MTM (Methods-Time Measurements).

For example, one tire company allotted 11½ seconds for a worker to punch in or punch out at work:

Identify card	.0156
Get from rack	.0246
Insert in clock	.0222
Remove from clock	.0138
Identify position	.0126
Put card in rack	.0270
	.1158

Just as a mechanical engineer studies a manufacturer's specifications in order to understand the capabilities of a motor, a human engineer tries to know a worker's motions by standard data. This is an attempt to create timed, predictable, consistent production action from human beings.

Under Taylorism, production and planning became the thrust of the workplace; personnel directors became only sounding boards for employee reactions. Managers and engineers ran the business; personnel directors and psychologists could only try to persuade the supervisors of the workplace to consider the neglected human element in order to reduce employee discontent.

25 | HAWTHORNE EXPERIMENTS: MAYO

AFTER TAYLORISM HIT ITS PEAK between 1900 and 1910, inherent problems caused it to fall into disfavor. The workers were degraded and worn out; management became disillusioned with its contentions.

Elton Mayo, an Australian professor of industrial research at Harvard, came forward with a system which would be dominant in the 1920's. He believed that an adaptive society was needed to accommodate the new technology: leaders must induce a willingness to carry out orders, and workers must be willing to cooperate.

Mayo maintained that factory work had to become satisfying. He felt this could be achieved if the administrators could create a "neighborhood effect"—a team atmosphere, in which small groups of workers could participate with management in reducing conflicts.

Mayo felt that management must learn new social skills, including the "capacity to receive communications from others in such a fashion as to promote congenial participation in a common task." He thought that unions would interfere with this cooperation between management and the workers, although unions in the 1920's were not widespread and had little strength.

PHILADELPHIA

In 1924 Mayo studied high turnover among mule spinners in a textile mill near Philadelphia. While turnover in most departments was 5% to 6%, it was 25% in the spinning department. The men had to walk 30 yards or more to tie up the threads of the spinning frames. The job had very low status; one worker said: "It doesn't take brains—just strong legs."

Mayo gave one-third of the men two 10 minute breaks in the morning and two in the afternoon. While the workers had never before exceeded 70% of the quota, they now made 80%.

Then, because the supervisors thought the workers should "earn" their rest periods, production dropped back to 70%.

But when there was a sudden rush order to get out, the president called on Mayo to take charge. During the rest periods, the machines were shut down and supervisors and workers rested. Morale went up; absenteeism diminished; production increased. The men were allowed to choose their rest periods and alternate with each other. Production reach 86½%, and years later the president said turnover never exceeded 5% to 6%.

Mayo concluded that work efficiency was negatively affected by pessimistic reveries resulting from monotony, and by postural fatigue and impaired circulation from the repetitive movements.

What Mayo didn't understand was why production also increased for the other two thirds of the men in the other department who were not used in the experiments.

Later, he reasoned that the visible research project demonstrated to the workers that their problems were not being ignored. Also, the president, who was very popular, had taken the workers' side against the supervisors. And third, a crowd of solitary workers had been transformed into a group with social responsibility. Social changes were being made in the factory.

Mayo's system failed for two reasons: in his efforts to meld the interests of workers and management, Mayo did not realize that a cooperation defined by management would be at the expense of the workers. And when he created the neighborhood effect in the factory, he did not realize that each worker brought in his own ethnic, religious and ideological views. Still, many of Mayo's points remain valid in industrial relations today.

THE HAWTHORNE EXPERIMENTS

A classic series of studies of work behavior took place at the Western Electric Company's Hawthorne Works in Cicero, Illinois, from 1924 to 1932. The manufacturer of telephone equipment had an enlightened management and was non-union. Thinking that lighting was affecting worker production, the company ran its first experiment in 1924 to determine if there *was* a relationship.

The outputs of groups of workers were checked daily as their lighting was gradually increased or decreased. Production went up and down in some groups; gradually increased in others; and increased and then stayed level in others. There was little relationship to the lighting being either bright or dim. Interestingly, production in the control group increased even though no change was made in its lighting.

The investigators concluded that lighting was only a minor factor affecting an employee's output—and that the many other factors involved would be difficult to isolate in a large department with many workers.

The company called in Elton Mayo and his associates, who conducted experiments for five years. The official report is the book *Management and the Workers,* by F. J. Roethlisberger of Harvard and W. J. Dickson of Western Electric.

RELAY ASSEMBLY TEST ROOM

For the first and major experiment, six experienced women workers were chosen to work in a separate room where they could be closely observed. They assembled relays at the rate of about one unit a minute. This task was chosen because the work was repetitious, no machinery was involved, and the short production time allowed fluctuations in output to be noted immediately.

The two-year experiment was divided into thirteen periods to test how varying rest periods would affect production. The first three periods were mainly to get the women (unmarried, in their early 20's) used to the test room.

First period (5 weeks) The women remained in their large department of 100 workers, but their individual outputs were tracked.

Second period (5 weeks) The women were given time to get used to working together in the new test room.

Third period (8 weeks) A separate wage incentive program was established for the group. Their earnings were determined by their own production, not by the large department.

Fourth period(5 weeks) The actual experiment started. Their superintendent cautioned them to work at a comfortable rate. The women were invited to have two five-minute rest periods; they voted to have them at 10:00 am and 2:00 pm.

Fifth period (4 weeks) They were given *ten*-minute breaks.

Sixth period (4 weeks) They were given *six* five-minute breaks, even though they didn't favor the short breaks.

Seventh period (11 weeks) They were given a 15-minute break in the morning with lunch furnished by the company, and a 10-minute break in the afternoon.

Eighth period (7 weeks) Given a choice, they quit ½ hour earlier.
Ninth period (4 weeks) They quit one hour earlier in the afternoon.
Tenth period They went back to the full-length day.
Eleventh period (9 weeks) They went on a five-day week, having Saturday mornings off.
Twelfth period (12 weeks) They returned to their original 48-hour week with no rest periods.
Thirteenth period (7 months) They worked 48 hours with a 15-minute morning break and a 10-minute afternoon break.

The result of this two-year experiment: there was no correlation at all between working conditions and hourly output. *In every case, the women's hourly production was higher than in the initial three periods.* In every case, total daily output increased as well (except in the ninth period, when they quit an hour early). And when they reverted back to the full work week with no rests, their hourly output was somewhat lower but their weekly output hit a new high.

How are these results to be explained?
• This was a cohesive group of unmarried women. Two friends were allowed to choose the other four members to make up the original group. During the experiment, two left the group—but their replacements adjusted very well to the group. The women became good friends—celebrating each other's birthdays, and meeting socially outside of work. It was fun to work together.
• They knew they were key figures in the project. Their suggestions were sought, and they met with the superintendent.
• According to company policy, workers could talk quietly with each other if it did not interfere with the work; but in the test room, the women could laugh and talk as much as they wanted. They felt as if they had no supervision, and worked without anxiety—even though observers watched them all the time.
• Morale remained high. Their attendance in the test room was four times higher than it had been previously, and was over three times as good as that of the other women in the department.
• Because the women's performance determined their earnings, and their output increased 30%, their pay was a source of pride.

INTERVIEWS
Between 1928 and 1930, supervisors from other departments interviewed 21,000 of the 40,000 employees at Hawthorne. The employees were asked what they liked and disliked about their

jobs, working conditions, and supervision. When the interviewers learned that the workers wanted to talk about what was on their minds—not just about the questions asked by the interviewers— the plan was changed to allow the workers to talk freely. The interviews had positive benefits for all parties involved: the workers felt that the company was really interested in listening to them; the company found many conditions that needed correcting; and the supervisors became more sensitive to the workers' feelings.

But the interviewers found it difficult to evaluate the complaints. A worker complaining about smoke and fumes would then talk about tuberculosis in his family and his fear of contracting it; a worker complaining about low rate of pay would then talk about his wife being in the hospital and his worry about her future health and the hospital bill; and a worker complaining about the officious way his foreman gave orders would then talk about how domineering and old world his father had been toward the children. The workers often could not separate work from their other life; they brought many feelings and attitudes to work with them.

One particular practice that an interviewer discovered eventually led to a later experiment. In one department, the workers had to make adjustments to many small parts in a unit. The workers had led management to believe this job was complicated, although it was quite simple; the workers, in effect, had put a fence around the job. When anyone brought in a unit that didn't work right, a worker in this department would fool around with it for two hours to prevent anyone outside from finding out what he really did.

This work group had developed two leaders. One leader would deal with outsiders, answering technical questions. The second leader took care of internal problems by training newcomers and controlling output.

In spite of strong worker control in the group, some workers insisted on transferring out—possibly because of divided loyalty between the group and the company.

BANK WIRING ROOM

As a result of this finding, the company set up a third study between 1931 and 1932.

The Bank Wiring Room was a separate room where nine wire-men, three solderers and two inspectors worked on large units (along with an observer, who had no authority). The company expected all bank wirers to make 914 connections an hour, or 7,312 a day. However, the men felt that 6,000 connections was a fair day's work. Four men met the company's standard, four fell far short, and one exceeded it. The men also did unauthorized things, such as making unjustified day-work claims for their low output some days; trading jobs between soldermen and wiremen; and talking and joking excessively and indulging in horseplay.

Their work behavior and standards of production were similar to that of many work groups: do not turn out too much and be a ratebuster; do not turn out too little and be a chiseller; do not tell on your fellow workers and be a squealer; and do not act importantly and be a big shot. They utilized many strategies:
• If a worker got out of line, another worker would "bing" him—hitting him on the upper arm. In an extreme case, they would ostracize a worker.
• If an inspector got out of line, they would drop solder or screws into his test set so that it short-circuited, or they would pull out his tester plug just far enough so that it wouldn't work. In one unusual instance, they got the inspector transferred.
• They maintatined a uniform output level so as to discourage supervisory tampering. Most of the production was done in the morning, so they could slack off and easily finish their quota in the afternoon.

The results of Hawthorne experiments of fifty years ago have recently become clearer as the years passed. They established that there is something more important than hours of work, wages and physical conditions—something which increased output no matter how physical conditions changed.

The Hawthorne studies showed that the factory, in addition to its economic function of producing goods, has an equally important function of creating human satisfaction. But the two functions are intertwined; if the human organization gets out of kilter, no efficiency system can correct it and improve production.

Motivation can never be understood on a purely individual basis; the key to worker behavior lies in the social groups found in the factory. If management disregards the human factor, and measures only with the stop watch, fatigue and monotony may erupt—a fearful and unnecessary human waste.

26 | QUIET: PEOPLE AT WORK

MANAGEMENT PEOPLE GENERALLY THINK OF MAN as a rational being who is concerned with maximizing his economic gains.

But workers generally determine what constitutes a fair day's work, and refuse to go beyond this amount—even if they can make more money by doing so. It makes no difference whether the plant is unionized, or whether it is in the United States or abroad, or whether the workers trust or distrust management; although there are exceptions, the pattern prevails.

Even Frank Gilbreth, the creator of MTM (Motion-Time Measurement) noted: ". . . nothing can permanently bring about results from scientific management and the economies that is possible to effect unless the organization is supported by the hearty cooperation of the men. Without this there is no scientific management."

Workers know that they are human, and that they have needs like everyone else. A worker needs to be socially visible, to feel he somehow belongs; he needs to locate himself in social space.

If management attempts to control worker behavior in ways incompatible with these needs, workers will push back by cutting their output. They use this tactic to protect themselves against attempts to deprive them of security, predictability, opportunity, status, and so on. It gives them a satisfying feeling that they are exercising some control over their workplace.

Most workers want to belong to work groups; they enjoy the interaction with others, and gain a feeling of stability and security. But some workers who have low sociability like to work alone. A study of 25 Swiss machine shop workers showed that ten preferred working alone, four liked to work with others, four said they would work with others depending upon who they were, and seven felt others were useful in their work.

A worker who is required to stay silently at his work station is worse off than in prison; in prison, at least, he can sit down and talk to others. Workers try to overcome the restraints of their "warden" by making the workplace more sociable. But some managements, unaware of worker needs (or callous to them), respond by tightening their oppressive supervision—thereby compounding the effects they are striving to avoid.

The reward/punishment system is often used to shape behavior in the workplace. Under piecework, if you have high production, you earn more money; if you have low production, you earn much less. If you are accepted by the workgroup, you bask in their acceptance; if you are not accepted, they may shun you.

Various scholars report that workers are bored and unhappy in their work. On the other hand, reputable poll takers report that workers are satisfied. Yet both of these conflicting claims are true.

Many jobs *are* boring and unsatisfying—but the worker himself can be very ingenious and creative in surmounting the deficiencies of the job. If the task is burdensome, he tries to make it less so. If it is repetitive and monotonous, he tries to make it more interesting. If he has an inventive frame of mind, he thinks of ways to improve the efficiency of the job. He seeks the friendship of his co-workers to make the atmosphere more pleasant.

Faced with a difficult situation he can't change, the worker adapts to it with as many accommodating devices as he can invent. Where he can, he talks to fellow workers; where he can't talk, he signals other workers and lets his feelings be known. Where he can, he trades off with other workers to meet quota; where he can't, he paces himself so he gets over quota for a while and then eases off again; or he starts easy, then attains good production, and then eases off.

The worker creates ingenious games. He handles materials with varying rhythms as if he were conducting a Beethoven symphony. He daydreams. He is in an everlasting fight to retain his mental health.

While many psychologists say happy workers must find fulfillment in their work, some workers do not look upon their work as enriching their lives. Rather the opposite: they deliberately choose *not* to find enrichment in their work. They think of the material things they can do for their families; this emphasizes their role as head of the family. They plan activities for their leisure time; this gives them some control over their lives.

Some young workers find work to be just like their school years, when they had to do what the teacher told them. Others are fortunate in finding work that fits their personality. Still others are fortunate in finding skilled jobs in which their ability is challenged and appreciated.

A telephone operator who operated an old-fashioned switchboard with lines and plugs complained to management that she had too much work to do. In response, the supervisors checked on her—and discovered that her switchboard was lit up like a Christmas tree. They did not know that she had arranged to call herself; all the trunk lines were alive with incoming calls, which she heroically tried to complete.

When she was not being checked on, she would plug her trunk lines directly into "information"—her most common incoming call—so that she had only to flick a switch to complete the call.

She was very kind in furnishing a writer with very confidential information she had overheard from labor relations. This finally forced the director of labor relations to install a separate phone that did not go through the switchboard.

None of this interfered with her lively avocation of taking horse bets to be placed with a bookie. She had achieved the ultimate: a job that didn't control her—she controlled the job!

PIECE RATES

The piecerate system is geared to an acquisitive, competitive, individualistic worker. But workers belong to work groups that are important to them and have a real influence on their behavior. The problem is reconciling a system made for individuals with a situation in which workers operate in groups.

A time-study man studies an operation scientifically, and then sets a rate that is not so tight that the men will not work at it—yet not so loose that the workers can turn out all that is required early in the shift.

But factory workers have an arsenal of hidden jigs and fixtures that can be used to do the job faster than the rate to which it was timed (as Taylor well knew). These devices are a tribute to the ingenuity of the American workers. They show a knowledge of machine operation that could be exceedingly valuable to management—but the knowledge is carefully hidden so that it may be used in the battle against the time-study man.

A new worker will not be taught the skills and secrets until he is accepted as trustworthy by his fellow workers. The acceptance may be rapid or slow, depending upon the nature and secrets of the particular group.

To the worker, making out on production is a game. He speeds up to avoid boredom, then has time left over for himself.

Two centuries ago, the liberal owner of a Scottish textile mill, Robert Owens (founder of the Consumer Cooperative movement), tied yellow ribbons on the machines of workers who produced less than average, green ribbons on the average machines, and red on machines that produced above average. Within two months, all of the machines had red ribbons.

RATE BUSTERS

Melville Dalton chose 84 workers in a southern city (all with seven or more years experience) and studied them for a two-year period. There were nine rate busters who exceeded the 150% ceiling of the group; 50 others who made the 150% ceiling, and 25 others who made only 100%.

The rate busters were Republican (most workers were Democratic); Protestant (most workers were Catholic); came from higher economic levels; and were sons of skilled workers or farmers. The rate busters did not participate in any groups on the job or in the community, and were very individualistic.

A SYNDICATE

In a study by Donald Roy, a syndicate of employees was formed to circumvent management's attempt to change rules and systems.

Inspectors, tool crib men, time checkers, stockmen and setup men need to interact daily with machine operators. The operator had to get his work orders from the time checker; then he had to give this order to the crib tool attendant to get his blueprint and tools; then the setup man did his part, followed by the inspector. If anyone had stuck to the company-required procedure, hours would be lost each day.

Instead, the employees cooperated in evolving their own system of shortcuts and rule infractions so that everything could move smoothly without delay. This enabled the workers to get their work time in, and even get credit for time they did not deserve.

A PAJAMA FACTORY

Two experiments in a pajama factory in Virginia in the 1940's compared the effectiveness of democratic discussion versus authoritarian request.

Employee morale at the pajama factory was low, output was poor, turnover was high, and employees were hostile toward management. Four groups of production workers were chosen for the study. The first group was told to work in the usual way and given a new, higher rate. Groups two and three were asked how they could help reduce costs and simplify the process; they were told they would be trained before a new rate was set. The fourth group used a modified form of group discussion.

Group one never produced over 50 units, and 17% of these workers left their jobs within 40 days. Groups two and three achieved a rate of 74 units and none left. The compromise fourth group produced 69 units.

The company now brought in group one, which had filed a protest with the union that the rate was unfair, and treated it in the same way as groups two and three; it reach 73 units with no further protest.

In a second experiment, where the average was 60 units and never exceeded 75 units, the workers were asked to discuss the problem of production and decide on a future target. They decided on 84 units an hour, and finally stabilized at 87 units. But the company found that the control groups would not produce more than they originally had—even though the company told them, asked them, ordered them and lectured them to produce more.

PAINTING TOYS

William Foote Whyte tells of a company making wooden toys. Eight women painted the toys as they went by on a line of hooks. Since the women were not making the time the company thought they should, a consultant met with the women and had them discuss the problems of their jobs. They said that three large fans to circulate air around their legs would help. While this did not seem to be important, the fans were installed—and they did seem to help.

At the next meeting, the women said they could not work at high speed all day. So a control dial was installed next to a woman who seemed to be the leader. After a week, the women agreed on a medium speed for the first hour of the day, fast for the next 2½ hours, and slow for the half hour before lunch. All afternoon the line ran fast except for the last 45 minutes, when it ran medium.

The women turned out 30% to 50% more product than the time-study man had figured. However, they were making more money than many of the skilled workers—who demanded that the inequity be adjusted. In response, the superintendent ordered a return to the original speed (which was slower than the fast rate). Within a month, six of the eight women had quit; several months later, the foreman quit.

The factory system is a social system made up of mutually dependent parts. A drastic change in one part of the system— even a change that is highly successful, such as the toy painting— may generate conflict in other parts of the system. Grievances are not always between workers and management; they may, as in this case, be between groups of workers—between day workers and incentive workers, between different shifts, etc.

FLEXITIME   Workers can start work and stop when they please, so long as they work a core period (say, 11 am to 2 pm) during the day. This enables them to avoid rush-hour traffic, to synchronize their schedules with working spouses and to get children off to school (a feature that may be very important to women workers). This works in larger offices. It has worked successfully in 3,500 West German firms. Absenteeism has been reduced in American firms that have used it.

REDUCED WORK WEEK   Some small and medium-sized companies have four-day weeks with ten-hour days. Efficiency has held up, and absenteeism has dropped. Some workers like it, and some don't. Perhaps single persons like it, while mothers of school children might not.

In a 1973 experiment in a textile mill, 100 employees went on a three-day, 36-hour week; a six-week vacation was also allowed. Production improved, and absenteeism dropped a third.

ELIMINATING REPETITIVE OPERATIONS

Indiana Bell Telephone directories require 17 to 21 separate operations to complete, with each worker responsible for a separate operation. The jobs were rescheduled, with each worker being given the responsibility for more operations; some workers were given a complete directory to compile.

Mistakes dropped substantially, promotions were earned, and job turnover was reduced.

In a company which formerly produced electric hot plates by having each worker do a separate step, the process was changed so that each woman assembles an entire unit. Production rose 47%; rejections fell from 23% to 1%; absenteeism fell from 18% to 1%.

A voltmeter factory broke the line down into groups of six to ten persons; each group assembled the product from beginning to end. Production soared, absenteeism went down, and quality improved.

In a famous 1932 study in England, women who threaded embroidery needles were dismayed when told their quota was being increased from 900 to 1,200 per day—but elated when told they could go home when they had met their quota. Most of the workers managed to reach their quota and leave a few hours early each day.

BREAKING UP THE ASSEMBLY LINE   Norway and Sweden have taken major steps to improve the quality of work. Volvo and Saab have broken the routine assembly line down into smaller groups who complete an entire engine. Production costs are somewhat higher, but are offset by savings in absenteeism and in keeping skilled workers.

THE GAINES PLANT

General Foods started a worker participation plan in the early 1970's at the highly automated new General Foods Gaines dog-food plant in Topeka, Kansas. With minimum supervision the workers made job assignments, scheduled breaks, interviewed job applicants, and even decided pay raises. They are treated like managers: they make management decisions, and use the same plant entrance and parking places as management.

A few problems arose. Jealousy and competition developed between teams on different shifts. Voting on other workers' raises proved to be a delicate matter, and has been eliminated. The workers would like to have a bonus system, but management fears the ripple effect of such an innovation throughout the company.

The plan is meeting its goals of efficient production and satisfied workers—but it has changed somewhat. General Foods has added seven management positions to the Topeka plant to get a tighter handle on it. Other plants are using the Topeka plan, but dropping certain elements of it.

Most of the changes have been imposed by management. The

innovative system is a threat to the conventional way of supervising. Managers and professionals in engineering, personnel and financing see the Topeka plan as a power threat to their capabilities and interests. Perhaps bureaucracy inevitably will win this challenge to an interesting concept.

Workers have ideas and abilities that could greatly increase production—but these are neither requested by management or volunteered by workers. If the aims of both could be joined, both labor and management would benefit.

LIFETIME EMPLOYMENT

The Japanese lifetime employment system may help persuade American management and workers to consider working toward a common aim. The company is committed to a permanent job security for employees; in return, the employees are committed to the welfare of the company. Quality circles allow all employees to contribute ideas to help increase productivity and quality. Decisions are by consensus, so all are committed to projected future actions. Even under adverse business conditions, the large companies go to extremes to keep their labor force intact.

Japan, of course, has its own unique history, traditions and values. But the success of Japanese companies in getting their employees to work toward corporate goals presents a challenge to other countries. American firms could benefit from adapting crucial elements of this proven system to their labor relations system.

27 | SEARCH FOR THE HAPPY WORKER

IN A MONUMENTAL STUDY, the Survey Research Center, University of Michigan asked 1,533 workers of all occupational levels to rank the importance of various aspects of work. The response:

1. Interesting work
2. Enough help and equipment to get the job done
3. Enough information to get the job done
4. Enough authority to get the job done
5. Good pay
6. Opportunity to develop special abilities
7. Job security
8. Seeing the results of one's work

Wouldn't you assume that most workers would rank job security and good pay as their primary concerns—rather than 5th and 7th in importance? Therefore, how was it possible for the Michigan study to come up with the ranking it did?

Part of the answer lies in the interviewing method, the way the question was framed, and the selection of people to be interviewed.

If a worker is asked whether he has a good job, he may say "No" if he is asked while on the job; "Yes" if he is asked at home; and "So-so" if he is asked on the street. How he feels as a member of his group at work or as the head of his family is important.

If you asked workers whether they wanted a percentage wage increase or a cents-per-hour increase, the skilled workers would choose a percentage increase. If you asked them whether seniority or seniority/ability should govern choice of jobs and other privileges, the senior workers would choose seniority.

A more important perspective on why the obviously important factors of security and pay were not highly rated in the Michigan survey is given by Abraham Maslow's hierarchy of needs, the best-known classification of human motivation.

The most basic needs are to satisfy hunger and thirst. After these comes the need to feel secure. Next is the need to be accepted and loved. Finally there is self-actualization: the need to realize your potential.

Similar priorities can be applied to a job. If the basic needs of good pay and security are met, then we can focus on less-essential needs such as interesting work.

When we choose a job (if we have that luxury) we go through a checklist: job security, so we won't be laid off; pay that is competitive with similar skills in the community; day work, so we won't have to work nights or a rotating shift; a job not too far away, so we won't be worn out fighting traffic or paid out buying gas; work that is not too physically hard or unduly repetitious, is not dangerous, and does not involve harassment from supervisors.

Money is the main payoff for working, and the obvious reason why people work. Pay may be the only evidence by which a worker can assess his importance to his place of work. If workers receive the going rate in their industry or their community, they take money for granted and rate other factors higher; when they receive less than they think they should, they rank money at the top.

Job security is also a critical component of work. A highly motivated worker wilts to nothing when faced with a layoff. Surveys show that the working class chooses certainty of income over more money, while the middle class chooses more money with less stability.

Job security is so essential that some unions buttress it by negotiating clauses to protect employed workers. These involve attrition, early retirement, Supplemental Unemployment Benefits (SUB), and severance pay. The automobile industry has been a model in this regard. SUB costs about 10¢ an hour; since some payments may run as high as 95% of wages, inverse seniority is requested so that senior employees are allowed to go first. SUB plans cover only 4% of the workforce; few unions do not consider unemployment to be much of a threat, but most unions simply have not been able to introduce SUB into their industry.

Beyond the basic needs of pay and security, there is less certainty about other factors. An analysis of 300 studies in the United States shows that:

• Different people react differently to job changes.

- The greater a worker's skill, the greater is his desire for an enlarged job.
- There is no positive relationship between job change and productivity.
- If job enlargement does not have other benefits, such as wages, it may have no positive effect.
- There is no correlation between satisfaction and motivation.
- When motivation is based on rewards, job satisfaction is a by-product.

Polls have consistently shown that workers like their jobs. Back in 1947, Roper asked 3,000 factory workers about their jobs. Two-thirds said their jobs were "interesting," 23% said "all right," and only 7% said "dull." In many studies since, on the question: "Are you satisfied or dissatisfied with your work?" the dissatisfieds have generally been below 20%. The Gallup Poll showed 90% satisfied in 1963, and 83% satisfied in 1971.

Yet we know that many workers are dissatisfied with their jobs. When workers were asked: "What type of work would you try if you could start all over again?", those who would choose the same work are pretty much as we might suppose: university professors, 93%; lawyers, 83%; white-collar workers, 46%; skilled auto and steel workers, 41%; blue-collar workers, 24%; and unskilled workers, 16%. It is logical to assume that workers with high-status, well-paying jobs would like their jobs much more than do people with lower-paying jobs.

- Of higher paid workers, 8% were dissatisfied compared with 20% of low-income workers. As the saying goes: "I've been rich and I've been poor—and, believe me, rich is better."
- The older a worker is, the more satisfied he is with his job—regardless of income. Only 6% of workers over age 55 were dissatisfied, compared with 25% of those under 20.
- Workers in small towns respond more favorably to management, while workers in larger cities are more alienated.
- Unmarried women were three times as dissatisfied with their jobs as were married women; as they become older, they become five times as dissatisfied.
- Blacks are twice as likely as whites to be dissatisfied with their jobs.
- In their middle years, blue-collar workers become more dissat-

isfied with their jobs than do white-collar workers—possibly because their wages have not increased as much over the years.

• Mental health was best among workers who are high in education and occupation; it was poor among those who are low in education and job status. (Surprisingly, an educated man who holds a low-level job has good mental health.)

Where the skill level is high, mental health is good—no matter what level of education or type of personality the worker may have. Half of the skilled workers showed good mental health; only 10% of the repetitive machine paced workers did.

Among a group of 1,000 telephone operators, one-third of the group accounted for two-thirds of the absences, mostly from respiratory problems. Those highest in absenteeism were lowest in their psychological outlook; they were more unhappy, resentful and frustrated, and suffered from 12 times as many respiratory illnesses as the others.

There is a popular myth that a worker who retires will soon drop dead. A four-year study of 1,260 older men found that the health of men who retired was likely to improve—and that the health of men who continued working was likely to decline.

Over half of all men in one study said they would keep working even if they didn't need the money. In another study, when asked what they would do if they inherited enough money to live comfortably, 80% said they would continue working (because they would feel lost or bored or go crazy). Yet a number of working families receiving huge payments in lotteries in New York and New Jersey have chosen to retire. In England, some who had quit after winning in the pools later returned to work.

A large proportion of workers say that they like their work because it keeps them busy They would dislike not working because they would have nothing to do with their time; they don't like being idle.

Many workers such as physicians, teachers, and policemen rationalize their occupations as being a service that furthers the happiness and well-being of their fellow man. The soldier regards himself as a preserver of freedom, and the lawyer sees himself as a defender of the judicial system.

28 | BONUSES: FOR WHOM?

IN THE 1,100 COMPANIES LISTED on the New York Stock Exchange in 1970, the top executives received additional compensation equal to 49.2% of their base salaries. And a 1974 study found that 74% of the manufacturing companies paid their three top officers on an incentive basis; the median bonus was 40% base pay.

Thus, top management—which already has the motivation of the highest salaries and personal achievement—is given yet another money inducement in the form of bonuses.

In corporations, the stockholders benefit most from profits. Then come the managers, who also get bonuses based on profits. But the workers, who are lowest on the totem pole, benefit the least (or, generally, not at all) from prosperity. The hired hands, paid by the hour, rarely have income security; and if business slows, they are immediately laid off.

Incentive pay evidently motivates executives to superior performance. But the executives don't think this principle should apply to workers. This is why there is often mutual distrust between managers and workers in regard to each other's ability and worth. The manager says: "See how hard I work; follow my example." The worker responds: "Why should I?"

Workers essentially resent a system that gives a week-old stockholder more rights than a 30-year worker. (The Japanese are quick to point out that our corporate quarterly report is responsible for the poor growth and competitiveness of many corporations; it shifts attention from long-term viability to short-term financial benefits.)

The bonus system is not a natural choice in normal industrial relations. Management feels it is giving up something it doesn't have to, and workers have to trust management to reward them when they increase production.

Management rewards supervisors for their creativity and effectiveness. But when workers increase productivity, they do not benefit; on the contrary, some workers may lose their jobs. Efficiency enhances the interests of managers, but threatens the interests of workers. For this reason, workers have a disincentive to cooperate in improving productivity.

Basically, there is nothing wrong with the bonus system. Workers don't mind bending with the company's bad fortunes if they can also benefit in good times. Workers know they will have to suffer the bad, anyway—in layoffs and speedups.

Trust has to be developed on both sides. What has to be surmounted is management's fear that workers will restrict production. On the other side, workers fear that their efforts in increasing production will not benefit them—but may actually hurt some of them.

Every worker knows more about his job than does anyone else. And he has time to think about his job—time that supervisors never have. A worker whose ideas are considered, and perhaps accepted, is welded firmly into the fortunes of the workplace.

To succeed, a bonus system needs a truly democratic environment. The normal authoritarian factory system chills the creativity of participants. A bonus system is not easy to operate; it will not always work. But it is a valuable and viable system if management and workers think it is needed and whole-heartedly support it.

THE SCANLON PLAN

In the early 1930's, Joseph Scanlon was president of an emerging steelworker local. He worked for a company that was fighting for survival, encumbered by aging machinery. Company officials and the union committee agreed to a plan in which the workers could make suggestions to improve production—and each 1% inprovement would earn a 1% bonus for the group.

The plan succeeded. Scanlon went on to become research director of the Steelworkers' union, and later joined the staff of the Massachusetts Institute of Technology.

The Scanlon Plan is a philosophy of organization, a way of company life. It is flexible, but it requires:

• Workers must truly trust management. They must work conscientiously and give suggestions freely in order to reap the rewards of their contributions.

• Management must freely accept workers as equal partners, without jealously guarding its prerogatives.

Each month 75% of the productivity increase is paid in a group bonus, and the other 25% is held by the company as a reserve against any month when production falls below 100%. The unused part of the reserve bonus is paid out to the workers at the end of the year.

So many suggestions pour in from the workers at the beginning of a bonus plan that foremen and supervisors may feel it is a reflection on their supervision. But when both workers and supervisors are working together to increase efficiency, foremen no longer have divided loyalties and conflicting pressures.

Production committees regularly evaluate all suggestions; in one company of 300 employees, 1.050 suggestions were submitted in four years; 905 were accepted, 94 rejected, and 51 were awaiting further action.

It is important to have a simple understandable measurement; if the plan is poorly planned, it may not succeed. Most plans have been able to ride through a decline in sales or an adverse shift in product mix, because now the workers see the whole picture and understand the problem.

Although grievances are supposed to be handled in the normal manner, they often are not raised at all—or are settled informally—because of the general concern about production.

A bonus plan is a way of work on a problem. It is not a substitute for anything; the company should not propose it as a substitute for a wage increase, nor should the union exchange it for some concession. It is not a work speed-up. Workers don't work faster—they work smarter.

In a study of ten companies using the plan, bonuses for a two-year period averaged 17.4% of gross pay. Increased production and profitability have enabled companies to improve their standing in the market, and thereby make the workers' jobs more secure.

The labor cost in these companies varied from 20% to 55% of the cost of the product. It might seem logical to assume that where the labor costs are a high percentage of the product, the plan has a better chance to succeed. In fact, however, even in those companies where the labor cost percentage was low, many suggestions were submitted.

One study showed that nine companies using the bonus plan had average earnings; three had better than average earnings; and four were close to liquidation.

A likely situation for a bonus plan would be in the main industry struggling to survive in a small town. The onus is upon management and workers to devise a scheme to allow the industry to continue and prosper. This strong motivation should be enough to compel both parties to adopt and stick to the plan, because failure would be catastrophic to them and to the town.

LINCOLN ELECTRIC COMPANY

The most outstanding example of a company rewarding its employees for their productivity is the Lincoln Electric Company of Cleveland. It is the world's largest manufacturer of arc welding equipment, supplying 40% of domestic sales.

Starting in 1934 with a 26% bonus, it has paid a year-end bonus to employees almost equaling their regular wage. A non-union company, Lincoln pays its employees the government figure for the appropriate skill in the Cleveland area. Most employees are paid on piecework or group piecework basis.

• In 1974, with sales of $236 million, the yearly cash bonus was $26 million—an average of $10,700 per employee, or 90% of base wages. Some workers on the floor earned more than $45,000.

• In 1979, a $46½ million bonus was paid to just over 2,600 employees—an average of $17,884 (higher-paid management was included in the plan).

• For the past ten years, the bonus has ranged 90% to 104%.

Everyone who has been with the company for two years is guaranteed continuous employment with a minimum of 30 hours a week. There have been no lay-offs since 1951. Half of Lincoln employees are shareholders in the company.

One reason for the company's success is that everyone works very hard to attain the aims of the company. The company is very rational and conservative, with no frills. Savings are passed on to its customers to strengthen the company in the marketplace. Prices of some products have not increased over the years, and a few cost even less than years ago. James F. Lincoln, directing head of the company and brother of the founder, is a rugged individualist. He is critical of most managements, as his comments show:

• If those crying loudest about the inefficiencies of labor were put in the position of the wage earner, they would react as he does. The worker is not a man apart. He has the same needs, aspirations and reactions as the industrialist. A worker will not cooperate on any program that will penalize him. Does any manager?

• The industrial manager is very conscious of his company's need of uninterrupted income. He is completely oblivious, though, to the worker's same need. Management fails—i.e., profits fall off—and gets no punishment. The wage earner does not fail but is fired. Such injustice!

• Higher efficiency mean fewer manhours to do a job. If the worker loses his job more quickly, he will oppose higher efficiency.

• There never will be enthusiasm for greater efficiency if the resulting profits are not properly distributed. If we continue to give it to the average stockholder, the worker will not cooperate.

• Most companies are run by hired managers, under the control of stockholders. As a result, the goal of the company has shifted from service to the customers, to making larger dividends for stockholders.

• If a manager received the same treatment in matters of income, security, advancement and dignity as the hourly worker, he would soon understand the real problem of management.

• Continuous employment of workers is essential to industrial efficiency. This is a management responsibility. Laying off workers during slack times is death to efficiency . . .

From the beginning, an advisory board of elected employee representatives has met twice monthly with the company to bring employee issues to management, and to question company policies. The employee handbook defines their duties:

Board service is a privilege and responsibility of importance to the entire organization. In discussions or in reaching decisions Board members must be guided by the best interests of the Company. These also serve the best interests of its workers. They should seek at all times to improve the cooperative attitude of all workers and see that all realize they have an important part in our final result.

Lincoln has had brilliant success in fulfilling the basic security needs of its employees. Since the company is not unionized, it must exercise extraordinary care for the welfare of its workers.

However, the company's literature does not furnish any evidence that workers have an equal voice with management in regard to bonuses or related matters. If there is a lack of worker democracy, it flaws this otherwise most impressive financial arrangement.

29 | THE YOUNGER WORKER

THE WORK ETHIC IS NOT AS STRONG IN YOUNGER WORKERS as it is in older workers. Forty years ago (although it may seem current) an author of this book wrote:

The new worker lacks pride in his work; does nothing until told to do it; does not care if he works; has an independent, cocky, so-what? attitude; lacks respect; does not follow the tradition of a fair day's work for a fair day's wage; and feels that the world owes him a living.

Older workers, on the other hand, have a driving need for a regular job. This used to be attributed to their memories of having been unemployed during the depression. But today, few people of working age remember the depression—yet older workers still value the importance of a steady job.

The older worker has made peace within himself. He accepts his status in the community. He holds a better job at work (whether because of seniority or ability or favoritism) and can be depended upon.

On the other hand, the younger worker faces a host of problems. He hasn't acquired the discipline of getting to work every day on time. The fact that he may stay up late with the fellows or with his girlfriend doesn't help the problem.

He hasn't decided on the job he wants. If the economy is tight, he may be forced to stay on his current job even though he doesn't like it. But still he doesn't fear the possibility of economic insecurity, as did the previous generation of younger workers.

A whole new belief has come about that a person is entitled to a job, and should be paid if unemployed, and should have health care and even pension benefits as part of his citizen's rights.

Young workers today are brought up more permissively at home and in the schools. They talk back and question authority everywhere.

Some even question success. While it is often the college-trained person who says that what is important is that one do his own thing, this view of questioning the aim of success is confined to the young.

For years it has been known that workers who are strong supporters of the company are also strong adherents of the union; these are often the older workers. Similarly, the workers who question and challenge the company do the same to the union; these are often the younger workers. The most valid explanation is that a worker's regard for the company and union is determined largely by his stake in the job, and by the ability of the union to affect that stake.

Typically, a young person gets a job and adopts the attitudes of the younger workers. He doesn't know whether he will stick to the job. He becomes a bothersome worker, challenging the supervisor on occasion, and having a problem of absenteeism. He is also a troublesome union member, challenging all established rules of the game, and insisting that changes be made now.

Then he marries and settles down some, because of his new status—but not completely, because his wife also works. He still is independent, and he'll not refuse a drink with the fellows.

We might expect that the increased family income would bring the young worker into the establishment—but it doesn't. We can only hypothesize that since he is not able to support his family by himself, he has a diminished image of himself.

Then comes a child, and the die is cast. His wife must stay home with the baby, and the decision is made for him that he has found his life's work. The future of his job now becomes important, because he accepts his new responsibility.

This establishes his stake in the job. He becomes more concerned with the fortunes of the company and his position in the company.

As he grows older, his stake in the job increases—so his conservatism increases as well. He becomes a strong union supporter, because he knows the union protects his interests on the job. These interests change as he passes through the stages of maturing. While the children are growing up, medical benefits are paramount; when the children leave home, shorter hours and vacations become more important; finally, retirement benefits take priority.

With time, therefore, young workers become old workers—and

take on their attitudes. This process is repeated anew each generation.

But every generation is not the same. During the 1960's, youth was in revolt. The Viet Nam war and the draft were protested. College graduates chose not to work for big business; some lived in communes. Now, in the 1980's, college students are searching eagerly for educational programs leading to job possibilities.

But the decline in the work ethic may be rooted mainly in the change in governmental entitlements, and the subsequent change in family living.

Only a generation ago, if a married child became unemployed for some time, his family moved in with his parents. Today, however, unemployment and welfare benefits are generally adequate to keep a family together in their own home.

When the government assumes responsibility for the welfare of families, the importance of work must suffer and erode. A pertinent example is the union contract, such as in the automobile industry, that allows certain employees to be laid off and still receive 95% of their wages. Is it now important if one works?

So the younger worker of today is different from his counterpart of a generation ago. It is the younger workers who want:

• More participation in management.

• More job enrichment. (In two studies in Pennsylvania and Kalamazoo, 73% of the workers under age 30 thought job rotation was a good idea, but only 42% of the older workers thought so.)

• More money, because they make the least.

Young workers, unlike older workers, do not believe in hard work and in pride of work. They have less favorable attitudes toward their jobs and their companies. They feel less favorable toward the community and the economy. But in time . . . they become older workers.

30 | THE WORKING MOTHER

THE LABOR FORCE IN 1980 ESCALATED TO 97 MILLION from 78 million in 1970, largely the result of the baby boom following World War II. This huge influx of 19 million new workers could have been absorbed into the labor force if industry had expanded greatly during this period. But in the period 1970 to 1980, the Gross National Product ranged from the highest-year growth of 5.8% to three years of negative growth, averaging 3.2% for the 10 years. Unemployment, which is 10% in 1983, will undoubtedly remain high until new and expanded industry can absorb the additional workers.

WOMEN IN THE WORK FORCE

Within this statistic of 19 million additional workers in the labor force lies a significant and pervasive figure: in 1980, 51.4% of all women were in the labor force—as compared to 42.6% in 1970. In 1981, 59% of all female high school graduates were in the labor force (it was 50% in 1971), and 69% of all female college graduates were in the workforce (60% in 1971).

And in the year 1981, 1.2 million more women came into the labor force. In fact, 7 out of every 10 who come into the workforce now are women. This leads to the prediction that women will become a majority of the workforce by the end of the century.

The 1980 figure of 51.4% of all women in the labor force totals 41,283,000 women (the men total 55 million) working or seeking work. They fall into three categories:

Married, with spouse present (50%)   23,097,000
Single, never married (61.2%)   10,340,000
Widowed, divorced, separated (41.1%)   7,846,000

Women (as are men) are more satisfied with their jobs as their age increases: 21-29 years, 78%; 30-39 years, 82%; 40-49 years, 88%; 50-59 years, 86%; and age 60 and over, 90%. The same applies to schooling: high school, 81%; college degree, 88%; graduate degree, 90%.

In 1982, the median earnings for women working fulltime was $238 weekly, which is 66% of the $363 median earnings of men. Currently, women unemployment is slightly lower than men, because men are largely in manufacturing and women in service-producing industries.

THE MARRIED WORKING MOTHER

In 1981, there were 25% more dual-earner, married-couple families (25.6 million) than in 1971. Sixty percent of all married-couple families with children under age 18 had both parents as wage earners.

The working married mother has certain problems to face, peculiar to her status as co-earner with her husband.

When a woman considers going to work, she must weigh four factors: (1) her net income after deducting taxes, child care, extra clothes, transportation, meals; (2) the redistribution of household duties, including shopping; (3) forgone leisure, because working women average 20 hours of housework a week; and (4) the psychic cost if the job is not pleasant.

Unless both husband and wife agree that she should work, her working will present problems. She may want to quit working and keep house, but her husband may insist that she keep working; or she may want to work, but her husband may want her to be in the home; finally, both may want her to be a homemaker, but a need for money may force her to work.

If the wife makes more than the husband, there is likely to be a shift in power. Actually, though, if wives were paid going rates for household duties, many women could claim to be the higher earner.

Even though the husband may agree to do some housework, most men are reluctant to do duties they don't like; many blue-collar workers resist doing any housework at all.

When it comes to child care, most fathers are not mothers. One group of fathers talked to their babies an average of less than one minute a day during the first three months.

There may be conflict over how the wife's earnings should be handled. Some parents have a joint bank account. Sometimes the husband pays all the basic bills and the wife pays the fringes. Sometimes they continually negotiate. Sometimes the wife tries to save her money.

MOTHERS WHO HEAD FAMILIES

The structure of families has changed dramatically in the last decade. Since there are now a million divorces yearly, the single-parent family is the fastest growing alternative to the conventional husband-wife form. While 61.8% of all women with children age 6 to 17 worked, 82.3% of *divorced* mothers with children 6 to 17 worked (this represents a 23% increase in 10 years).

But only 35% (2.5 million) of mothers with children, living away from fathers, received support in 1978; another million entitled to support received nothing. It is easy to understand why so many divorced mothers work.

Mothers who never married are only 5% of all working mothers. Having a child without marriage is not acceptetd in the white culture and only partially accepted in the Black culture. Many of these mothers are poor and less-educated and hold low status jobs when they work.

Where the husband is not present, the working mother has certain problems to face. First are her own personal, social and recreational needs. Then is the child care for the children while she is at work; this is accentuated because there are so few child-care centers, and often they are costly. And finally there is the absence of the male role model for the children growing up; the female child seems to have more difficulty developing the skills and understanding needed for heterosexual relationships. Working mothers tend to blame themselves for their children's discontent and unhappiness.

Guilt is the underlying hangup of many working mothers whose own mothers did not work. By choosing a different life-style, they are challenging their mother's values, social attitudes, and child-bearing practices. This creates a pervasive feeling of guilt when they face the uncertainty caused by their conflicting roles.

The employment of women outside the home represents one of the most important social changes in the United States in the past century. Where these working women head families, there has been a cultural lag of institutions, such as child-care centers and the courts, that do not seem to allow the single-parent family to attain equity and justice.

31 | THE ASSEMBLY LINE AND AUTOMATION

THE INVENTION OF INTERCHANGEABLE PARTS is generally credited to Eli Whitney (inventor of the cotton gin), who contracted in 1798 to make 10,000 rifles for the United States government. Any part of the rifle could be interchanged with the same part of any other Whitney rifle. This interchangeability was the basis of the assembly line.

In time, Whitney and others in the arsenal industry used powered machinery to produce interchangeable parts for small arms; the practice then spread to other industries. By the 1850's, the United States was the leader in producing milling machines, grinding machines and lathes. The turret lathe had a series of cutting tools mounted so that they could be used in succession on the product being made. The machine could be programmed so that a semi-skilled worker could perform half a dozen specialized operations rapidly and accurately.

In 1908, a demonstration of interchangeability drew worldwide attention in England. Three Cadillac cars from Detroit were taken apart. The parts were scrambled together; 90 parts were selected at random, thrown away, and replaced by stock parts. The three cars were then re-assembled, and all performed perfectly in a 500-mile run.

The assembly line is a logical way to put together complex products. As long ago as 1785, a water-powered grist mill in Philadelphia took in grain at one end, and delivered the finished flour at the other end. The New England textile industry used the assembly line to move textiles through various stages of treatment.

The slaughterhouse gave the assembly line a big boost. Overhead trolleys were necessary to move the huge carcasses. Then someone connected the trolleys by chains, and added power to form a continuous chain.

Ford's first Model T appeared in 1908. One worker could assemble the 29 parts of a magneto in about 20 minutes. In 1913, Ford put 29 men on an assembly line for the magneto, with each person putting on one part and hand-pushing it on rails to the next person; this reduced production time to 13 man-minutes per unit. Powering the line and raising it so that it was easier to work on reduced the time to five man-minutes per magneto.

The crankcase then went through the same experience. Within a year, assembly time was reduced to an eighth of what it had been.

The whole car was next. Soon, a car was coming off the assembly line every two minutes. Later, it became one car a minute. And Ford became synonymous with the production line.

Before the coming of the production line, versatile mechanics were needed to make things; now, only semi-skilled or unskilled workers were necessary to do limited tasks. What did the workers think of their work? They voted with their feet; in 1913, the turnover rate was 380%.

That same year, the Industrial Workers of the World (IWW) started organizing Ford, where $2.34 was the highest daily wage. In 1914 Ford made the astounding announcement that wages would be $5.00 a day. This took care of labor turnover. Ford said: "The payment of five dollars a day for an eight hour day was one of the finest cost-cutting moves ever made."

By 1924, two million Fords were being produced annually. Half of all the cars on roads of the world were Model T Fords.

Today's assembly lines make extensive use of automation. The forerunner was a French invention of 250 years ago. Between 1725 and 1745, three French inventors each improved on the others to produce the Jacquard weaving machine—which was to have tremendous influence on mechanical and clerical automation.

Cards were perforated by special machinery, then laced into a chain and pressed onto pegs on the cylinder of the weaving machine. This enabled the horizontal (warp) threads to be inserted and withdrawn at the proper times and places to mechanically weave the pattern. (The player piano is another use of this invention; perforations on a roll of paper cause the right notes to be struck at the right times.)

In the United States, the principle was adapted by Dr. Herman Hollerith in 1885 when he invented a machine for counting the punched cards used to tabulate the 1890 census. The information was coded in punched holes on the cards, and the machine could sort, classify and tabulate the bits of data. After improvements, these bits of information could be read and stored by electrical impulse. The computer has now become the chief instrument of mechanization in the office.

The punched-hole concept is used in the modern milling machine, controlled by a tape (which can be used again and again) to make complex designs. The tape determines the feeds and speeds, the cutters required, the coolants, depth of cuts, etc. Again, skill is taken from the worker and programmed into the machine.

A worker requires only four months of training to run a programmed milling machine whereas machinists require four years of training. Managements often "red circle" the tape jobs to keep trained machinists on them, and to prevent union complaints.

Other developments were converging toward the evolvement of the electronic computer: the slide rule, the mechanical adding machine (to be followed by the multiplying machine a generation later), and the mechanical calculator.

The first operative computer was Howard Aiken's Harvard Mark I in 1944. Two years later, an all-electronic computer was built at the University of Pennsylvania for the Army. John von Neumann did much to enable instructions to be encoded into data the machine could use. With this programming and feedback control, a computer could now direct a single machine or total production. When Bell Laboratories invented the silicon chip, eliminating the banks of vacuum tubes, the computer's size and cost were reduced tremendously.

Computers have caused clerks and bookkeepers to be replaced by keypunch and tabulating-machine operators. Office workers are undergoing a mechanization similar to that of production workers; indeed, the flow of information in offices has been likened to the flow of materials in manufacturing.

Many data-processing workers consider their work to be monotonous and repetitive, with no opportunity to exercise judgment; like factory workers, they see themselves as working for the machine. Absenteeism is high; they have to punch a clock, and are not allowed to converse; if they don't produce enough, they are fired with a week or month notice. So there is little difference between processors and factory workers. In fact, the American Management Association has said: "To be honest—we don't want people to take data-processing jobs as stepping stones to other jobs. We want permanent employees capable of doing good work and satisfied to stay and do it. The only rapid advancement for nonsupervisory data-processing staff is out of data-processing."

The robot differs from all other automation. It works like a human being in doing a number of tasks. It does only what it is programmed to do, but it generally does it better than a human does—and without getting tired. It can check its own work, and tell the boss by signal that it has made a mistake. It can, for example, identify the next car on an assembly line as one of four different models, and properly spot-weld it.

Robots were welcomed by everybody when they took over the handling of chemicals and performed work in high temperatures or dangerous conditions. But now that they are performing many routine tasks on production lines, workers see them as a threat to their job security.

But work has to fit a robot exactly. And since robots are expensive, they have to be used continuously in order to pay for themselves; their work week is seven days, 24 hours a day.

The United States is expected to be using 50,000 robots by 1990. However, ruthless competition in the auto industry may explode this estimate.

In Nagoya, Japan, the Yamazaki Machinery Works uses automation to turn out in three days what normally would take three months. The factory produces 1,400 precision components for metalworking implements each month. Instead of the 200 skilled workers formerly needed for this, there are ten or twelve on the day shift, with only one night watchman—even though the plant runs continuously. Eight-ton metal castings are milled and moved throughout the plant without human assistance. Under computer control (the only thing American), the 18 machinery centers choose proper drills (replacing them if they break) and advance the castings to the next machine. Workers are needed only to start each basic casting into the process, and sharpen the variety of tools each machine requires weekly. The $18 million investment is expected to be recouped in two years through cost savings.

32 | A STUDY IN STRESS: THE POLICEMAN

STRESS IS A RECURRING THEME OF THIS BOOK. Physical stress is more obvious, and its effects are more measurable; psychological stress is more insidious, and its effects are not as readily apparent.

When we think of stress at work, we tend to specify a particular problem—such as the relentless speed of the conveyer line, or the interpersonal problems of the public-aid caseworker. But stress is all pervasive: stress at work affects family life, and stress at home affects work behavior. Often, the pressures are so intermixed that they cannot be separated.

An air-traffic controller at a busy facility probably has the most stressful job there is. But even there, traffic is not heavy during certain periods, and scope workers spend some non-stress time answering phones and writing reports.

Since the police are often in the headlines, and most of us have strong feelings about them, police work is a good choice for seeing how stress really operates.

Hans Selye, who fathered the stress theory—and even chose the word stress to explain the human condition—considered police work to be one of the most hazardous occupations. He cites a long list of adverse conditions: shift work; long working hours; constant fear and anticipation of danger and death; confrontation with injury and violence; prejudice, suspicion and hostility toward police officers by the public.

Police departments are quasi-military organizations that try to control every facet of an officer's life: how he dresses, where he lives, the hours he works, the duties he pulls, the dangers he faces. There is little upward communication, and police have little influence on the hierarchy. The department focuses on obedience and control—and backs it up with reprimands, suspensions, and postponement of promotions. A policeman may become a workaholic in his efforts to succeed, and then recognize the futility of it all and become a burnout.

A police officer rarely spends time on truly dangerous work and professional criminals. There are long, dreary, boring nights on patrol. He spends much time on paperwork or the innumerable social problems of the community. He is required to make arrests for gambling, prostitution and drunkenness when the heat is on— and this hardly endears him to the public.

A policeman soon sees the criminal system as a travesty of justice, because of court extensions and plea bargaining and political interference. His advice is never asked for. If a case is dropped, he does not know the reason; or the court may give a light sentence or parole. If he believes in the system, let him arrest the beautiful people or the politically powerful. Why enforce laws the system obstructs?

The typical police officer regularly meets more people in troubled and conflicting situations than most of us do in a lifetime. He deals with people who are often in a highly emotional state, so he sees the worst of human nature.

He may have to use extra-legal methods to do his job. One policeman we know was assigned to watch for pickpockets at a railroad station. But the victims would never press charges, because they were catching a train soon for a distant point. Since the policeman was never able to get witnesses, he had to arrest the pickpockets on trumped-up charges.

Most of us can choose with whom we will associate; the policeman has no choice. Day in and day out, an officer is expected to swallow his emotional reactions and conduct business as usual. Police officers are expected to be controlled, calm and strong. We are shocked if an officer expresses feelings of pain and discomfort. Is it any wonder that many officers refuse to use the counseling available to them? Many think that seeing a shrink is tantamount to admissions of inadequacy and emotional incompetence. Some may release their burning anger by periodic brutality against undesirable transgressors.

When a policeman puts on his uniform, he becomes different from the rest of the world. It becomes a case of "us" against "them." He knows that there are those who hate his guts and are even willing to kill him. But he must function effectively in spite of his fears.

Shift rotations, overtime and court commitments can mount to over 60 hours a week; although pilots, controllers and train employees have regulated hours, police officers do not. And yet, when an officer responds to a call, he must make a quick evaluation of the situation and take the most appropriate action. In the absence of fixed formulas, he must be counselor, mediator, lawyer, enforcer.

But fatigue cripples his analytic and interpretive skills and impairs his decision-making. This may be why, when he deals with ethnic and racial groups whose lifestyle and body language he least understands, he is not likely to be compassionate—especially at five in the morning. Selye points out that when we are trying to defend ourselves against one stressor, we are less effective in protecting ourselves against other stressors; our problems are intensified.

An officer doesn't want his wife to know of his fears, lest he be considered weak; he doesn't want to frighten his wife by telling her of his narrow escapes. His wife may think that if she asks about his work, she may burden her husband with additional worries that may hamper his effectiveness. What results is a conspiracy of silence, with both of them constrained in their conversation. All communication is affected, and all kinds of problems become magnified and more difficult to resolve.

There are close physical and emotional bonds among policemen. Any attack against the police is taken personally by each officer. A wife soon learns that her husband has a special relationship with his partner; he discusses all kinds of intimate problems with his partner—often over a beer after work. The problem is much more acute if the partner is female. Eventually, a wife must come to grips with the fact that the police department family holds more interest for her husband than does his natural family.

Kirkham estimates that the divorce rate among officers is 75%; in another study of 100 officers, every officer declared that his work was causing significant marital difficulties. These tensions were attributed to schedules, jealousy, danger and social restrictions.

A number of police are on their third marriage by the age of 30. In one suburb with 13 officers, nine of them were getting a divorce during one three-month period. In an adjoining suburb, the police chief wrote in the local paper that divorce and alcoholism were the two main problems in his force.

People who have high self-esteem are relatively immune to stresses that bother other people; they can cope constructively with frustration. But the public perception of the policeman is low, and he knows it; he can do little to affect that image, no matter how exemplary his conduct may be.

Insults are often directed at the policeman's family as well as at himself. Many people are uncomfortable being with policemen socially, and they make a policeman's wife and children act defensively. Added to the internal pressures, these social stresses are hard to take. A perceptive spouse soon learns to patch up the wounds of abuse injected by the public. Many police forces ask spouses to take orientation sessions to help them understand the pressures to which policemen and their families are subject.

Police officers start their job in perfect health, and end with job-related disorders. The medical evidence of job stress is strong. There are high rates of stress-related digestive and circulatory ailments, including hypertension and heart disease. Coronary heart disease accounts for almost a third of all deaths nationally; stress is thought to be the leading cause, and may have as much impact as diet, smoking and lack of exercise together.

The suicide rate of policemen is 6½ times that of the average professional person. And giving up the identity of the badge also makes it difficult for them to cope with retirement; they continue to live their creed of "we serve and protect."

The television series *Police Story* and *Hill Street Blues* reveal with accuracy the personal problems of the police. The novels and movies of Joseph Wambaugh give a similarly true picture, as do *Prince of the City* and *Serpico*.

As an experiment, a white liberal university professor worked as a policeman in a patrol car in a large city. He found that he soon adopted many of the police attitudes that he had formerly criticized: cynicism, mistrust, hostility, racism.

What do you do when you answer a false alarm and a group of young Blacks greet you, with one hollering PIGS. It is just a false alarm, and you have other things to do, but it is an insult to you, you wonder how your partner expects you to react, and it is an insult to the department and community. You leave the car and advance on the group: "Anybody got anything they want to say?"

Now encouraged, one steps forward with a cigarette in one hand and a can of beer in the other: "I said it, man. Pig. P-I-G. You understand that?"

So you grab ahold of him, swing him to the car, and frisk him. The crowd growls and moves closer. Your buddy comes from the car with the shotgun cradled in his arm.

"You're arrested for being drunk in public. You must be drunk, or you wouldn't talk like that to the police."

So, once again, in a case not covered by the books, you handle a "no-win" situation that can go many different ways.

33 | DRINK AND DRUGS: DEVILS AT WORK

SOCIETY HAS FAILED TO EITHER PREVENT OR CURE ALCOHOLISM. In the early 1900's, attempts were made to control drunkenness by regarding it as immoral and criminal. National prohibition was tried in the 1920's, but that did not succeed, either.

Alcoholism then began to be thought of as a disease; now the World Health Organization, the American Medical Association, and the U.S. Public Health Department all recognize alcoholism as such.

The treatment of alcoholism has gradually shifted away from the medical profession. Psychological treatment evolved and now includes individual and group counseling by qualified persons who are not doctors. Therapists and counselors are often themselves former alcoholics who can command the confidence of their clients.

When an alcoholic recognizes that he has an illness, and receives treatment and rehabilitation, then he alone becomes responsible for controlling it. This is no different from the diabetic who has received medical care and counseling; he himself must assume responsibility for keeping his disease in remission by daily injecting insulin and testing his urine.

Alcoholism follows a predictable pattern. After someone becomes a social drinker, he learns that drinking diminishes the effects of stress and bolsters his ego. As he experiences more stress, drinking becomes an ingrained coping technique—so he continues to drink even more.

Although alcohol is a depressant on the nervous system, it has a paradoxical effect: as alcohol releases inhibitions, a person behaves as if it were a stimulant. A shy person becomes talkative, and a lonely person becomes part of the group. Drinking is accepted as a social lubricant; it can turn a colorless person into the life of the party.

Moderate consumption is legally tolerated and, in general, socially approved. On the other hand, someone who develops a dependence on alcohol receives little sympathy; he is criticized for his lack of will power and irresponsibility, and the assumption is that he doesn't want to be helped.

Drinking does make an alcoholic's life temporarily less difficult to face; it provides a tempting escape. But even after it becomes clear to everyone that the drinker is an alcoholic, he will say that he has no problem and could stop anytime.

Alcohol imposes a heavy economic burden on society, with the costs escalating each year. These costs include lost production, health and medical expenses, accidents, fires, violent crimes, and an overload of the criminal justice system. In 1971, they were estimated to total 25 billion dollars; in 1975, 43 billion dollars; and in 1976, 60 billion dollars.

About half of the 55,500 traffic deaths, and 68% of the one million traffic injuries, involve a driver or pedestrian under the influence of liquor. In half of all murders in the United States, the killers or victims (or both) had alcohol in their systems. The alcoholic is ten times more likely to die in a fire, 30 times more likely to be a suicide, and seven times more likely to be separated or divorced.

The problems that alcoholics impose on society are mind-boggling. They account for 70% of robberies and 50% of sex offenses. They are 30% of the sex victims, 70% of the assault victims, 70% of the assault offenders, and 60% of the child abusers. They inflict deep suffering on families, children and the community.

Alcoholism tends to run in families; as many as 80% of the children of alcoholic parents become alcoholics themselves.

Many alcoholics say that the first drink makes them feel much better—as if their bodies are inadequate until alcohol is introduced; then they attain "normalization." Scientists reject this claim, and point out that it gives an alcoholic a perfect reason not to seek a cure.

WOMEN DRINKERS   There are many explanations for the increasing incidence of drinking problems among women. Young women are drinking more with their boyfriends. Women in their twenties are experiencing more acute conflicts about their sex roles, and ambivalence over careers and traditional family roles.

Having been reared permissively, women hurt by divorce or who find the workplace stressful seek solace in alcohol. Married working women have significantly more drinking problems than do single working women or housewives. In their forties, women experience empty feelings, loneliness and depression. Women now live much longer, and try to dissolve their loneliness in alcohol.

The concentration of alcohol in the bloodstream determines how much we are affected; the more and faster we drink, the higher the concentration. Since women typically weigh less, have more body fat, and have a lower percentage of water in their system, they become intoxicated with smaller amounts of alcohol than do men.

Women drinkers deteriorate more quickly with liver and other problems, are hostile and aggressive, and are inclined to break off treatment.

If a pregnant woman drinks a great deal, her child may be born with all kinds of physical and mental impairments in proportion to the degree of drinking. Smoking adds a further physical risk to the baby.

YOUNG DRINKERS Drinking appears to be increasing among teenagers. There has been a downward shift in the age of the first drink, and an increase in the number of high school students who report getting drunk. Many youths use both alcohol and marijuana; this polydrug abuse is a prominent concern of health professionals.

CULTURAL PATTERNS National patterns of drinking reflect various cultures. Although both France and Italy produce and consume much wine, there is much more alcoholism in France. Yet, although Italian-Americans have a much lower rate of alcoholism than the national average in the United States, they have eight times the rate of the Italians in Italy—possibly because of American patterns of drinking (at times other than meals, and the use of liquor other than wine). The Irish-American alcoholic rate is three times higher than any other U.S. group, and 50 times that of Jews. Alaskans and Swedes and Scotch drink more, possibly because of being confined through long winters. Hispanics of both sexes report high rates of heavy drinking; however, Blacks report higher rates of abstention.

Even though drugs get greater attention than alcohol does, and law enforcers publicize drugs but not alcohol, alcohol is ten times as prominent and harmful. Alcohol is intoxicating, alters mood and behavior and produces sharp withdrawal distress—just as drugs do. Often, an alcoholic does not eat properly, and severe nutritional problems result—such as liver disease or peripheral neuritis. Alcohol has a direct toxic effect on the brain cells; by impairing circulation, it deprives brain cells of oxygen—and these can never grow back after they are destroyed.

DRUGS

The drug revolution which broke out in the mid-sixties has been one of the most important social changes in our times.

Every society has made use of some kind of mind-altering and mood-altering substances. In the past, whether the drug was alcohol or coca leaves, rules were generally clear as to where the drug was taken: in group rituals. Isolated use was discouraged.

In America, the Civil War was a turning point. Morphine was used as a pain killer, and hundreds of thousands of people became addicts; it was even labeled "the soldiers' disease." Morphine was available in all kinds of medications—even in patent medicines bought through the mail—and many middle-class people became addicted. By the end of the country, morphine, nicotine and alcohol were the most widely used drugs. (Nicotine and alcohol are not labeled as drugs, but they *are* drugs.)

Then morphine was declared illegal. Alcohol became illegal during Prohibition. During World War II, amphetamines were given to the armed forces of many countries to keep them awake and alert for long periods of time. After the war, amphetamine abuse broke out in countries such as Japan and Sweden; the drug had been tested and found to be fantastic.

In the United States during the 50's and 60's, socially rejected drugs such as marijuana, heroin and cocaine were secretly being abused by some minority groups and special-interest groups, but not the mainstream. The location of the Viet Nam war in drug territory, and the general rebellion of the time, had an influence on drug use.

At the same time, tranquilizers and oral contraceptives appeared. Major tranquilizers control the minds and behavior of severely emotionally disturbed people; they are so successful as chemical straitjackets that mental hospitals now house *half* the number of patients they once did.

Minor tranquilizers can tone down anxious, tense and despondent people. Drugs such as valium and librium soared in popularity as doctors became important pushers. Patients are as much to blame as doctors; most patients want to get something for their money so they can answer friends who ask: "What did the doctor give you?"

Drug companies advertise extensively in medical journals. Many doctors depend on drug companies to keep them up to date. Drug companies spend about $5,000 a year per doctor to promote their products. Tv got into the act; the woman of the house is pictured as the home nurse for in-house prescriptions—another drug pusher.

The oral contraceptive was another landmark drug. With family planning and careers as legitimate goals, women took to these drugs by the millions. The convenience of the drug overrode possible side effects; they supported the desired lifestyle.

The Pill solved a perpetual burden of women: the risk of pregnancy. At the same time, it aggravated the problem of drug use among adolescents—because the way older people use drugs influences the way adolescents use them. When adults use drugs to solve any problem or support any lifestyle, why shouldn't adolescents do the same? Looking at their parents, adolescents learn the key to a better life: better living through chemistry.

Older mainstreamers are offended by this accusation. They see a clear distinction between their drugs and those used by the younger generation. But the maturation process can easily be subverted by drugs—with each person choosing his own poison: acid (LSD), speed (amphetamines), or grass (marijuana).

MARIJUANA   One of the most important facts about marijuana is that the marijuana available today is five to fifteen times as potent as that of the 60's. And when boiled into "hash oil," it can be 60 times as powerful as the marijuana used in the past. These newer forms have not yet been studied in the laboratory, because of the ethical problems they pose—so we will discuss the less potent types of marijuana here.

Marijuana is a weed composed of many chemicals, some 400 of which are unique to the weed. A few have been studied in the lab; THC is the most important of these.

A marijuana smoker holds the smoke in his lungs for 10 to 30 seconds. He may build up the pressure in his lungs to force the smoke into the bloodstream; this is an excellent way to deposit carcinogens in the lungs and become more susceptible to bronchitis. Biopsies and autopsies of G.I.s in Germany show serious changes in lung tissues; another decade will show if such smoking patterns cause cancer.

Many social scientists are more worried about the effect of marijuana on sexual development, driving skills and intellectual development. Marijuana is heavily used and abused in the ages between 12 to 18, the crucial period in maturation. While scientists have worked with monkeys rather than adolescents, the results of large doses of THC have been worrisome: it inhibits the hormones that control sexual development, fertility and sexual functioning; and it may affect the placenta, contributing to fetal deaths, still births, and neonatal deaths.

When motorists were stopped for unsafe driving in California, 16% of them had THC in their blood. Medical examiners find that about 10% of victims of auto accidents have THC in their bloodstreams. The accidents could have been due to marijuana-caused impairment in awareness, sense of time and distance, peripheral vision and perception.

Students who try to "enrich" their school days this way can pay a heavy price. When the more potent drug forms are used, students have much less drive, lose interest in what is going on, and remember little of the learning that goes on in class. They have a short attention span, poor memory, and a limited ability to integrate material. When learning is turned off, negative behavior is soon turned on.

Fortunately, almost half of the students surveyed in 1981 realized that there is a great risk in regular use of marijuana. A large percentage recognized that the drug impaired their school performance and thinking.

PCP   One of the most surprising drugs being abused is PCP. Originally intended to be a general anesthetic, the side effect of serious emotional disorganization was found to be too severe. When PCP is used as an animal tranquilizer, for example, a cat may sit for 24 hours with no movement except for breathing and a back-and-forth movement of its eyes. Most intriguing is the spaced out look; the animal stares into the distance, oblivious to anything going on.

PCP is very unpredictable; frequent users have frightening experiences with it. Even with moderate doses, users often feel they are going to die: arms and legs become numb, eyes roll, muscles become rigid; the person becomes preoccupied with death. He may have a out-of-the-body sensation—thinking that he is floating near the ceiling, looking down at his own body. Some people actually find this experience pleasant. They enjoy being scared out of their wits, and are happy that they are close to death—and come back.

Violence and accidents are frequent among users of PCP. California has had many court cases in which people under the influence of PCP attacked and brutally killed others. There is a question of whether it is PCP itself that is responsible—or the violent-prone people who are attracted to PCP. Whatever the cause, the PCP user may have the delusion that the other person is a vicious animal attacking him.

Muscle rigidity and delusions combine to cause accidents. One user drove onto the freeway and stopped his van in the middle of traffic, causing a major accident—because he forgot he was on the freeway. Others have drowned in bathtubs and showers in only a few inches of water.

It is the astounding prediction of many drug experts that PCP represents the drug of the future. It is easy to manufacture; the ingredients are widely available; no Mafia connections are needed; and the mental and physical effects are substantial. The user knows he is on, and the elements of danger make the experience that much more exhilarating.

AMPHETAMINES   Amphetamines are stimulants that arouse the central nervous system. Their use has exploded over the past decades. All kinds of people have become pill poppers—students, truck drivers, diet fiends, bored housewives, executives fighting jet lag, sport figures. But adolescent pleasure-seekers pushed its use to epidemic proportions. In 1962, eight billion ten milligram amphetamines were manufactured—enough to supply every person in the United States with 40 tablets.

By 1970, Congress cut this production by passing the Controlled Substance Law. With amphetamine use declining, most of the pills now sold on the street are counterfeit, look-alike drugs.

A number of drug effects account for the popularity of amphetamines. Fatigue and pain disappear. Vitality, assertiveness, initiative, power, euphoria, and elation take over. Students can cram all night, truckers can drive all day, and football players can play aggressively even with injured limbs. Pleasure seekers inject amphetamines to enjoy marathon sex (20 hours is one claim) or play their horn for 10 hours. However, the drug reduces the user's ability to undertake complex acts or analysis, because the mind cannot keep up with the revved-up body.

A huge dose can trigger paranoia or violent behavior. Doctors have finally learned to differentiate between schizophrenia and similar drug-caused reactions.

When a person stops using the drug, withdrawal effects can be traumatically frightening; he becomes depressed, bone-tired and starved. Depression may reach suicidal levels; a user may sleep for 20 hours with continual troubled dreams. Intense hunger may be so strong that the user may insist on taking more amphetamines. Some users become so dependent they can inject one hundred times the normal dose of 5 to 20 milligrams.

BARBITURATES   Barbiturates are downers; they are widely prescribed to depress nervous system activity. A full dose at night can produce sleep; a reduced dose during the day can calm down a nervous person.

The same barbiturates can, in different quantities, reduce anxiety, sedate, induce hypnosis or kill. Barbiturates inhibit nerve signals, change the chemical balance, and relax various functions: heart rate, blood pressure, skeletal muscles. They interfere with our body's ability to use oxygen to produce energy; such interference prevents our nerves from carrying signals to our brain. Thus, barbiturates make it easier to sleep.

The fast-acting barbiturates (amytal, nembutal, secobarbital) are taken by mouth; their effects are felt within 20-40 minutes, and last four to six hours. Because of their speed, they are widely abused.

The slow-acting barbiturates (such as phenobarbital), take effect in about an hour, and last for as long as 16 hours. They are rarely used because their effects are both delayed and prolonged.

Moderate doses of less than 300 milligrams a day don't produce physical dependence—but they may generate psychological dependence on the drug's effects. With daily doses of at least 600 milligrams for a period of four to six weeks, the body *must* have the drug for the person to be able to function somewhat normally.

There are many hidden addicts among respectable middle-class people; a heavy user may receive prescriptions from a number of different doctors who do not know of the duplication.

Normally, people can fall asleep naturally by engaging in relaxing activities before bedtime; however, jet lag, a strange bed, or traumatic experiences can cause insomnia. But doctors too often casually and carelessly prescribe barbiturates for insomnia.

While there may be a need for a drug to cure insomnia, it should be used only for a brief period and then discontinued for a few days; the evils of the drug can then be avoided. It normally takes 30-60 minutes to fall asleep; barbiturates will do the job in 20-30 minutes. Is the risk of dependence worth the time saved?

A person's behavior with barbiturates may be similar to that with alcohol: he may be relaxed and mellow one minute, and irritable and morose the next. The following morning he may be slightly intoxicated and euphoric; then he may become temperamental, and his performance may be inadequate.

Driving under the influence of barbiturates can be as dangerous as under the influence of alcohol. One 200-milligram dose of secobarbital can impair driving skills for 10-22 hours.

While the effects of barbiturates and alcohol are different to the user, they appear the same to the observer: a heavy, sleepy look; a depressed, ill-tempered attitude; a jittery, excitable manner; slow thought; incoherent speech; failing memory; and weaving gait.

Thousands of people die of barbiturate overdoses each year because the stomach doesn't eject the drug by vomiting, as it does when too much alcohol is taken. If barbiturates are taken regularly, they remain in the bloodstream for long periods; this adds to the overdose risk.

Tolerance develops rapidly, with a high level being reached in two weeks. Larger doses have to be taken for two reasons: (1) barbiturates stimulate the production of enzymes which inactivate the drug; and (2) the nervous tissue becomes accustomed to the drug, so larger doses are needed to be effective. Since a user needs higher and higher levels to attain the desired effects, he comes closer and closer to a lethal dose. Abrupt termination of barbiturates after addiction also can lead to death.

COCAINE   Cocaine is obtained from the coca shrub, which

grows in Peru and Bolivia. Before cocaine was chemically isolated in the 1850's, the coca leaves themselves were chewed. Indians of Peru and Bolivia still chew the leaves regularly, ingesting about 360 milligrams of coca each day.

Cocaine first appeared in a number of tonic and patent medicines. Testimonials for its pleasant effect were received from popes, monarchs, authors, and presidents of the United States. Since 1903, cocaine has not appeared in Coca Cola; only the flavor of its leaves does.

By the 1960's and 1970's, cocaine had become the champagne of drugs. It is commonly snorted by the beautiful people, who have an aversion to injection. A cocaine paste, called free base, now allows it to be smoked; however, the original euphoria is soon followed by such an unpleasant state that the user immediately has to smoke again. Prolonged smoking causes serious personality changes and respiratory problems.

Snorted cocaine can reach the blood plasma in three minutes, and will persist there for four to six hours. Cocaine is a local anesthetic that constricts the blood vessels, and can block a nervous impulse for 20 to 40 minutes. However the psychological effect remains for only 15 to 30 minutes.

But these effects are powerful. Cocaine is one of the most powerful anti-fatigue agents known. It produces an intense feeling of mental and physical power, well-being, and euphoria. Users say it is like a climax a thousand times stronger than that found in intercourse.

Freud, for one, claimed that cocaine caused his mind to be clearer and more brilliant, and allowed him to work for countless hours. After recommending it to a friend who subsequently ruined his life, Freud stopped advocating it.

While the body doesn't develop a physical need for cocaine, psychological dependence is so intense that compulsive use is difficult to avoid.

HEROIN   Opium is contained in the sun-dried milky substance that oozes from certain types of poppies. This can be boiled and chemically treated to produce morphine. Morphine can be processed further into heroin, which is more potent and addictive. A few weeks of frequent use can make a person addicted to heroin. But after a single heroin shot, morphine is just as effective—since the body converts heroin to morphine. However, heroin is what is sold on the streets.

Only a few people treated medically with morphine go on to abuse the drug; addiction most often follows experimentation with a peer group. Most medical patients think of morphine only as a medicine to be taken when ill; when morphine is discontinued, some feel an urge to continue its use, but dismiss it after the medical regimen is over.

Most veterans returning from Viet Nam who had used pure heroin were able to drop it; only 7 to 10% slid back and some of these may have been drug users earlier. Many of the current street bags contain so little heroin that it is difficult to get a full-blown addiction; addiction, therefore, isn't so much a chemical problem as it is a people problem.

Smoking or eating heroin does not produce the "rush" effect; it must be injected. Users dissolve heroin in water, heat it in a bent-handled spoon, draw it up into a syringe, and inject it into a vein (if it is not collapsed) or under the skin (skin-popping). The opiate is rapidly distributed to various tissues. Most of the dose is excreted within 24 hours. Methadone, on the other hand, accumulates in the body; this is one reason for its success in treating heroin addiction.

To understand opiates, it is necessary to understand pain. Pain has two components: a conscious awareness of a pain-producing stimulus, and an emotional reaction to the stimulus that is accompanied by behavioral responses.

A person in pain who is given an opiate will still be aware of the pain—but it will no longer bother him. He will relax, and may even sleep. In this way, fear, tension and suffering can be blotted out by opiates; the sensation of pain remains but the emotional reaction to the pain is killed. Anxiety seems to intensify pain; by reducing the anxiety level, an opiate can render the pain tolerable.

TREATMENT There are four basic approaches to treatment of opiate addicts: therapeutic communities, methadone maintenance, outpatient (drug-free) programs, and detoxification.

Therapeutic Communities These are fulltime, drug-free residential programs. Synanon, started by Deterich in 1958, has served as a model for such programs. Here, the ex-addict is provided with a substitute family in which he is reborn and moves up the steps to maturity. In this warm, supportive atmosphere, he is stripped of the bad coping techniques that led to his addiction. Through a positive system of rewards, he gradually feels more competent and successful. This requires that complacency and game-playing be shattered through criticism and verbal attacks; he reaches maturity through self-examination.

Methadone Maintenance   Rehabilitation is the goal, with methadone substituted for heroin. Addicts are first helped to build a stable way of life—obtaining jobs, maintaining homes, achieving community standing. Then the discontinuance problem can be attacked—and the stakes are now higher; the addict's achievements make him strongly motivated to battle his craving. However, many scientists call the program a cop-out; by substituting one addictive drug for another, they say it leads to a long life of addiction.

Outpatient Drug-Free Programs   These range from having a patient sleep at home and spend his days at a therapeutic center, to less formal rap sessions and personal counseling.

Detoxification   This is the process in which an addict is taken off the drug. Patients are given gradually decreasing doses of methadone until they lose their physical dependence on heroin. With some order now brought into their lives, they are now more interested in long-term treatment.

How successful are the programs? The record has been poor. Of 1,900 opiate addicts treated at Lexington from 1952 to 1955, 90% relapsed. One bright light: older addicts were more successful in abstaining, evidently because they matured out of the habit.

Recent studies are more encouraging. In therapeutic communities, two-thirds of those completing the program were still abstinent a year later. Those who stay a reasonable time in the methadone program show marked improvement.

But the drop-out rate is high—as high as 50% in some programs. However, sometimes as many as 30% to 40% of the drop-outs become abstainers.

While progress has been made in the treatment of opiate addiction, the effectiveness is still not sufficient, and many addicts are still not being treated.

INTERVENTION AT THE WORKPLACE

While it is easy to detoxify an alcoholic, it is very hard to get him to stay on the wagon. Alcoholics Anonymous is an effective national program, but it reaches only a small percentage of alcoholics. Any program requires the support of others to pull the alcoholic through the relapses and suffering.

A revolutionary—and successful—change in the approach to treating drink and drugs has been through early intervention at the workplace. For example, this service has been available since 1972 to 80% of all federal employees; 100,000 of them have sought treatment.

Occupational alcoholism programs are based on four assumptions:

1. The best way to identify an employee's alcohol problems is by the supervisor's awareness of poor performance.
2. Alcoholism should be regarded as a medical problem at the workplace.
3. Regular disciplinary procedures for poor performance should be suspended while the subject is seeking treatment.
4. Returning to adequate job performance is a major criterion of success.

THE INLAND STEEL STORY   The 1975 Big Steel national agreement provided for alcoholism treatment; drug addiction was included in 1977. Inland Steel has an effective program for its 25,000 employees (at capacity) in East Chicago, Indiana.

Referrals to the program come from the supervisor, from the union, from the labor-management committee, or from court officials. The program has three separate phases:

• A hospitalization program of three to four weeks, used only when indicated and necessary. To be effective, it must be followed by the other two phases.
• A 90-day program of active one-on-one treatment. The participant meets his counselor once a week for three or four weeks, and then every other week for the next two months. This leads into group therapy and Alcoholics Anonymous or Narcotics Anonymous programs.
• A follow-up program of one-on-one counseling over the next nine months. The participant is called in after 30, 60, 90, and 180 days.

The program uses many free agencies, and as many as 160 Alcoholic Anonymous programs in the district. Latinos (Spanish speakers) comprise a significant percentage of the workforce and are not responsive in English-speaking groups; a Spanish-speaking therapist deals individually with them, handles their group sobriety sessions, and refers them to Latino AA groups.

There are generally 120 participants undergoing active treatment in the 90-day program at one time. The percentage of women patients has increased, as has the percentage of women in the workforce. White-collar subjects have a better recovery rate—possibly because they have been wiser in covering their condition, and realize that they do not have union protection. Two-thirds of the participants are primarily alcoholics who may take some drugs; the other third primarily use a specific drug, though they may take other drugs or alcohol. Drug users require tighter control, because they are more manipulative and evasive.

The goal is to return patients to their jobs with an acceptable level of absenteeism, job attitude and job performance. The company's 83% record of success is comparable to those of similar programs.

If other related problems are discovered during the course of counseling, they are dealt with directly or referred to appropriate agencies. These include mental health problems, homosexuality, impotence, and serious family sexual problems. Financial and legal counseling are also furnished, if required.

As of now, company connected programs are more successful than any other kind. Given the fact that drugs (alcohol) are here to stay, we need many, many more of them.

But will we get them? That remains to be seen.

34 | PRODUCTIVITY: THE JAPANESE MODEL

HOW COULD THE OVERPOPULATED ISLANDS OF JAPAN, with 115 million people (half the population of the United States), on less land than Montana, jump in three decades from wartime defeat to high-technology leadership—in spite of importing all of its oil, all of its iron ore, all of its aluminum, and two-thirds of its wood?

Japan now has the world's second largest industrial capacity, surpassing that of the Soviet Union. It leads the world in percentage of students who complete high school (90%). It prints as many copies of books and newspapers as the United States does, though it has half as many people. It has the lowest infant mortality rate and the longest life expectancy in the world.

The United States suffers in comparison. Long known as the carmakers of the world, Detroit automakers lost more than four billion dollars in 1982; 320,000 autoworkers were unemployed. Japan increased its car sales in the U.S. from 800,000 in 1975 to 1.9 million in 1980, taking 23% of our entire domestic market before accepting a voluntary quota.

What happened? For years, our carmakers regularly polled car buyers. But while many said that they wanted to buy small cars, they continued to buy large cars (which cost only a little more and were more comfortable and prestigious).

Then the tripling of gasoline prices in the late 1970's forced the U.S. buyer to buy the car he had always said he wanted. But the Detroit carmakers were geared to make big cars with low gas mileage, while the Japanese had cost-competitive, well-engineered cars with high mileage.

The losers of World War II—Germany and Japan—now have the strongest economies. This shows that the discipline of its people could be redirected to competitive production. Germany and Japan were soon to challenge our steel companies because they went directly to the new oxygen furnaces. Of the world's 22 largest modern blast furnaces in 1978, 14 were in Japan and none were in the United States. This is a sorry statistic for the world's leading producer, the only major nation to come out of World War II with its production capability intact.

National productivity is a measure of the total goods and services produced, divided by the employee hours required to produce them. It is the entire output of the economy (houses and cars built, steel produced, operations performed, etc.) divided by the total hours of all persons working.

Productivity is increased mainly by technological improvements and increased capital investment. Management planning and supervision is next in importance. The energy, skill and intelligence of the workers are very important, but productivity depends more on how the people are used.

The United States productivity grew at an average annual rate of 3.3% from 1947 to 1967. From 1967 to 1977, it averaged a 1.6% increase. Starting from a low production base, Japan had an average annual production growth of 10.2% from 1960 to 1973.

Japan has succeeded in taking over the radio, television, and hi-fi industries; has surpassed the Swiss watch industry; has done in the British in motorcycles. the Germans in cameras and opticals, and most others in items such as pianos and snowmobiles. Japan can build ships 20% to 30% cheaper than anyone else, and builds 50% of the world's ships; it would build more if other countries didn't subsidize their own waning industries.

By 1975, through a combination of improved technology and worker reliability and skill, a Japanese auto worker could produce five and a half times as much as his British counterpart and twice as much as a European. A Japanese steelworker could produce two or three times as much as an English steelworker.

The United States, the world's most capitalistic nation, endorses the free market system—in which private industry controls production and distribution (both domestic and foreign) without interference from governments.

But most nations don't operate that way. The Western European governments own and operate many major industries. Major foreign sales handled by a government agency are likely to become a government issue. Even Japan, with its privately owned industries, has a strong interest in foreign sales—because governmental agencies have a powerful guiding and nurturing hand.

North America, Western Europe and Japan agree that a relatively free distribution of products between their nations is necessary for the well-being of all. They have found that taxes, quotas and other restrictions placed against imported products (to give domestic products an advantage) are counter-productive; their citizens have to pay more for imported products, and the country whose products are taxed often reciprocates by discriminating against *their* products.

For the past three decades, these nations have adopted the General Agreement on Tariffs and Trade (GATT) to regulate the free flow of products between them. However, Japan has been slow in letting in products that are competitive with their own— although it has eliminated some of its discriminatory practices.

The tortuous trials between Japan and the United States are illustrated by the 64K RAM (Random Access Memory), a small chip that can store 65,536 separate bits of information.

In 1981, competition from Japanese firms (who had captured 70% of the world market) dropped the cost of the 64K RAM from $23 to about $5. The U.S. Commerce Department alleged that the chips were being illegally dumped (sold at a price lower than production costs). In response, the Japanese trade agency warned Japanese firms to be above reproach in their marketing methods in the United States in order to avoid new restrictions. So the Japanese slowed their chip exports to the United States.

The result? The following year, 1982, the U.S. Department of Justice announced it was investigating six Japanese firms for conspiring to limit their exports to the United States in order to prop up chip prices. One hand knowest not what the other hand doeth.

Loans have recently become an important element of foreign sales. A major source of contention is government subsidization of interest on loans. The GATT policy is that a country bidding on sales to a foreign nation may offer a loan at an interest rate no lower than the selling nation's own market rate. The United States has an Import-Export Bank which provides low-interest loans that are competitive with those of other countries; however, it must follow the GATT rules.

Japan has come late into the modern world; in 1868, Japan

still had over 250 local feudal lords. In its transition to capitalism, Japan borrowed from Europe and America to build her present industrial and political systems. The Allied occupation after World War II created democratic changes on its political and social institutions. The large trading companies were broken up; after the occupation ended, however, they gradually recombined to assume their present large and powerful positions. Mitsubishi is the largest of the industrial, banking and trading conglomerates; its 28 divisions had sales of 123 billion dollars in 1981, and it had bank assets of about 103 billion dollars.

A destroyed city can be rebuilt under a master plan that calls for a better design than the original. Similarly, a national industrial plan can call for a rational rebuilding of industry that avoids wasteful features that may have developed in earlier years. Japan wisely chose to develop industries which had high potential in foreign markets.

In the United States, on the other hand, trade has been geared to domestic markets. Of late, some industries have been in danger of being smothered by foreign competition; textiles is one such industry, with Japan making early inroads. But Japan knows that Korea and Taiwan, with comparable technology and low wages, are overtaking it in certain areas. So Japan has directed its research efforts and workforce at those areas where its skill and technologies place it in a strong position. The United States could learn a lesson from Japan in how to utilize the strongest assets of our economy, so that we can develop a trade policy that welcomes the future instead of mourning the past.

Japan has a potent economy because it has powerful government agencies that plan and implement rational industrial strategies. These agencies help create and support strong companies with great competitive potential.

The Ministry of International Trade and Industry (MITI) knows a great deal about various industries throughout the world, and therefore knows the potential for growth. MITI arranges for Japanese companies to become involved in a budding industry, and helps them by importing technology and arranging favorable loans to cushion the early costs and risks.

In this way, Japanese industries were built up after the war. Since the basic industries had government backing, the larger companies could guarantee their employees long-term employment. The industries are based on long-term aims rather than short-term gains. Financing is from banks rather than stockholders; this reinforces the companies' long-time goal of viability rather than immediate profit. Since employees virtually never leave a large company, the company can spend many years training them—knowing that the investment will be returned. In the United States, which has a more mobile workforce, highly trained and experienced people tend to be lured away by other companies.

The commitment of a Japanese company to its workers is a key reason for the commitment of its workers to the company. This has enabled Japan to achieve high productivity and superb quality control.

Japanese workers in major companies earn as much or more than do American workers. On the other hand, Japanese workers work longer hours than we do, receive minimal social security benefits, have poorer living conditions. And over two thirds of the workers are in smaller companies, where they do not enjoy the guarantees that employees of the large companies have.

One statistic speaks well of Japan's embracement of capitalism and democracy: the earnings of workers in the highest 20% of the salary scale are only 4.3 times as high as those in the lowest 20%. In the United States, the difference is 7.1 times.

The character of the Japanese labor movement was also revealed in fifteen interviews the author had with labor leaders:
• Each union is nationwide, organized on an enterprise basis.
• Each fulltime labor leader is paid as if he were still working for the company. For example, a union leader who has 20 years of job seniority might be paid the salary of a section chief, even though he holds a low-level union job.
• When contract renewal approaches, members pay strike dues regularly. The union pays each member strike benefits equal to the amount he paid into the fund; they know it will be three half-days of token walkouts.
• Three of the people interviewed were labor leaders at the start of World War II. All three were exempted from army service because of what the authorities called "dangerous thoughts." The authorities did not want them to contaminate the other conscripts with their dangerous ideas about the rights of rank-and-file people.

35 | WORKERS AS MANAGERS?

THE GOVERNMENT OF THE UNITED STATES is directly and indirectly involved in so many aspects of our lives—education, research, health, job training—that many Americans think this country is no longer capitalistic. On the contrary, it still remains by far the most capitalistic nation in the world. Strong corporations continue to resist encroachment on their prerogatives by strong unions.

But the winds of change are blowing.

Gigantic AT&T has a statement of principles in its union contracts providing for "employee participation in the decisions which affect their daily work and the quality of their worklife."

The 1982 negotiations between the UAW and Ford took place during the worst period of the auto industry, with Ford losing a billion dollars a year. The union made financial concessions to the company, but the contract shows a new Japanese influence:

• None of the 94 bargaining units will close during the life of the contract, unless sales volume dips to a certain point.

• There is a goal of lifetime employment. All employees with 15 years of service come under "the guaranteed-income stream"; in two plants, protection will be given on an experimental basis to the most senior 80% of the workers.

• An employee involvement program will enable employees to participate in the decision-making process (and the top UAW negotiator will make two presentations yearly to the Ford board).

• Profit-sharing and a contract reopener will go into effect if sales volume reaches a specified peak.

American unions are more effective than other developed countries' unions in collective bargaining. Still, our unions lag behind the others when it comes to the involvement of workers in management and the exercise of union power beyond the workplace.

The unions of western Europe are affiliated with political parties, and have won codetermination and similar rights of representation on the boards of corporations. In Germany, the codetermination law covers all companies with over 2,000 employees (copied after the earlier coal, iron and steel "parity" system) with fulltime worker membership on managing boards. Workers hold half of the seats of corporate boards. In Austria, Norway and Luxembourg, a third of the board seats are reserved for workers. France allows non-voting labor observers on boards. Sweden requires board representation by workers if a company has more than 25 workers.

Yugoslavia has had worker control for over two decades. Yugoslavia has a Socialist (communist) political system but a market (capitalistic) economy. But neither the socialistic ideology nor the workers' councils enabled the workers to shift any power away from the managers.

In Italy, the union would not agree to the firing of 9,000 redundant employees at the Montedison petrochemical complex in 1982, which would have saved the company an estimated $180 million annually.

Because of the retention of unneeded employees in state-owned companies in Germany, England and France, it is really impossible to ascertain if they are dumping their products in the United States when, for example, they sell us their steel. Should they figure the necessary cost of producing the product—or the actual cost, which includes the wages paid the redundant employees?

Unions in the United States have consistently opposed any worker representation on boards of directors. They feel that collective bargaining permits them to influence companies in the way they want—while the European model would weaken the role of the union and dilute worker solidarity. The election of UAW President Douglas Fraser to the Chrysler board was simply to protect the union's investment—a wage reduction to enable the company to survive. Even during World War II, when Americans were motivated by the war effort and worker participation was supported by unions, management and government, the concept did not succeed.

What follows is a look at work in Sweden, paraphrased from *Democracy on the Shop Floor?* by Eric Einhorn and John Logue.

By 1970, Sweden had had twenty years of full employment.

Most workers avoided unattractive, regimented jobs. Absences from illness reached 15%, and turnover sometimes exceeded 100%. The harmful consequences of absenteeism, unreliability and poor workmanship persuaded companies and unions that job redesign might be a way of reducing worker dissatisfaction.

Saab and Volvo replaced automobile assembly lines with team assembly in some plants. Such teams also eliminate the foreman, train new employees, do quality control, and repair machinery. The system is more flexible and more humane than a production line. There are buffer zones for units at each end of a work group—so the team is not pressured to start and finish at specified times; if it fills the next buffer, the group can rest for an hour or more.

Savings through reduced absenteeism, better-trained workers, elimination of supervision and more stable production have more than offset the higher costs of self-managed assembly teams. Saab figures it has recovered its investment in the new facility in two and a half years.

But an auto manager says: "Managers are trained to be authoritarian. It makes us feel secure to run things that way. Anybody who believes in order prefers the assembly line over the teams. You go out on the floor and what do you see? A bunch sitting and talking, another group playing cards, others reading, asleep. It's enough to make a manager feel insecure."

The Swedish blue-collar unions are closely allied with the Social Democrat party, which held power from 1932 to 1976. The current government is continuing the Social Democrats' programs (the S.D. returned to power in 1982).

Sweden's functional socialism—which socializes some functions of ownership without transferring title—splits rights in various ways between management and labor. Plant managers are now responsible to the employees, in addition to their board and stockholders.

Most workers in Sweden are more interested in the organization of work and in making jobs more pleasant than they are in wages. One reason for this attitude is that half of any wage increase would go to the government in taxes.

Half a dozen special acts of legislation were passed in the 1970's to cover employees. The Work Environment Acts of 1974 and

1978 take safety and health responsibility away from government inspectors and places it in the hands of safety stewards. These stewards are worker representatives, paid by the company, who have the right to shut down any production that poses an immediate danger; this happens about a hundred times a year.

The 1974 Act On Security of Employment places an obligation on companies to retrain employees. When the huge ship-building company in Gothenburg was nationalized in the late 1970's, excess employees were guaranteed employment for two years. Rather than permit overmanning, the union won job retraining, academic courses, and special projects using the ship facilities. Of the 1,300 redundant manual employees, 41% were hired by other firms, 21% were rehired by the shipyard, 10% took early retirement, and the rest took sick or disability pay. Not one was left unemployed; national policy is to keep unemployment below 2%.

The 1977 Employee Participation in Decision-Making Act requires the employer to continuously furnish the union with information on production, economic status, and personnel policy—and the union can inspect the company's books. In some shops the union, in effect, exercises veto power over management appointments. All managerial decisions—even making new investments—are subject to collective bargaining. *The union's interpretation of contractual provisions for worker influence and employee rights is binding until the labor court rules to the contrary.*

Sweden is not the United States; its system of labor relations is not ours; and it has full employment and a responsive government to impel the country in the direction it has taken. But perhaps the Swedish model will spread.

Einhorn and Logue write: "All Americans are democrats in theory. It is just our practice that is schizophrenic. Democracy stops at the office door and factory gate. Outside, you are a citizen. You speak your mind, vote as you see fit, run for office. Inside, you are a subject of managerial absolutism."

The question is: for how long?

AFTERWORD

36 | THE MANIPULATORS

PEOPLE CAN BE DIVIDED INTO THOSE WHO MANIPULATE, and those who are manipulated. The manipulators have a deep understanding of psychology (including the principles described in this book) that helps them exert a degree of control over other people.

Manipulation can be good or evil, depending on who is doing what to whom. It can be as harmless as a host getting his last guests to leave so he can go to sleep . . . or as despicable as a chimney-repair ripoff of an elderly homeowner. In the workplace, many workers and union representatives use manipulative techniques for practical purposes.

This chapter describes several out-of-the-ordinary cases of manipulation. Some are illegal or unethical; some are perfectly legitimate; and some are in a gray area. We are not suggesting that anyone emulate the seamier practices; we are suggesting that you study them in order to gain a greater understanding of human behavior. This understanding can help you refine your own manipulative skills in legitimate areas.

THE BIG CON

A long-fabled character is the confidence man, ably described in David Maurer's 1940 book, *The Big Con,* and the 1973 Academy Award-winning film, *The Sting.*

Improved communication and sophistication have exposed the mystique of this aristocrat of crooks since his heydey from 1880 to 1920. He uses remarkable ability to exploit the gullibility of man while operating the short con (taking what money the victim had on him) and the big con (which required a few weeks to build up the mark for big stakes). When the FBI conducted its ABSCAM against members of Congress, it used a professional confidence man to generate the credibility of the plot.

The film *The Sting,* starring Robert Redford and Paul Newman, accurately tells the story of the Big Con. You remember the plot: Redford being wronged by a nasty character, and with the help of Newman conceiving an elaborate plan to right the wrong—and also line their pockets. The various steps necessary to set up and play and fleece the victim are even listed on the screen in old-fashioned screen titles.

Since the nasty character was to become the victim *(putting the mark up),* he was enticed by allowing him to make some money through returns at a fake Western Union office *(playing the con).* He was then led *(roping the mark)* to the ultimate ploy *(telling the tale).* They allowed the victim to make money *(giving him the convincer)* by winning on a remote horse race, with the returns coming over the wire in "the store." He was then lured to the ultimate coup *(giving him the breakdown)* for which he had obtained a large sum of money *(putting him on the send).*

Then, in an elaborate and fast-moving finale, the victim loses all his money *(taking off the touch),* but is afraid to go to the authorities because a murder occurs *(blowing him off).* Nor would it have done him much good, because they would have bought protection *(putting in the fix).*

The Sting is a great film, with its scenes and music evoking the mood of the turn of the century. But it also tells a sociologically sound story, built on the sequential steps that confidence men had found necessary to hook and lure and fleece a victim.

INDUCING CONFESSIONS

The Supreme Court's Miranda decision requires that a suspected criminal be advised of his rights before he can be questioned—including his right not to talk without his lawyer present.

Prior to the Miranda decision, policemen had developed psychological interrogation techniques that enabled them to obtain many confessions. Although there is a general awareness today that suspects don't have to talk, these techniques are worth reviewing because of their demonstrated effectiveness.

It is difficult to break a hardened criminal; it is much easier to get a confession from someone who has been arrested for the first time. He is very fearful. He is undergoing a new and terrible experience. He wants to talk to someone. If the interrogator is understanding and sympathetic, he is more likely to talk.

Most people have an innate urge to talk. When their reputations are challenged, they feel compelled to defend themselves—by telling the truth, or by lying if need be.

The police officer knows all he can find out about the crime and the suspect before starting the questioning. Conditions in the room encourage the suspect to speak freely: no interruptions; no shackles; the policeman is in civilian clothes, and is alone with the suspect. The questioner sits close to the suspect—and even touches him on the shoulder or hand—so that thoughts and feelings will flow freely.

The policeman assumes that the suspect hasn't told the whole truth. He controls the investigation; he doesn't let the suspect interrupt the questioning. Since he is trying to identify with the suspect's feelings, the policeman minimizes the moral seriousness of the crime, and suggests that others may have moral responsibility for the crime. The policeman tells the suspect to tell the truth to ease his conscience.

Some specific techniques have often proven effective:
• The policeman questions the suspect about another crime of a lesser nature that occurred at the same time, hoping he will name his confederate as an alibi.
• When he knows certain information about the suspect, the policeman asks questions about these irrelevant matters to see if he will lie.
• The policeman calls attention to the suspect's internal signs of guilt: dry mouth, trembling internal feeling, throbbing head—and to his averting his gaze, his claims that he is telling the truth, and his claims that he does not remember important events.
• Where there is an accomplice, the policeman plays one against the other (they are kept separated all the time) telling the weaker suspect that his partner is planting all the blame on him.
• The good cop, bad cop technique involves one officer who is so threatening that the suspect is grateful to talk to a second officer who is sympathetic and understanding.

An understanding of the suspect's internal feeling of guilt shaped by his moral training, his general feeling of helplessness engendered by the oppressive police-jail system, and the easy solution of his dilemma urged by the policeman's sympathy make it clear why these techniques have led many suspects to confess.

JURY SELECTION

The composition of a jury can determine whether a defendant is convicted or released. Therefore, by selecting jurors whom they believe will vote their way, the opposing attorneys can influence the outcome of a trial. This is why jury selection sometimes takes longer than the trial itself. One court case took five months to select the jury.

The prosecuting attorney's objective is to see that the accused is convicted, while the defense attorney's objective is to get the defendant released—even though both attorneys are officers of the court and are serving the cause of justice.

Prosecutors try to get jurors who are upholders of the law: men, Republicans, prosperous persons such as bankers, engineers and accountants, Germans, army officers.

Defense attorneys try to get jurors who have compassion and understanding of human frailties: women, Democrats, poorer people, social scientists, minorities.

HUSTLING

W. C. Fields popularized the saying: "Never give a sucker an even break." Fields should know. He was a proficient poolplayer, and his father owned a poolroom; he used a pool routine in his vaudeville act.

There are hustlers in pool, bowling, tennis and golf. Card-playing is not included on this list, because poker and other card games involve luck and perhaps cheating in addition to skill. Real hustling involves skill and deception.

If you're hustling, you encourage your opponent to play and to bet against you by allowing him to believe he is a better player than you are. Say you're playing pool. You bet $5 a game. You win the first game with a flukey last shot. The sucker wins the next game. You agree to raise the ante to $10 a game. You string the sucker along with your ragged playing, which makes him look good. You may have to allow him a handicap to continue. Finally, you start playing for big stakes—and take him to the cleaners.

The 1960's film, *The Hustler*, gave a very accurate portrayal of pool playing and hustling. It caused a minor revival of pool and billiard playing, which had steadily deteriorated since the 1920's, by lending it some stature and legitimacy.

Bobby Riggs was an acknowledged tennis hustler who performed on television. He was a top player who would give other players a handicap to play him.

Hustling requires use of the short con—getting the sucker to play and keeping him playing. It is based on a weakness of human nature: a person thinks he is better than he actually is, and likes to test himself (and maybe has a little larceny in his heart as well).

SHOPLIFTING

Stores don't know exactly how much money they lose through stolen merchandise—but it runs to millions of dollars each year. Much shoplifting is thought to be done by employees of the store, with supervisory help leading the way.

Professional shoplifters, called "boosters," are watched closely and are prosecuted with vigor. Many boosters work with others, but some work alone. Some use booster boxes or store bags to conceal the merchandise. Others use booster skirts or bloomers.

Professionals have certain rules—for example, "Never grift on the way out." This means that when they have taken the item they come for, and see something else they want, they leave the store and get rid of the first item, then return for the other.

Most of the shoplifters are amateurs, who are called pilferers.

Most shoplifters are women—since most shoppers are women. They do not think of themselves as thieves—but when they are caught, the shame makes them stop. Few are arrested.

Shoplifting is high among younger people, who may continue until arrest forces them to question their morality.

Shoplifters who belong to the dominant social group tend to be noticed less by security personnel; people who look "respectable" are approached cautiously. In many stores, Blacks are watched more closely and are arrested more frequently than whites.

If people don't plan to steal, they usually won't—even if they are given the opportunity to do so. In a ten-day test using very attractive small merchandise, with no salesperson present, not a single item was stolen. This shows that pilferers are sophisticated and determined, rather than impulsive.

CARD PLAYING

When money is involved, it pays to know who you are playing

cards with. Card sharks have special ways of communicating with each other by body and voice signals. These are so subtle and ordinary—a way of holding a cigarette, or breathing, or scratching an itch—that they cannot be detected. The first letter of a conversation can determine the suit—such as "Have you got a match?" for hearts. The position of face-down cards on the table can represent ace, king, queen, etc. Feet can touch other feet. In the world bridge championship of 1965, the British team was accused of such signaling, although the charge was never proved.

A gambler can put his hand on his chest with the thumb spread to indicate: "I'm going to take this game; anyone want to go with me?' If another player places his right hand on the table, thumb down, this means "yes." Or the other gambler may hit the table with his fist; this means: "Never; I discovered this sucker first."

When their livelihood depends on such a simple act as putting cards on the table, gamblers will spend endless thought and practice on ensuring their success.

THE FORTUNE TELLER

How does a fortune teller seem to know so much about her customer's private life?

First of all, the customer is subject to manipulation—having placed enough credence in the fortune teller to go to her.

The fortune teller categorizes her customer: her age, the way she dresses, her wedding ring (or the reddened finger where the ring was), and who she comes in with—so she can peg her as to her possible problems.

Fortune tellers are practical psychologists; they know that everyone has problems, and that all people want to think the best of themselves. They know that as people go through various periods of their life—courting, marriage, children coming, children leaving—they have similar problems.

The fortune teller knows that if her customer is young and out-going, she's probably worried about one of her boy friends (or *the* boy friend). If she's young and quiet, she may wonder why she doesn't have a fellow. If she's over 30 and married, she's concerned about her husband, her children, or perhaps money. If she's not married, perhaps some friend—male or female—has not behaved right. Older women always worry about their children or grandchildren.

The fortune teller uses character analysis to elicit clues. "You have suffered from being too generous" is sure-fire; everyone has suffered to some extent, and for what better reason than generosity? Subtle flattery is an effective tool in winning the client over.

As the fortune teller looks into the crystal ball, she may say: "I see a man drinking, and he is with another man. I see a woman in the background, but she isn't you." The customer's eyes may widen with interest, or narrow with concern—providing more clues. If the fortune teller pauses, the customer may prompt her (and later forget she volunteered the information). It is human nature for people to hear and remember those things they recognize as features of their ideal self—and to forget anything that's not on target.

The fortune teller gets little clues of interest or frowns or tenseness to guide her on her probing way. If she succeeds in locating the problem, she gives her customer the reassurance she wants: "If you continue to treat him in a loving way, he will return to you as he has done before."

CHALLENGING THE CORPORATION

People are intimidated by big, impersonal institutions such as banks, hotels, and supermarkets, and even government offices. This is why they sometimes allow themselves to be hasseled. They stand in long lines, wait interminable lengths of time, allow themselves to be seated where they can't see or hear. They shrug it off with: "You can't fight City Hall."

But you can. Institutions are vulnerable to customer complaints—but rarely have to worry about them because people seldom complain.

Suppose that a single clerk is on duty where there are facilities for three clerks to handle the people. To get action, just address all the people in a voice loud enough for management to hear: "Well, it doesn't look like this hotel wants our business. They treat us like cattle." Some people will look at you curiously, others with sympathy; some will avoid looking at you. The main thing is that the manager will come rushing over, wanting to make concessions in order to stop the noise. Clerks may be sympathetic to the plight of the people they are serving—but cannot help them under current orders.

Often, the problem is caused by a supervisor's edict to cut

expenses or get maximum work out of his people. It is fruitless for the clerks to protest. But the challenge of one customer has more weight than that of a dozen clerks.

AN INCIDENT

One summer, a labor leader and his wife went to Greece, where they made various side trips from Athens. When they returned to their hotel in Athens the second time (where their entire booking had been paid for in advance), the manager of the hotel wouldn't accommodate them—saying there wasn't anything he could do for them. So the wife—a psychologist—suggested they get their pajamas from their luggage, change into them, and sleep on the sofas in the reception room.

The manager became very excited and finally put them up at a nearby hotel.

On their last few days in Athens, they filed a complaint with the government tourist bureau. The hotel manager was required to attend. After being admonished by the judge, he told the couple that anytime they returned to Athens they would be welcome as his guests.

Back in the United States, the couple received an official apology from the Greek government. Yes—it does pay to protest improper treatment.

NOT TALKING

An effective tactic for a union representative in negotiating (i.e., discipline) is not to talk. When someone expects you to respond, and you don't, he may get flustered and keep on talking.

Since you want to draw him out as much as you can without making any concessions yourself, this is one way to do it. You can devote your full time to listening. You don't have to think about arguments you will use, but devote your full time and attention to what your opponent says and the reasons and nuances behind what he says.

However, if you adopt a refusal to talk as a regular technique, your opponent may adopt a strategy to cope with it.

One labor leader always takes a clipboard into talks with management—with the phrase DON'T TALK lettered at the top of the board.